CHINA'S REGIONAL
DEVELOPMENT

CHINA: HISTORY, PHILOSOPHY, ECONOMICS

CHINA'S REGIONAL DEVELOPMENT

EDITED BY DAVID S G GOODMAN

Routledge
Taylor & Francis Group

LONDON AND NEW YORK

First published 1989 by Royal Institute of International Affairs

2 Park Square, Milton Park, Abingdon, Oxon OX14 4RN
711 Third Avenue, New York, NY 10017, USA

Routledge is an imprint of the Taylor & Francis Group, an informa business

First issued in paperback 2016

The publishers have made every effort to contact authors/copyright holders
of the works reprinted in *China: History, Philosophy, Economics*. This has not
been possible in every case, however, and we would welcome
correspondence from those individuals/companies we have been unable to
trace.

These reprints are taken from original copies of each book. In many cases
the condition of these originals is not perfect. The publisher has gone to
great lengths to ensure the quality of these reprints, but wishes to point
out that certain characteristics of the original copies will, of necessity, be
apparent in reprints thereof.

British Library Cataloguing in Publication Data
A CIP catalogue record for this book
is available from the British Library

China's Regional Development
ISBN 978-0-415-36152-1 (hbk)
ISBN 978-1-138-99128-6 (pbk)
China: History, Philosophy, Economics

CHINA'S REGIONAL DEVELOPMENT

edited by
David S.G. Goodman

R

ROUTLEDGE
London & New York
for
THE ROYAL INSTITUTE OF
INTERNATIONAL AFFAIRS
London

First published 1989
by Routledge
11 New Fetter Lane, London EC4P 4EE
29 West 35th Street, New York, NY 10001

British Library Cataloguing in Publication Data

China's regional development.
    1. China. Regional economic development.
    I., Goodman, David S.G., *1948–* II. Royal
Institute of International Affairs
338.951

    ISBN 0-415-03510-4

Library of Congress Cataloging in Publication Data

China's regional development / edited by David S.G. Goodman.
        p. cm. — (Chatham House papers)
    Bibliography: p.
    Includes index.
    ISBN 0-415-03710-7 (U.S.)
    1. China — Economic policy — 1976– 2. Regional planning — China.
I. Goodman, David S.G. II. Royal Institute of International
Affairs. III. Series: Chatham House papers (Unnumbered)
HC427.92.C4655 1989
338.951–dc19   88-39741
                                     CIP

To John Gardner,
teacher and friend

Contents

Contents

Contributors

Shaun Breslin is a lecturer in the East Asia Centre, University of Newcastle upon Tyne. His current research is a study of the impact of economic modernization on politics in Shanxi.

Terry Cannon lectures on Third World development at Thames Polytechnic, London, and is editor of *China Now*. With Alan Jenkins he has edited *The Geography of Contemporary China: the Impact of Deng's Decade*.

Peter Ferdinand is a lecturer in the Department of Politics, University of Warwick. He has written on politics in the USSR, Yugoslavia and China, and is the author of a forthcoming comparative study of the three political systems.

David S.G. Goodman is Professor of Asian Studies, Murdoch University, Western Australia. He is the author of *Centre and Province in the People's Republic of China*, and *China's Provincial Leaders*.

Maurice Howard is an independent China consultant.

Richard Kirkby is Director of the China Services Centre, Sheffield City Polytechnic. He is the author of *Urbanisation in China*, and is currently involved in research on China's urban economic development.

Michèle Ledić is a research fellow at Birkbeck College, London. She has been a Senior Lecturer in Economics at the University of Zagreb, and worked in the research departments of the World Bank and Shell International. She is currently engaged in research on China's foreign trade and energy.

Martin Lockett is a management consultant with the John Lewis Partnership. He was formerly a Research Fellow at the Oxford Institute of Information Management in Templeton College, and a Lecturer in Social and Economic Studies at Imperial College. He is the author of *Organizations as Systems* and co-author of *The China Challenge*.

David R. Phillips lectures in geography at the University of Exeter. His research interests include the social and economic development of South-East Asia, Hong Kong, and China.

Anthony G.O. Yeh is in the Centre of Urban Studies, University of Hong Kong. Together with David Phillips he is the editor of *New Towns in East and Southeast Asia*.

Preface

Since late 1978 the Chinese Communist Party (CCP) has tried to steer the People's Republic of China (PRC) into a large-scale restructuring of its political practices and economic system. Deng Xiaoping has described this new era of reform as 'the second revolution', so fundamental does he regard the potential consequences. The goal is economic modernization, and the aim of this volume is to present a non-national perspective on its prospects.

The PRC is often portrayed as if it were a homogeneous and unified entity. Such a description was misleading but understandable when access to China was limited, sources of information were exclusively CCP controlled, and an attempt was sometimes being made to implement policies uniformly across the country. However, in the 1980s when the economy has become more complex, politics have become more pluralist, and even the CCP explicitly recognizes that the size of the PRC imposes severe restraints on central government, there is an obvious need to look beyond national-level portrayal and to highlight the regional dimensions of China's development.

Moreover, two characteristics of the reform era emphasize the importance of regional development, particularly for countries and enterprises wishing to do business with China. One has been the 'open policy' whereby the PRC hopes to use the prospect of a 1000-million-strong market and its primary products to attract the new technology and administrative skills it requires for its modernization especially from the west and Japan. The second has been the PRC's current emphasis on 'regionalization' — the development of market-oriented, rather than bureaucratically-controlled, patterns of economic development.

This volume has resulted from the work of a study group organized by the Royal Institute of International Affairs, which met through the winter of 1987–8. In contrast with other approaches to the subject of China's reform era, the emphasis is very definitely on the present and the future (rather than the past and the present). Moreover, its primary concern is with development rather than regions, and with the practice rather than the theory of regional development. Thus, unless otherwise specified, where the terms 'region' or 'regionalization' are used they refer, not to any specific region but rather to the more generalized phenomenon.

The structure of this volume follows very closely the pattern of seminars held at Chatham House. The first chapter presents an overview of the prospects for China's regional development, as well as a consideration of current regional policy and its historical background. Next there are five chapters which examine various dimensions of, and constraints on, regional development. These cover the regional dimensions of politics and administration, economic and financial levers, foreign trade, transport and communications, and energy. The final four chapters are case-studies of the prospects for development in specific regions of the PRC: one for each of the three large planning regions designated under the current Seventh Five-Year Plan, and a chapter on China's Special Economic Zones.

No book on China's regional development could hope to address its topic without benefit of maps, and this volume has attempted to meet that need. In addition to a general map of China (p. xv), there are maps depicting physical features, the various regional systems (military, administrative, provincial, economic), the railway system, mineral deposits, and other regionalizations adopted since 1949. These are contained in a separate appendix of Maps. For those less familiar with the complexities of contemporary China, a chart of the administrative hierarchy in the PRC is included (p. xvi) and a glossary of Chinese terms used in the text (p. 195).

With only three exceptions, *pinyin* has been used as the system of transliteration from Chinese into English. The exceptions are Tibet, Inner Mongolia and the Yangtze river, all of which are probably more readily recognizable in those forms than as Xizang, Nei Menggu and the Changjiang, respectively.

Any enterprise of this kind necessarily owes a debt of considerable magnitude to others. The authors would collectively like to acknowledge the assistance and stimulation of their many kind friends in China itself, as well as those who participated so vigorously and usefully in the series of seminars held at the Royal Institute of International Affairs in connection with the preparation of this volume. The staff of Chatham House, in particular, Laura Newby, Brian Bridges and Pauline Wickham, have facilitated the project greatly with their usual encouragement and efficiency. Thanks are due to Professor Cole (of Nottingham University) and Frank Leeming (of the University of Leeds), both of whom graciously allowed use to be made of their cartography. Finally, a debt of gratitude should be expressed

to ICI, GKN and Standard Chartered Bank, who have generously supported the study of China at Chatham House.

David S.G. Goodman
Murdoch University, Western Australia

Abbreviations

AAR	Average annual growth rate
AFP	Agence France Presse
bdoe	barrels a day of oil equivalent
CCP	Communist Party of China
CITIC	China International Trust and Investment Corporation
CNA	China News Agency (Taipei)
CNOOC	China National Off-shore Oil Corporation
CPPCC	Chinese People's Political Consultative Conference
EPZ	Export-Processing Zone
FYP	Five-Year Plan
GATT	General Agreement on Tariffs and Trade
GDP	Gross Domestic Product
GNP	Gross National Product
GVIAO	Gross Value of Industrial and Agricultural Output
GVIO	Gross Value of Industrial Output
JPRS	Joint Publications Research Services
LPG	liquified petroleum gas
NCNA	New China News Agency daily reports
NCNA(E)	New China News Agency daily reports, in English
NIC	Newly-Industrializing Country
NPC	National People's Congress
PLA	People's Liberation Army
PRC	People's Republic of China
RMB	Renminbi [Chinese People's Currency]
SEZ	Special Economic Zone
SINOPEC	China Petrochemical Corporation
SWB	*BBC Summary of World Broadcasts, Part III, The Far East.*
SWB-E	*BBC Summary of World Broadcasts, Part III, The Far East, Weekly Economic Supplement*

China: Province-level administrative divisions, Special Economic Zones, and fourteen open coastal cities (1984)

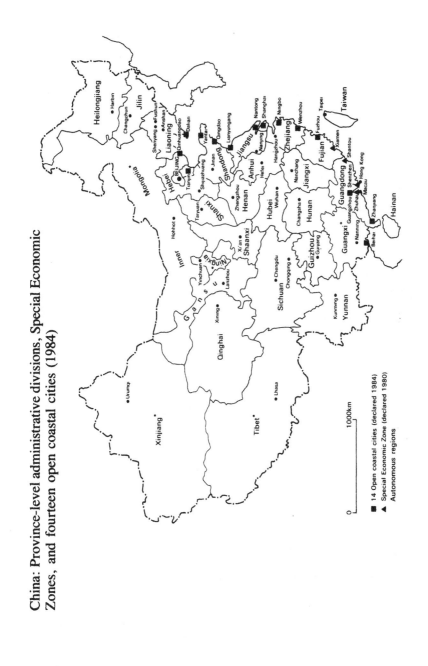

■ 14 Open coastal cities (declared 1984)
■ Special Economic Zone (declared 1980)
▲ Autonomous regions

The regional administrative hierarchy in the People's Republic of China

[Large administrative regions: formally in existence, 1949–54 and 1958–67]

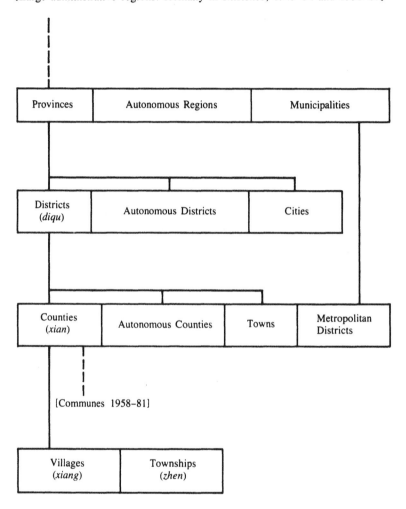

The title 'Autonomous' indicates that the area has a significant population of at least one minority nationality.

Chapter one

Introduction

Richard Kirkby and Terry Cannon

There is no nation on earth which can claim complete equity in the distribution of economic and social well-being throughout its territory. Regardless of political system and style, there is even considerable dispute about the virtues of encouraging a more equitable spread of income-earning opportunities. It is often argued that it is better to concentrate productive activities in the places where they seem most profitable, and then to redistribute the higher rate of surplus generated. These issues are currently a matter of some debate in China.

China has a population and a land mass of continental proportions — throughout recent centuries its population has been between one-quarter and one-fifth of the global total — yet at no time has more than a fraction of its present 9.6 million square kilometres of national territory ever been exploited for human needs. A central aim of the post-1949 Communist leadership has been to delineate the geographical bounds of a unified nation-state and to ensure its gradual consolidation. Thus for the first time in Chinese history the great wildernesses of the border regions to the west and north-east have been brought firmly into the ambit of national policy.

The PRC's precise objectives and means in pursuit of a regional policy, and the consequences, have been largely neglected by western scholars. For the most part, the regional dimension has been overlooked because of the particular absence of information, even by the standards of Chinese studies in general. During the Mao period, the regional impact of national policy was not usually writ large — indeed, a central objective was deliberately concealed. Only today is it becoming clear that for over three decades of the People's Republic, national security was a paramount criterion of all macro-level investment and population location policy. The data now coming to light, as discussed in detail later, suggest that Mao's vision of an appropriate peacetime polity for China after 1949 was dominated by war planning.

The innovations of the post-Mao era are breathtakingly bold. China is not the first socialist or centrally-planned economy to inaugurate a reform programme. But nowhere have changes been so sweeping and rapid, concerning so many people and so much territory. In the pantheon of Soviet-style 'socialist construction', China is the first nation to make a distinct break with those keystones of Stalinist planning — high accumulation, emphasis at all costs on heavy industry, and the primacy of productive over non-productive capital investment. Today, as in the past, the new economic strategies have definite intentions and implications in regional terms. The threads may be tangled, and frequently pulling in opposing directions, but at least they are now explicit in the pluralistic weave of policy.

The remarkable transformation of China today bears the heavy weight of the past; its ultimate success depends greatly on the extent to which the regime can capitalize on the huge and inchoate mass of inherited productive assets and infrastructure. In order to fulfil its present purposes of modernization and growth, the Beijing government must in particular learn how to integrate into its ambitious new plans the defence-related installations imposed at staggering costs by the Mao era on a geographically hostile hinterland. How the present rulers now utilize the military-industrial legacy of the 1960s and 1970s will be a key factor in the success of national economic development into the twenty-first century.

The physical setting

In comparison with the United States and Europe, a far higher proportion of China's territory is at high altitude. Chinese schools conveniently divide the country into five relief groupings (Map 1). First, some 20 per cent of the land consists of high mountain areas, with average elevation of 5,000 to 6,000 metres — forty peaks being over 7,000 metres. Areas of high plateau account for a further 20 per cent, with average height above sea level of between 1,000 and 2,000 metres. A further 15 per cent of territory is classified as mountains of middling range; and 10 per cent is described as hill country. The remaining 35 per cent of China's land area consists of basins, low plateaux and plains.[1]

Rainfall declines markedly from the south-east of the country to the north-west, accounting for the vast sweep of arid lands and sand desert of Xinjiang, Gansu and Inner Mongolia (Maps 2 and 3). The huge territories of Tibet and Qinghai also have little rainfall, and can be described as 'cold deserts'. Across the continent of China temperatures vary enormously, with winter conditions in the sub-tropical areas being mild and frost free, while in the north-east the Siberian influence keeps the average to $-30°C$. Soil, slope and rainfall conditions provide the constraining factors on cultivation even where mean seasonal temperatures are favourable.[2]

China's long history has seen most of the present-day national territory under imperial jurisdiction at some period or other. However, for the majority (Han) people, the Middle Kingdom has always been regarded as the lands bounded to the north and north-west by the Great Wall: within this northern limit are useful — and defensible — territories. Of the 65 per cent of the land classified as mountains, plateaux and hills, almost none of the first can be used for agriculture, while the plateau areas provide some limited poor pasture. Hilly areas are partially cultivable, depending on slope, soil and aspect. Of the 35 per cent designated as basins, low plateaux and plains, that in the west of the country is generally too arid to be of use. Unsurprisingly, although one-third of Europe is cropland, and even one-fifth of the United States, merely one-tenth of China is considered cultivable.

A glance at a physical map will reveal one further determining feature of China's development: the steps of relief descend from the west and north-west down to the east and south-east (Map 1). The vital importance of eastern China is reflected in the fondness of China's geographers for the Aihui-Tengchong (north-east to south-west) line — from Aihui *xian* in Heilongjiang to Tengchong *xian* in Yunnan (Map 7). To the left of the line are the great outer reaches, traditionally sparsely inhabited by the non-Han peoples and today including four of the five Autonomous Regions (Xinjiang, Tibet, Ningxia and Inner Mongolia: see chapter 10) as well as Qinghai and Gansu. Here is 60 per cent of China's territory, all the highest mountain chains and plateaux, the deepest basins and greatest deserts. Yet even after huge programmes of transmigration, this western belt accounts for a mere 6 per cent of China's population. To the right of the line there are many poor, remote upland areas; but essentially heartland, eastern China has all the great fertile river valleys and plains, a climate favourable to agriculture, and one thousand million people (see Map 4).[3]

Three further points are worth noting about the physical setting. First, although poor communications and technologies almost entirely prevented their exploitation before 1949, the great hinterland regions do hold enormous natural wealth: there are now known deposits of nearly every useful mineral. There are precious metals, forest and water resources, and significantly — in terms of Beijing's determination not to cede any of the border territories — uranium for China's nuclear defence, power and research sectors (Map 12). In short, with sufficient attention to communications and labour, to the west of the Aihui-Tengchong line there does exist great potential for major industrial development.

Second, despite the migration of millions from the Han east, the western regions are the traditional homelands of many of the minority peoples (see chapter 10). This has had a bearing on the military-strategic policies of the CCP since 1949, for there is not always an identity of interests between the various minority groups and Beijing.

Third, in the past the focus of foreign penetration and economic activity, such a crucial platform for contemporary development, was overwhelmingly eastern. This included the communications infrastructure, the new railways, and improved inland waterways essential to trade and exploitation of resources. By 1948 over 90 per cent of all modern sector industrial units, employment and motive power lay in just eight ex-Treaty ports.[4] A more telling measure of the overwhelming domination of the coastal provinces could hardly be required.

Regional policy in the Mao era

Although the CCP's main preoccupation in 1949 was how to deal with China's nascent urban industrial culture, the guerrilla heritage did provide the CCP with some ideas about development strategy which were pressed into service after the Liberation. The Long March described a great western arc, impelling the eastern revolutionaries deep into the interior. Eyes were opened to the potential both of the efficacy of the deep retreat stratagem, and of the rich natural resource base of their country. The red base areas of Jiangxi, and more particularly of Shaanxi, also impressed upon the party the necessities and virtues of regional self-reliance — not merely in food production, but also in simple industrial goods and war *matériel*.

The CCP's ascent to national power was preceded by an involuntary exile from the great cities and rich agricultural lands of coastal China. This exile thrust the Communist forces deep into the mountainous interior. The process of the revolution, therefore, had a mainly non-coastal (and rural) locus, leading to misinterpretation on the part of some foreign analysts regarding the ultimate purposes of the CCP. But although a native anti-urbanism (and thus anti-easternism) was always present, the party leaders never harboured any illusions about their ultimate goal: the rapid industrialization of the nation. In its pursuit they would build on the natural and man-made resources bequeathed to them by history, regardless of their regional disposition. Crucial in the minds of China's new rulers was not only the pace of industrial growth, but also the defence of the revolution against all challenges — principally external but also internal. These overall preoccupations and purposes have guided all national development policy since 1949, and underlain much of the often-violent intra-party struggle which has taken place.

The manifest unevenness in the distribution of China's productive forces and population has occasionally been discussed by the CCP in terms of the ideological objectives of socialist construction. But so have many others, when the real debate is about the practicalities of certain courses of action as against others. In the assessment of political or economic opportunities and constraints, the birth-marks inherited by the CCP have been a constant and major feature; a pragmatic sense of urgent need has therefore usually been the ultimate determinant of major policy.[5] It is true that at such times as the Great Leap Forward, the voluntarism of Mao Zedong was to the fore, and ideology was given a free rein. But taking the whole four decades of Communist party rule, such phases as the Great Leap Forward are aberrations. Pragmatism has been the guiding factor, despite the rhetorical and ideological gloss of the day.

As far as regional equity is concerned, it is possible to find the occasional official statement to the effect that uneven patterns of China's space economy are ideologically unacceptable to a socialist society. But never in the Mao period is the theme of regional equity *per se* elevated to a matter of principle and policy. What is evident is the fear on the part of practical decision-makers that these (inherited) patterns are irrational. If not handled with care, they may be dysfunctional in terms of the over-riding national, economic and strategic goals of the moment. At any conjuncture, the optimum regional policy is therefore that which most efficiently serves the grand ends of rapid industrialization coupled with the vigorous defence of China.[6]

Policies and consequences

No sooner had the Communist armies swept southwards and won nationwide power than, in the face of perceived foreign threats, leading voices within the party were sensing the need for another great tactical retreat. In late 1949 the new mayor of Shanghai saw his development programme for the great metropolis in these terms: 'We must evacuate the population of the city systematically and transfer factories to the interior wherever possible.'[7] While this proved quite impractical, the thrust of his concerns was echoed by the architect of China's First Five-Year Plan (FYP), 1953–7: 'Our present task in urban construction and hence industrialization is not to develop the large cities on the coast, but to develop medium and small cities in the interior.'[8] The efforts to concentrate new investment on the non-coastal provinces were integral to the all-important First FYP. Of the 700 backbone projects of the Plan, over two-thirds went to the non-coastal provinces. This included almost all the key projects built with direct Soviet assistance. All told, the First FYP despatched 58 per cent of China's total industrial investment to the non-coastal provinces: by its end, the civic leaders of coastal cities such as Shanghai or Guangzhou (Canton) had changed their tune, and were openly bemoaning the neglect in state investment.[9] In 1956 some adjustment was suggested by Mao in his *On the Ten Major Relationships*.[10]

None the less, the policy of directing the bulk of industrial investments to the inland regions was sustained throughout the following two decades of Mao's dominance over Chinese politics. In the Second and Third FYPs (1958–62, 1966–70) the level of the mid-1950s was either equalled or surpassed; only in the Fourth FYP (1971–5) was there a slight diminution. Whatever one's assessment of the Chinese development experience, this remarkable situation testifies at least to the effectiveness of Chinese central planning.

National development policy has been influenced by two broad sets of issues. The first is the CCP's perceptions of economic rationality. The second group revolves around the party's perception of national security needs. This latter has been far and away the most influential factor in Chinese regional policy since 1949.

The industrial revolution, pursued with relentless determination by all factions of the CCP, has required a huge supply of minerals and fossil fuel. For Mao as for Stalin, the rate of growth of national iron and steel output seemed at times the sole criterion by which socialist advance should be judged. From the First FYP on, a huge commitment was made to the construction of fully integrated iron and steel works, the training of technical expertise through the establishment of special institutes of iron and steel research, and to the organization of a huge bureaucracy concerned solely with the rapid expansion of that key sector. Much of the effort was put into developments in the coastal regions — for no modern socialist city could hold its head up high without its own steel-making facilities. This explains the huge plant in Beijing (Shougang) and in Nanjing (Meishan), both based on reasonably nearby supplies of iron ore, coal and limestone. In other coastal locations, especially Shanghai, supplies had to be brought in from some considerable distance. A number of giant works were also quickly established in the interior, both where substantial reserves of raw materials were available, and (for non-economic reasons which will be considered shortly) where they were not close at hand. In the former group are Wuhan in Hubei Province, Baotou (Inner Mongolia) and Panzhihua (Sichuan); in the latter, the provincial-owned plant at Lanzhou (Gansu Province), the Urumqi works in Xinjiang Autonomous Region and the Chengdu complex in Sichuan. It is striking that of the provincial capitals of the non-coastal provinces, by the mid-1960s all except Lhasa had its medium- or large-scale iron and steel works. None had existed on the eve of the First FYP, when China's total steel output was just 1.35 million tonnes (mt). (By 1978 it was over 30mt and a decade later that figure has almost doubled.)[11]

The petrochemical complex around the Daqing oilfield in the Siberian wastes of Heilongjiang epitomizes the policy of developing vital heavy industrial bases at the point of mineral extraction. Daqing has grown from nothing in the early 1960s to one of China's major urban agglomerations, now having a total population of three-quarters of a million.[12] The Guizhou coalfield, administratively centred on the new municipality of Liupanshui, is yet a further example; as is the rapidly growing nickel extraction complex of Jinchang in the wilds of Gansu province. There are many more such instances of the state not shirking from the huge investments required to open up mineral resources in remote desert or mountain regions.

Although agriculture (and the 'key link' of grain in particular) was just as crucial, the party judged that as long as growth in total output kept pace with the expansion of China's population, state intervention should be less in terms of investment and more in terms of the firm hand of bureaucratic direction. The aim was to ensure that, whether by material, moral or coercive inducements, the state procurement monopolies mobilized the maximum possible agricultural surplus. In the absence of external sources of development capital, the 'primitive socialist accumulation' process — as applied by the Soviet Union to finance its massive industrialization of the early 1930s — was adopted. As well as providing food and a ready source of labour for the burgeoning industrial centres, agriculture supplied a very high proportion of inputs for China's new industry (taking industry as a whole, perhaps 40 per cent by value; and for light industry, as much as 70 per cent).[13]

In so far as state intervention in agriculture had a regional connotation, it was most markedly through the efforts to transfer population and capital resources to the north-east, Inner Mongolia, Gansu and Xinjiang. *The National Programme for Agricultural Development* laid out ambitious plans to open up and settle 100 million *mu** of marginal land to extensive crop production and grazing.[14] Such grand targets were often stated during the Mao era. However, there was little to show for them, and those state farms established in such areas were generally miserable failures.

National security and the 'third line'

The second and more significant aspect of development during the Mao era — the perception of national security needs — had a powerful implication for regional policy. The remarks of leaders about de-urbanization and retreat to the interior cited earlier were not wilful dreaming for a return to the familiarities of the guerrilla warfare years. They were founded on a sense of acute isolation imposed by the western powers — led by the United States — after the Liberation of 1949. Throughout the 1950s, and to a lesser extent the 1960s, China considered itself in an undeclared state of war with the United States. The Korean

*See Glossary for this and other Chinese terms.

conflict, the Taiwan Straits crisis, the troubles in Tibet, and the border war with India, all fed this perception. The extreme de-urbanist and dispersionist proposals, including those of Mao himself (in 1960 he called for a 'complete evacuation' of the eastern cities)[15] were, of course, never implemented in China. Such experiments had to await the sub-Maoist Khmer Rouge's appearance. Yet China's industrial investment was determinedly and consistently steered away from the coastal regions during the more than two decades of Mao's dominance, and exploitation of the interior's natural resources was only a subsidiary aim.

The overriding objective of this policy was to furnish the interior provinces with their own basic industrial infrastructure in order that they might stand alone in the event of external attack or internal counter-revolution. To the Maoist leadership, the policy became even more imperative after 1960, when China was facing not one but two super-power enemies. From 1964 on, with the US involvement in Indo-China, and particularly after the border fighting of 1969 with the Soviet Union, the dispersal policies took prime place on the now secret agenda of China's development programme. The map of China was notionally divided into 'three lines' (*san xian*), or regions. The first of these was the vulnerable eastern seaboard, and the north and north-eastern border areas; the second, an intermediate or buffer belt; and the third line was the inaccessible redoubts of several interior provinces. After the 1969 Sino-Soviet conflict, the *san xian* policy was particularly emphasized, and the old slogan of the guerrilla warfare years — 'Disperse to the mountains and caves' — was the battle cry of a ferociously implemented mass campaign. Specifically, it was to dislodge large numbers of military-related research and production units from the north and north-east of the country and remove them — often lock, stock and barrel — to the 'Third Line'.

It is necessary at this point to describe the *san xian* effect in some detail, for it is a key factor in efforts to reform, reinvigorate, and reintegrate China's industrial economy during the 1980s and 1990s. At present, outsiders are still limited in their knowledge of the *san xian* phenomenon; the first references began to appear in official (and public) sources only in 1983, for instance, in the analysis of economic geographers.[16] When in mid-1987 a major front-page article on the subject appeared in the party newspaper, *People's Daily*, it was the signal to the Chinese that the tenets of Mao's military philosophy were to all intents and purposes dead and buried.[17] This article took the form of an interview conducted by journalists visiting the State Council *San Xian* Bureau, which is apparently still operating from Chengdu, provincial capital of Sichuan. According to other sources, the beginnings of the policy proper were in 1959–60, when Marshal Peng Dehuai was put in charge of *san xian* projects.[18] The final breakdown of relations with the Soviet Union occurred in 1963, and it is no coincidence that 1964 is the year when the *san xian* project is said to have taken on real momentum. A further upturn came in the early 1970s, following the clashes with Soviet troops on the north-east border. It is reasonable to assume that after Mao's death in 1976, the direction of resources towards the Third Line began to dwindle away.

Most remarkable in the 1987 revelations are the details of the staggering scale of the *san xian* commitment. Throughout the period of *san xian* it is claimed that 200 billion yuan RMB were put into military-related factories, research institutes, and transport infrastructure. This produced fixed capital assets of 140 billion yuan. The Cultural Revolution period (1966–76) accounted for 117 billion of the grand total;[19] to place this figure in context, aggregate state investment nationwide in capital construction throughout this same period was just 274 billion yuan RMB.[20]

It is no coincidence that Sichuan was chosen as the heart of the Third Line; it was precisely Sichuan to which huge numbers of factories and military enterprises were shifted from the eastern provinces in the face of the Japanese invasion of the late 1930s. But according to the new sources, the following provinces were also now targeted (in order of importance): Guizhou, Yunnan, Shaanxi, Gansu, as well as western Henan, western Hubei and western Hunan. In all, 29,000 state enterprises were built up throughout the region, with a huge work force of sixteen million. This latter figure constituted almost one-third of the total national state payroll in the mid-1960s, though both the number of units formally run by the military and their total employees are much smaller (160,000 and 1.07 million respectively — the latter figure of course excluding troops stationed in actual defence of the *san xian* installations).[21]

The great Panzhihua iron and steel works in the mountains on the Sichuan-Yunnan border region is a celebrated *san xian* project, subordinate to the Ministry of Metallurgical Industries rather than the military. Here, twenty-five years ago there was nothing, and now Panzhihua is China's fifth largest works, producing around two million tonnes per annum. Other examples are the large number of research institutes coming under the China Academy of Sciences, such as the Institute of Optics, which was forcibly removed from Changchun in the north-east to a small county seat in the hills of northern Sichuan.[22]

According to official accounts, the Third Line became a 'complete and self-sufficient industrial system' with a 'strong backbone of science and research'. *People's Daily* has listed the main sectors involved in the following order: the nuclear industry (very significant, connected to regional supplies of uranium); the metallurgical sector, especially iron and steel but also non-ferrous (for example, Guizhou's copper); aerospace and aviation (for example, the vital complex west of Xian); electronics; chemical engineering; and machine building.[23]

One vital aspect of the *san xian* programme was, in the absence of navigable waterways and long-distance highways, the securing of both internal and external communications. During the late 1960s, the fantastic construction feat of the Chengdu-Kunming railway was completed under Lin Piao's military jurisdiction. Other specifically *san xian* railways — many of them no less spectacular than the Chengdu-Kunming — were also built. The seven main routes include the Sichuan-Guizhou, Guizhou-Kunming and Hunan-Yunnan railroads — in all, no less than 5,000 kilometres of track (see chapter 5).

Evaluation of all those tremendous defensive works is just beginning to enter the public realm. The majority view is that, in the age of inter-continental missile warfare, it was a huge and unnecessary burden on the Chinese people — comparable to the worthless investment in the labyrinthine air-raid shelters and tunnels which are now crumbling away under every city of the coastal region. The mayor of Panzhihua recently described the steel-making projects there as representing a rare success in the Third Line policy.[24] What is certain today is that there cannot be any reverse movement: for better or worse, China is stuck with the great *san xian* system and all commentators agree that the main issue today is how to maximize use of past investments by reintegrating the *san xian* industrial and scientific infrastructure with the modernization programme of the 1980s and 1990s.

The legacy of the Mao era

Although during the Mao era regional policy was dominated by discussion of 'coastal' and 'interior' provinces, other regionalizations were used for a variety of purposes. Military regions (Map 5) were formed on the basis of provincial divisions: the main intention in their delineation was to enhance military-industrial autonomy in the event of hostilities (for instance, the Chengdu military region grouped Sichuan with a rear base area provided by Tibet). In addition, there were six administrative regions first utilized in the central planning of the 1950s (Map 6). After 1958 the six regions became little more than a convenience for statistical tabulation.

As already indicated, the most significant element in regional policy from the early 1950s right through to the mid-1970s was the consideration of defence, the distinctive regionalism of the *san xian* base being its most prominent feature. Overall analysis of the regional consequences of policy have been attempted on the basis of the available data.[25] This shows that central direction, particularly in terms of non-agricultural capital construction, has somewhat shifted the relative distribution of

10

productive forces, population (and urban population in particular) to the interior provinces. However, the share of the huge and far-flung border provinces of the west and north-west has hardly increased, though there have been very significant increases in relative terms because of the low base points.

For the purpose of present analysis it is important to consider some of the organizational problems left over from the Mao period which now present a barrier to the modernization of China's economy. A key constraint is the over-verticality of the administrative and industrial system which is itself a fusion of traditional Chinese patterns and the Soviet planning system adopted in the 1950s. The conflict between 'lines' (*tiao tiao*) and 'areas' (*kuai kuai*) — the exercise of vertical authority within a single bureaucracy, as opposed to horizontal co-ordination across several — is not new: indeed, it was identified by Mao as one of the malformations which the Cultural Revolution was supposed to erase. But, conversely, it was precisely Mao's overweening emphasis on self-sufficiency in general, and regional self-enclosedness (for defence and food supply in a situation of poor communications), that produced the many distortions which still confront the reforming, post-1978 regime. In industrial affairs, the Mao policy of 'small but complete', namely, self-sufficiency even within a small subregion, has been a target of widespread criticism. But changing matters in an entrenched bureaucracy is not simple, despite China's news media of the early 1980s repeatedly parading the more ludicrous cases. One such concerns two adjacent plants, the first producing a huge excess of oxygen as a by-product, but blowing it off into the atmosphere, and its neighbour requiring oxygen, but because it came under a different (bureaucratically vertical) order, there was no way that the two enterprises could co-operate. Or take the case of Hongjiang, a township in Hunan province: here, the local leaders attempted to construct an integrated iron and steel plant. This having failed for lack of raw materials, they then decided on that other symbol of modernity — motor production. Two vehicles were finally assembled after a year's heroic effort, but unfortunately the front wheels fell off as they emerged from the end of the production line.[26]

In fact, the iron and steel industry typifies these kinds of problems. As the 1985 World Bank study shows, its dispersed development went a lot further than providing almost every provincial capital with a plant. Briefly, China now has almost 2,000 state and collective enterprises in that sector, from tiny works producing only 5,000 tonnes per annum to the giant plants like that at Anshan, with over 7 million tonnes. Not surprisingly, the measured cost of production also varies enormously — from around 140 yuan RMB per tonne for the large works to more than 300 yuan for the small ones. As indicated earlier, much of the reasoning behind the steel industry's structure and location was economically logical — utilization of heavy and untransportable local supplies. But the obsessive concern with steel as the 'key link' in nation-building for the quasi-war economy of Maoist planning meant that an outdated military rationale was the governing factor. Many new medium-sized or even large iron and steel plants were, consequently, located at great distances from their source of supplies and from their markets.[27]

The implications of modernization

The Chinese leadership has today accepted quite a large measure of conventional wisdom of the World Bank type regarding the structure and organization of a modern industrial nation. A number of factors, most of them having an implication for regional policy, are called for. Modernization demands a high level of regional specialization, a recognition in policy of inter-factory and inter-regional comparative advantage (economies of scale and linkage). Competition immediately becomes an indispensable flux which must flow throughout all levels of the system.

The same general principles apply to human resources: the labour market (for a variety of purposes stringently controlled during the previous era) must be freed. That requires greater specialization in terms of skills, and a geographical mobility of the labour force. On the international front, modernization requires an integration with the dominant world economy — principally with the capitalist world but also with the other centrally planned economies. Of course, since 1978 China's linkage with the world economy has been transformed, and the scale of foreign trade in proportion to GDP is now comparable with that of many other countries. As indicated in chapters 4 and 7, the 'open door' policy has a very powerful regional impact; that is largely by design, but its tendency to overconcentrate modern-sector investment in the eastern coastal belt is beginning to raise some disquiet among politicians and planners. Many measures of current economic reform hold within them forces which are both 'agglomerative' and 'dispersing', and the implication in terms of the future balance of the regional economic map is as yet unclear. It is obvious that the greatest brake on a radical transformation of the country's economy lies in the physical impediments of China's geography. Clearly, it is only the organizational barriers that are susceptible to direct action, and upon these the CCP seems determined to mount an all-out assault.

The inauguration of four Special Economic Zones (SEZs) during the late 1970s (chapter 7) represents the first efforts to establish new 'horizontal' arrangements in the Chinese economy. Subsequently, fourteen other coastal cities were granted similar special status. 1983 saw the establishment of the super-region of the Shanghai Economic Zone, initially incorporating 74,000 square kilometres with ten cities — an area contributing over 20 per cent of China's gross industrial output (see Map 10). In 1988, a new SEZ was created for Hainan Island.

Numerous other amalgamations have been formally announced, covering large swathes of the coastal and inland regions; very few of them involve the peripheral provinces. The new zones in the coastal area are intended primarily to serve as technological centres of expertise, building on their direct export potential. On the other hand, new regional organizations have been established in order to strengthen key areas of the economy such as the metallurgical sector (the massive region led from the city of Chongqing in Sichuan), and the energy sector. The outstanding example here is the Shanxi (north west) Energy Base, approved in late 1982 (Map 10). This regional grouping — covering large parts of neighbouring provinces — contains 60 per cent of China's proven coal reserves and currently produces about half of the nation's total coal. A major external component is also present in the development of the Shanxi (north-west) Energy Base. Today oil provides around one-fifth of China's export earnings (chapter 6). The significant foreign investment put into coal extraction and surface movement within Shanxi, and the new rail link to the coast some 700 kilometres distant which is specifically to assist the supply of coal to Japan and other customers, indicate current thinking about the future importance of coal. These matters are discussed in detail in chapters 5 and 8.

A further effort of the early 1980s aimed at promoting comparative regional advantage lay in the measures to develop metropolitan growth poles — the twin concepts of the 'central city' and the 'economic centre' (chapter 2). Partly to facilitate these two growth-pole concepts, the central authorities forced through an almost complete dismantling of the traditional prefectural (*diqu*) administrative divisions of provinces, strengthening the polarity of those cities which had already annexed counties, and giving a new hinterland base to many more that had not previously been permitted to take over rural counties. Understandably, at this time it was Shanghai with its huge share of the nation's industry, and its excellence measured by return on capital, which was promoted as the national model.[28]

As noted earlier, many of the new regional arrangements announced in the early 1980s appeared to be piecemeal. They did not swiftly lead — in the case of the SEZs in particular — to the desired economic outcomes. The SEZs fell short of central government's high-tech, export-oriented intentions, providing instead greater linkage between the inland and the coastal regions, for much of the SEZs' marketing relations were (and remain), 'inward-looking'. This was of course an unintended outcome. Some coherence began to emerge in 1986, with the details of the Seventh FYP.

The Seventh Five-Year Plan

The *ad hoc* regional groupings created during the early reform period lacked any sense of a central, strategic master-plan connecting the overall economic objectives (mainly articulated in terms of increases in output, sector by sector) with the regional means of achieving those objectives. This deficiency was identified relatively early by Zhao Ziyang — then China's Premier, and now party general secretary. The result was the first real effort ever in the five-year planning process to specify clearly the regional ramifications of projected economic advance.

The Sixth FYP (1981–5) had seen many novel arrangements linking the production and marketing spheres both among and within regions. For example, the record shows that 66,000 contracts of association were signed between enterprises in different sectors and regions over the five-year period.[29] From 1983 on, the key slogan of the new 'anti-vertical' trend became 'horizontal linkage'. This sums up the government's determination to 'break through' organizational and regional barriers — a direct assault on the legacy of self-sufficiency at all costs and all levels of the organizational and regional hierarchy.

The key decisions on structural and regional reform were taken at the Third Plenum of the Twelfth Central Committee in October 1984 (*The Decision on Reform of the Economic Structure*). In March 1986, the First National Conference on Urban Economic Reform developed the political and theoretical basis for the new policy thrust. Here, Zhao Ziyang characterized the entrenched barriers between departments and regions as the 'main obstacle to the development of China's socialist commodity economy'. Shortly afterwards, the Sixth National People's Congress convened, and the details of the already current Seventh FYP (1986–90) were laid out. The Plan considers the Chinese economy in terms of Eastern, Western and Central regions. These differ somewhat from earlier tripartite divisions (Maps 8 and 9).[30]

The Eastern Region covers eleven provincial-level units having direct access to the coast, with a population of some 400 million. Its role will be to focus on technological modernization of traditional industries and technical improvement to existing plant, relying where necessary on imported equipment and expertise. The Eastern Region should also develop production of new high-tech and quality consumer goods both for domestic use and for sale on the world market. The region should build upon the foundations offered by the SEZs, the fourteen special coastal cities, and the various other 'open areas' (in 1986 there were three). It should also train large numbers of personnel in modern production and management techniques, with a view to serving other parts of the country as well as the Eastern Region itself.

The Central Region has eight provinces and the autonomous region of Inner Mongolia. It accounts for 370 million Chinese. Its particular function in the Seventh FYP is to accelerate the development of energy resources — oil and electricity (mainly hydroelectric power as well as coal). The Central Region should also concentrate on the development of non-ferrous metals, building materials and other appropriate mineral extraction and processing.

The Western Region embraces nine provincial-level units, including three of China's five autonomous regions. It should be noted that of these nine, only Sichuan is today relatively well-developed in agriculture and industry. The Western Region accounts for about 230 million people — and at 5.3 million square kilometres its area is half as large again as the other two regions combined. Its assigned purpose in the Seventh Plan is to concentrate on expanding agriculture, forestry, animal husbandry (on its extensive pasture land) and transportation. Where there is a national need the Western Region should also develop energy and mineral resources. It should not try to develop modern consumer goods production much beyond what serves local needs and (ethnic minority) tastes.

Three further elements of the regional dimensions of the Seventh FYP deserve highlighting. First, the question of links: the objective of 'horizontal linkage' is a far more extensive and complex interrelation of enterprises across the three main regions. The impulse is to come mainly, but not entirely, from the richer, more technologically advanced areas of the east. To enable this, transportation and communications must be greatly improved (chapter 5). Moreover, the plethora of regional groupings which emerged haphazardly after 1978 must itself be rationalized, in order to accelerate co-operation and integration on the national scale.

In this context, three specific 'networks' are mentioned in the Plan (see Map 10 for an indication). There is to be a national network, including the Shanghai Economic Zone, the North-eastern Economic Zone, the Shanxi (north-west) Energy Base, the Beijing-Tianjin-Tangshan Zone and the great South-western Zone, which includes Guizhou, Yunnan, Sichuan, Guangxi and the leading centre of Chongqing. A second network is of smaller economic zones linking provincial capitals, designated ports and cities along vital communication lines such as the Yangtze cities, or the vital railway from the coast to Urumqi in the north-west (soon to be extended to the Soviet Union). The 'central cities' with their annexed counties, coming under the respective provincial governments are regarded as a third network. In almost every province the administrative changes have now been completed to encourage this level of economic region to develop. Within each level or type of those three associations, there are many smaller transverse geographical and administrative arrangements already in place (at least on paper), and more are to be entertained in the future.

Second, since the publication of the Seventh FYP, party and state leaders have demonstrated their further determination to strengthen the eastern, coastal belt as a base of technological excellence. The concept of horizontal linkage is seen not only to extend the ties between coastal, interior and border enterprises; there should also be a second 'fanning out' from the coastal belt — towards the world market. To this end, the Seventh National People's Congress (NPC) in April 1988 announced the creation of China's first new province for over twenty years: the South China Sea island of Hainan. The object is to create an export-oriented zone open to the world. Even more significantly, the NPC announced the decision to open up the entire coastal belt (320,000 square kilometres with a population of 160 million) as a super special economic zone.[31] Additionally, it should be noted (as discussed in chapter 4) that the coastal belt is obviously going to benefit even further in the future from Overseas Chinese connections and capital inflow.

The third important feature of the Seventh FYP is its explicit discussion of, and recommendations regarding, the great *san xian* region (discussed in the Plan's chapter 20, part 3). The Plan calls for a fundamental reorganization of the *san xian* enterprises, both in their internal workings and in their linkage within and outside the region. One hundred major enterprises are earmarked for thorough revamping, and there must be many mergers and closures. A recurring theme in the CCP's self-advertisements of recent years has been the peaceful intent of China in the world. This is evidenced, it is claimed, by the reduction in the armed forces of one million. It is also seen in the 'civilianization' of numerous military-dominated industries.[32] Missile plants are now turning out wash-basins and motor-bikes for the masses, and even the air force is playing its part by using its planes to enter into competition for civil services with the flagging state carrier, CAAC. Such propaganda is merely the visible tip of a sharp struggle going on within the leadership, and with army chiefs, over the need to mobilize the massive *san xian* industry, infrastructure and scientific resources in the service of China's modernization drive.

Finally, the beginning of this chapter gave consideration to the ideological preconceptions of the CCP in dealing with the regional question. The conclusion was that, notwithstanding the rhetoric about concerns of spatial equity, the physical, historical and security constraints facing the People's Republic have always been paramount. It has been argued elsewhere that China's greatest (spatial) divide — that between town and country — not only survived Mao, but was necessary to his programme of industrialization.[33] Ironically, it has been the post-Mao leaders (in the past considered to have the least interest in the plight of the rural population) who have done most for the countryside. In the past decade, agricultural procurement prices have been markedly increased, and the peasants have been allowed to enrich themselves in numerous ways, not least through the vast system of rural non-agricultural enterprises fostered by the government in the 1980s.

A further new departure which benefits agriculture in general, and poor rural areas (most but not all of which are in the interior and border regions) in particular, is the open acknowledgement of rural poverty as a serious issue. Almost daily there is news in the Chinese press of meetings, schemes for rural poverty abatement, the signing of loans to poor counties, and so on. Currently, backward rural regions are receiving substantial material assistance through a number of state programmes; many of these rely on loans from the UN World Food Programme, the International Development Association (IDA) and the Asian Development Bank (ADB). Many such loans are tied to agriculture, but others are not, and the fact that the Chinese authorities direct them to remote areas is therefore all the more significant.[34]

China's currently emerging pattern of regional and trans-regional organizations presents a confused picture. But the Chinese economy — and, on the evidence of the recent party and state congresses of 1988, the country's politics too — is becoming more mature. The new regional dimensions of the present reform period reflect that maturity, confusing and sometimes contradictory though the picture may be. The appearance of new spatial arrangements of the Chinese economy is long overdue and, in an age in which the location of productive activities is no longer crucial to national defence, a much-altered economic map of China can be expected by the year 2000. The thrust of present policy is to allow some people to reap the benefits of economic reform before others. Current plans suggest that this principle is to be applied to China's regions, and it is therefore likely that regional differentials in economic growth will, in the medium term at least, become more pronounced.

Notes

1 For a good account of China's physical make-up and constraints, see Cole, J.P. (1985) *China 1950–2000: Performance and Prospects*, University of Nottingham, mimeo, chapter 3.

2 Leeming, F. (1985) *Rural China Today*, Harlow: Longman, chapters 2 and 8.

3 Kirkby, R.J.R. (1985) *Urbanisation in China: Town and Country in a Developing Economy, 1949–2000 AD*, London: Croom Helm, and New York: Columbia University Press, pp. 135, 260.

4 Paine, S. (1981) 'Spatial Aspects of Chinese Development: Issues, Outcomes and Policies, 1949–1979, *Journal of Development Studies*, vol. 17 (January), p. 150.

5 See Marx's (1875) *Critique of the Gotha Programme* in, for example, K. Marx (1974) ed. D. Fernbach *The First International and After* (Harmondsworth: Penguin).

6 For an interesting (and pragmatic) discussion of the regional question in socialism, see Zhu Zhuo (1980) *Renkou yu jingji (Population and Economics)*, no. 3, pp. 16–17.

7 Cited by Salaff, J. (1967) 'The Urban Communes and Anti-City Experiments in Communist China', *China Quarterly*, no. 27, pp. 83–4.

8 Li Fuchun, cited by Lin, C. (1971–2) *Urbanization and Economic Development in Communist China*, Independent Research Paper, Massachusetts Institute of Technology, p. 23.

9 Kirkby, *Urbanisation in China*, op. cit., pp. 136–40.

10 *Selected Works of Mao Tse-tung*, vol. 5 (1977), Beijing: Foreign Languages Press, pp. 284–307.

11 *Tongji nianjian* (1983) p. 245.

12 According to the *Tongji nianjian* of 1985 (p. 86), the non-agricultural population of Daqing was already over 0.5 million.

13 This was an oft-remarked evaluation of Chinese economists in the late 1970s.

14 *National Programme for Agricultural Development, 1956–67* (1960) Beijing: Foreign Languages Press, p. 16.

15 Cited by Friedman, E. (1979) 'On Maoist Conceptualizations of the Capitalist World System', *China Quarterly*, no. 80 (December) note 35, p. 826.

16 Xu Xueqiang *et al*, (1983) *Jingji dili (Economic Geography)*, no. 3, pp. 205–12.

17 *People's Daily*, 8 June 1987.

18 It is surprising that Peng Dehuai was given this task, as his bitter dispute with Mao of 1959 had deprived him of his position as Minister of Defence. The great Mao slogan of the time was 'Prepare for war, prepare for natural disasters, and do everything for the people'.

19 Li Wenyan (1987) *Changing Industrial Allocation and Industrial Management in the People's Republic of China*, Paper presented at conference 'Urban and Regional Development in Britain and China', University of Manchester, 26–28 November, pp. 3–4.

20 *Tongji nianjian*, 1986, p. 370.

21 In 1979 one of the authors travelled the Chengdu-Kunming railway. Every bridge and tunnel was still heavily guarded by the PLA and local militia.

22 Private source.

23 *People's Daily*, 8 June 1987.

24 'A Whiff of Prosperity comes to Mao's "Third Line"', *The Guardian*, 29 September 1987.

25 For example, Kirkby, *Urbanisation in China*, op. cit., chapter 5.

26 Ibid., p. 156; further discussion of the question of regional linkages and tensions is to be found in chapters 2 and 7.

27 World Bank (1985) *China: Long Term Development Issues and Options*, Baltimore: The Johns Hopkins University Press, p. 80.

28 *Ta Kung Pao*, 23 April 1981.

29 The Seventh FYP's regional elements are well summarized in 'New Ways for the Regional Economy', *China News Analysis*, no. 1311,

1 June 1986. The following discussion draws on this account.

30 *Beijing Review*, vol. 31, nos 17 and 18, 25 April and 2 May 1988.

31 'Five-year plan draft sets goals for regions', *China Daily*, 31 March 1986.

32 This trend is countered by another. China's current emphasis on the export of manufactured goods has led in recent years to an enormous expansion in the supply of arms to Third World nations — highlighted by the reported supply of the Silkworm missiles to Iran. China is now among the world's leading arms exporters, and the Third Line plants are doubtless playing a vital role.

33 Kirkby, *Urbanisation in China*, op. cit., chapters 1 and 2.

34 An excellent analysis of rural poverty issues is to be found in the World Bank report, *China: Long Term Development Issues and Options* (Baltimore: The Johns Hopkins University Press, 1985), chapter 5. The Party Central Committee and the State Council issued a directive in October 1984 'calling on the whole nation to help change the outlook of poverty-stricken areas as soon as possible'. See also 'Shandong helps its poor areas', *Beijing Review*, no. 48, 1 December 1986, pp. 21–4.

Chapter two

Political perspectives
David S.G. Goodman

An essential part of the CCP's drive to modernization in the PRC during the 1980s has been the pursuit of regionalization. Regionalization in this context does not necessarily entail any specific kind of administrative region as, for example, the PRC's provincial or county levels, or its special economic or development zones. Indeed, it could refer to any or all. Rather, regionalization refers to the development of the economy through co-operation, exchange and the operation of market forces in localized economies. This process is described as regionalization because of the emphasis on spatial development, but equally important is the condition that economic management should be based on economic and not administrative or political grounds. The development of localized economies is often seen as resulting from what are described as 'horizontal relationships'. This term has been used to emphasize the interaction of market forces and economic decision-making for economic reasons, as opposed to the operation of administrative fiat in the vertically organized environment of a command economy.

The concern with regionalization, then, is an essentially middle-range preoccupation. Various administrative measures have been taken during the 1980s to assist that process, including, in particular, the almost wholesale introduction of decentralization; the development of economic management structures separate from the state administration's hierarchy; and the encouragement of urbanization, especially of small and medium-sized towns and cities as the centres of localized economies. However, the political consequences of these measures are far from clear. Two fundamental sets of questions confront anyone interested in the PRC's future regional development. One is the potential impact of regionalization on local autonomy. At first sight it seems possible that the decentralization and incipient pluralism of the 1980s could result in a challenge to Beijing as the centre of China's political system, as well as to the power of the CCP. The other is the impact of the current political and administrative infrastructure on future regionalization. New patterns of economic and bureaucratic interaction are promised, but all the proposed changes must meet the challenge of entrenched bureaucratic interests and practices that have developed since at least 1949.

Decentralization and regionalization

Decentralization and regionalization have been constant and explicit goals in the pursuit of economic modernization since the Third Plenum of the Eleventh Central Committee of the CCP in December 1978. Decentralization has been used to refer to two distinct processes. The first is the delegation of management powers in the administration of economic activities from a superior to a subordinate level within the state administration's hierarchy. The recent decision of the Ministry of Communications to place the management of all ports (except Qinhuangdao) that were formerly under its direct management under the jurisdiction of the respective local authorities by the end of 1988 is a clear example.[1]

However, decentralization since 1978 has also implied the exercise of greater autonomy for each enterprise, even within the local authority. Regionalization is in many ways the corollary of greater enterprise autonomy. A major part of the current economic reforms amounts to the replacement of bureaucratic command as the determinant of economic activity by market forces, and an understanding of economic rationality. Enterprises are thus, in general, being encouraged to move away from the previously hierarchically organized channels of command (associated with the mechanisms of the command economy and 'the plan') towards co-operation within their economically determined regions.

The need for decentralization and regionalization as an antidote to the systemic faults of the command economy were clearly articulated in the PRC during the mid-1950s, when the leadership of the CCP decided to abandon its attempts to adopt a Soviet model for development. However, the ascendancy of Mao Zedong and political radicalism in 1957 denied the validity of such measures until 1976. A form of decentralization that effectively centralized economic management at the provincial level was adopted. Despite the re-emergence of six supra-provincial CCP regions during the early 1960s (Map 6), local 'self-reliance' rather than regionalization was the order of the day. Shortly after Mao's death, and even before the Third Plenum of 1978, it became clear that significant sections of the CCP's leadership were turning back to earlier remedies. At the National Conference for Learning from Daqing in Industry, held in May 1977, Yu Qiuli discussed the creation of 'economic regional systems', a view which was later elaborated in a report from the State Planning Commission.[2]

Decentralization was seen as desirable in the PRC, not simply because it had in some sense been a command economy, but also because of its size — in territorial as well as human terms. Overcentralization led to inefficiencies, not only because of bureaucratization, but also in the promotion of policies which were inapplicable or inappropriate to all local conditions. One spectacular example from the Great Leap Forward may be cited. At that time, under Mao's encouragement, 'deep ploughing' was promoted as a national good. In Guizhou the ability to extend the area of 'deep ploughing' was publicized as a major advantage of com-munization, particularly in the mountain areas. Guizhou has very little arable land, is generally very hilly, and has a very shallow topsoil. It goes without saying that the results were disastrous and unpopular.[3]

On the other hand, the introduction of decentralization is not without its problems. Too much local autonomy may challenge the authority of the CCP and lead to a constant drift away from the goals set by central government. This, of course, was precisely the accusation levelled at Mao's opponents during the Cultural Revolution. However, it is not a concern that disappeared with the Cultural Revolution, or that has been ignored in the current drive to decentralize. For example, the People's Bank of China complained recently that provincial-level local authorities were not fulfilling their obligation to purchase state construction bonds: 'The cold response by localities to the subscriptions of state bonds was attributed by the spokesman [for the People's Bank] to their departmental selfishness'.[4]

A similar problem of uncontrollability confronts the CCP in its desire to increase enterprise autonomy. If the rationale for decentralizing (and maximizing) enterprise management is economic, then there should be little surprise if the enterprise produces a profit without regard to the social good. None the less, there have been almost constant complaints during the past five years — not always without justification — that innovative or enterprising managers have engaged in 'economic crimes'. The corollary, as one conservative critic of the current decentralization measures put it, is that corrupt officials or managers can simply claim to be reformers.[5]

Regionalization is necessarily entailed by a programme of decentraliza-tion, for without it the latter cannot work efficiently. It too faces the CCP with problems of control, not least because the regions in question are economically determined and not the result of political or administrative decision. None the less, if any new pattern of economic regionalization is to be effective, it must come to terms with two fundamental aspects of the administrative hierarchy through which the CCP works. The first is that the PRC's administrative hierarchy is not, for the most part, a twentieth-century, let alone a post-1949 creation. On the contrary, the boundaries of its administrative divisions — in particular its counties and provinces — are historically determined. They result from repeated social interaction that was established well before modernization, and are likely to describe a local economy, communications network and political culture. Second, the PRC's largely pre-modern hierarchy of administrative-territorial units has, since 1949, been staffed by cadres who have developed their own administrative style and political skills based on that hierarchy. All these factors may, of course, facilitate regionalization under many circumstances. However, where the boundaries of new economic interaction conflict with current administrative divisions or practice, there is likely to be a contradiction between the political and the economic imperatives of the old and new orders respectively, at least in the short term.

Economic management and urbanization[6]

Apart from financial reforms and in addition to decentralization, there have been two fundamental administrative reforms during the 1980s designed to encourage the PRC's regional development. One has been an increasing differentiation between the structures of economic management and the state administrative hierarchy; the other has been urban-centred regionalization. (Financial reforms are discussed in chapter 3.)

A major reform has been the separation of economic management from the state administration. This has been not a complete divorce but rather a recognition that not all economic activity need be managed through the state administration, as was overwhelmingly the case before 1978. The state administration is now seen to have other important functions to execute, not the least of which is the regulation of economic activity; economic management particularly at county and village levels has passed out of the hands of local government and into the hands of the enterprises themselves. This reform is important, not least if regionalization is to develop outside the influence of the state administrative hierarchy, which defined the territorial boundaries of economic activity from 1949 until the 1980s.

Starting in late 1985, each province has established an experimental county to implement decentralization and the separation of economic management from state administration on a trial basis. For example, in Shandong the experimental county has been Laiwu. Subordinate to the county-level is the township-level, and subordinate to that in turn is the village-level. In Laiwu the powers of seventeen of the former twenty-two bureaux and departments of the county people's government have been devolved to village level with the county no longer exercising any direct routine leadership. At the same time no township or village government is directly responsible for economic management any longer. The county exercises regulatory powers over both enterprises and subordinate townships and villages, and this is reflected in the five county-level departments which were not decentralized. These were the county bank, and the departments of the county people's government concerned with public security, taxation, industrial and economic management, and prices.

At the basic level, individual enterprises have been encouraged to establish 'horizontal relationships'. Rather than depending on the state administration for investment, raw material supply and distribution of the finished product, factories, businesses, and other economic concerns, are directed to the market-place in terms of 'mutual co-operation'. The intention is that enterprises should make their supply, production, and distribution decisions on the basis of economic rationality and not simply administrative convenience.

From a wider perspective, the central government has positively encouraged several economic development zones — such as those of the Pearl River Delta, the Lower Yangtze, and the Bohai Rim — that cross provincial boundaries. In this case the intention is once again that economic co-operation will emerge separately from the hierarchy of the state administration, but the emphasis is on co-operation over relatively large areas in the more developed parts of the country. In addition, co-operation within these zones is meant to extend to the development of their economic infrastructure, particularly for transport and communications. The Bohai Rim Co-operation Area, for example, includes fifteen cities and districts (*diqu*) in the provinces of Liaoning, Hebei and Shandong, as well as the Tianjin metropolitan area. Some 258 agreements were reached between enterprises in the Co-operation Area during the first fifteen months of its operation.[7]

A further significant consequence of this reform has been the designation of several large metropolitan areas (Chongqing in 1983; Guangzhou, Shenyang, Harbin, Xian, Dalian (Luda) and Wuhan in 1984; Qingdao in 1985; and Ningbo in 1986) as in effect economic provinces — directly subordinate to the centre for all economic affairs. In budgetary terms these metropolitan areas are treated like other provincial-level units. They each have an agreement with the centre that stipulates the levels of tax in their area, the ratio of dispersal of revenue from the metropolitan area to the centre, and the period the agreement will be in operation — some are for three years, others for five. These cities are described as being at the 'semi-provincial level' (*fushengji*). Although economically independent, in political matters they are subordinate to the provincial committee of the CCP.

The potential for confusion and difficulties resulting from this functional duality are great. There have been some interesting political consequences, particularly where individuals and organizations within the new metropolitan-area economic provinces (but not necessarily concerned with economic affairs) have demanded general parity of status with the full provincial level. For example, the mayor of Ningbo would previously have ranked at the same level as the director of a department in the

Zhejiang Provincial People's Government but, after Ningbo's redesignation, could reasonably have claimed to be graded as governor of the province. In the event, the compromise solution was that this position was now to be regraded as the equivalent of a vice-governor of Zhejiang. This is a pattern which has been repeated in all nine cities, with a series of wholesale promotions raising individuals on average about two grades.

Promotions are clearly significant in personal terms; however, the creation of economic provinces has even more significant resource implications, since organizations within redesignated metropolitan areas may find themselves in the position (or claim the right) to participate at a higher level in the political hierarchy. Thus, to take an academic example, through the redesignation of Wuhan the local Academy of Social Sciences finds itself able to operate alongside provincial academies. Needless to say, these changes have hardly been welcomed by the already established provincial-level units.

Table 2.1 Number of cities and towns at different levels of the administrative hierarchy in the PRC, 1949–85

Year	Districts (diqu)	Counties (xian)	District-level cities	County-level towns	Total urban administrative units
1949	215	2,180	55	68	123
1976	211	2,136	86	99	185
1977	214	2,152	97	90	187
1978	210	2,138	101	89	190
1979	209	2,137	103	110	213
1983	178	2,080	144	142	286
1985	165	2,046	162	159	321

Sources: Data for 1949, 1977, 1983 and 1985 from *Administrative Handbook of the People's Republic of China* (*Zhonghua renmin gongheguo xingzhengquhua shouce*) (Guangming ribao chubanshe: Beijing, 1986); and for 1976, 1978 and 1979 from the annual publication *Guidebook to the Administrative Divisions of the People's Republic of China* (Zhonghua renmin gongheguo xingzhengquhua jiance) (Ditu chubanshe: Beijing, 1977, 1979 and 1980 respectively).

The special treatment of nine metropolitan areas as economic provinces, designed to encourage regionalized growth, highlights the second characteristic structural reform of the 1980s — the importance of urbanization. Regional development is to be based on urban centres, not only at the provincial level, but at all levels of the administrative hierarchy. One notable reform to have been introduced almost totally throughout Jiangsu, and partially in Liaoning since 1982, has been the introduction of the 'city district'. These have replaced districts (*diqu*) in the administrative hierarchy above the county, but below the province.

In those areas counties are now subordinate to the new 'city districts'. Although such a radical measure has on the whole not been followed elsewhere, there has been a general growth and upgrading of cities and towns in the administrative hierarchy, as Table 2.1 demonstrates.

Since the 1982 census the PRC has in fact calculated its urban population on a different basis from before that date. The result is that it is now claimed officially that about 40 per cent of the PRC's population is urban, as compared to approximately 18 per cent before 1982. Though some urbanization has undoubtedly taken place, these figures exaggerate the change. Most of the population still live where they did before 1982; it is the designation and boundaries of towns which have grown. None the less, the change in presentation and of emphasis is significant. Urban areas are now seen as the centres of the new localized economies.

Local autonomy

For a number of reasons, both political and economic, it seems possible that regionalization could contribute to an increase in local autonomy at the expense of central government. Both Chinese and western commentators, recognizing the strength of local cultures and communities, have highlighted the potential centrifugal consequences of regionalism, decentralization, and emphasis on the role of local government. Certainly, regionalism — as a political identification — is an inherent part of Chinese political culture. Individuals identify strongly with localities, particularly counties and provinces. Third- or fourth-generation Chinese in Hong Kong, Taiwan or the USA will still talk about counties in the PRC as their 'native place'. Even the CCP was largely a federal organization of regional branches for the first four years of its existence.[8] As a result, the establishment of a centralized polity immediately after 1949, and the CCP's apparent ability to permeate and control society, are often regarded as among its most remarkable and significant achievements.

However, regionalism — in the sense of a political identification with the region — clearly could and has been utilized as an integrative device rather than as a symbol of parochialism. In the early years after the establishment of the PRC, when the CCP's consolidation of power was its main concern, regionalism was positively fostered. Nation-building and political reintegration were seen as a two-stage process. First, there was local reintegration; then the localities were reintegrated into the national whole.

Moreover, local government is not necessarily an instrument for the expression of local autonomy. On the contrary, regional bodies — particularly for regions that transcend the more traditional provinces and counties — have rarely been designed or acted as instruments for the articulation of regional interests. For example, in three separate periods of the PRC (1949–54, 1958–66, and 1976–8) a supra-provincial regional administrative framework was established. Solinger has convincingly argued that on each occasion the intention and the effect was a high degree of centralization. Those regions were administratively efficient because their boundaries conformed to provincial boundaries. However, they were agents of centralization because they imposed new patterns of interaction on the constituent provinces, not least through leaders whose loyalty to the centre was considered unassailable.[9]

The CCP's use and control of leaders clearly provides devices for central control of localities. One such crucial device has been the informal 'inspection tour'. At least once a year (normally during the summer break) top-ranking CCP cadres will visit the provinces. Their visits have the dual aim of monitoring the performance of currently implemented policies, and of bringing news about new developments. Peng Dehuai's celebrated tour of his home province during the disastrous second winter of the Great Leap Forward is a good example of the first. Mao Zedong's sweep round rural China between February and early summer 1958 illustrates the second. Everywhere he went, embryo rural people's communes (both larger and more collectivist than even the largest agricultural producer co-operatives) sprang up soon afterwards. However, the appointment of local cadres throughout the state administration from above and through the CCP is clearly its most important device for centralized control. It is a power exercised for the most part through the personnel department of each unit in the state administration.

This is not to argue that there is no local autonomy. On the contrary, there is considerable local autonomy; indeed, without it the political system could not survive, given China's size and the consequent variety in human and physical environments. The conflict between central control and local autonomy is too often too sharply portrayed. Both are relative concepts and can, and do, coexist. Any drive for local autonomy in heartland China has always been mediated by the recognition that its legitimacy lies in a united China. Thus even the provincial independence movements and warlords of the early twentieth century justified their actions in terms of the doctrine of 'partial peace': they were establishing the 'just order' in their localities only temporarily — until its re-creation nationally.

Even in the period since 1949, the extent of the CCP's central control has been tempered by large elements of local autonomy made manifest in two aspects of the decision-making process. The Chinese talk about the dangers of 'cutting with one knife' when they want to refer to the practice of trying to apply a single policy uniformly throughout China. In fact this has happened remarkably little, for ever since the CCP's guerrilla days it has been an administrative principle that localities should 'do the best according to local conditions'. Communization (1958) and decollectivization (1980–2) are the two most famous exceptions that prove the rule, and even in those cases policy implementation was not characterized by a high degree of uniformity. In general, the centre lays down the broad goals and mechanisms of a policy for implementation, but the locality provides the detail. Inevitably this provides local leaders with the power not only of delay, because of special local circumstances, but also of implementing policies in ways that may not originally have been intended. The reorganization of the Hainan party and state administration leadership in 1985, after what was *ex post facto* judged to have been an inappropriate use of resources — profiteering from the import of manufactured goods rather than capital investment — is a recent case in point.

There is also a local dimension to the national decision-making process which results from its experimental and incremental nature. Usually, before any policy is adopted nationally it is implemented on a trial basis, sometimes in one, sometimes in more, areas. Depending on the results of those trials, more experimental areas may be chosen until national policy implementation follows. Undoubtedly it has often happened that trial areas have been selected in order to achieve desired results. In that process, alliances seem to develop between local and national leaders, initiatives may be implemented locally as a form of kite-flying before they are ever seriously discussed in a national policy-making forum, and adept local leaders quickly rise to national political prominence. A recent and spectacular example of such a scenario may be associated with Zhao Ziyang's promotion of economic reforms in Sichuan, when he was first secretary of the provincial CCP there (1976–80) shortly before he became Premier.[10] It is all the more remarkable because Zhao's programme of economic reforms in Sichuan was almost identical to that first proposed by Li Jingquan to the first session of the eighth CCP congress in 1956, when he was first secretary of the Sichuan CCP committee.[11]

The local dimension to the national decision-making process entails that there is an essential variability to the extent and exercise of local autonomy. Just as it is an oversimplification to regard central control and local autonomy in constant and perpetual conflict in China, so too it would be wrong to imagine all localities to be equally autonomous. That they are not necessarily equally willing to exercise their relative autonomy has been demonstrated by the demands made of central government by local leaders during the 1980s. Some — mainly those from the wealthier areas of East and South China — have argued for less central control and greater local autonomy. However, others such as those from Shanxi and Shandong (discussed later in chapters 8 and 9) have specifically lobbied for greater central involvement. For its part, central government has recognized that not all localities are equally able to exercise autonomy. For example, as Ferdinand indicates (in chapter 3), in budgetary planning it has adopted different ratios with different provinces for the distribution of revenue as between centre and province.

The extent and exercise of local autonomy is thus not an automatic feature of Chinese political life, but depends rather on each area's relationship with other localities, with the centre, and with the nation as a whole. Recent research has pointed to the significance of several factors: a locality's political cohesion and integration, its economic importance, and the personal connections of its leaders.[12] Physical distance seems less important than political distance. On the whole, it appears that localities which are politically distant from the centre have greater autonomy than those whose existence looms larger — for whatever reason, be it defence, a substantial national minority population, or the importance of economic output — in the centre's political mind. Thus, despite the physical distance, Tibet and Xinjiang in the far west of China are in fact politically closer to Beijing and thus less autonomous than provinces such as Shanxi or Shandong.

Bureaucratic inertia

Just as variable as the impact of regionalization on local autonomy is the influence of the PRC's bureaucratic structures on the emergence of regionalization. In particular, there are likely to be constraints on the emergence of economic regionalization where there is a need for new patterns of administrative behaviour that conflict with previous patterns of political regionalization. Conversely, where new and old patterns coincide, then past practices are likely to aid economic regionalization.

The willingness and ability of administrators to follow new patterns of organizational behaviour required by economic developments is clearly of crucial importance in the emergence of economic regionalization. Of necessity, any new administrative system is based on what went before, and must employ a considerable number of the same staff. These have their set bureaucratic procedures, their established channels of communication (formal and informal), and well-entrenched workplaces. It is not impossible to change all this, but it does require a herculean effort of political will. Moreover, it is not helped by the physical and spatial problems facing administration, of which communications is probably the most severe. For example, there are estimated to be considerably fewer telephone lines available in the whole of China than in the London telephone area. The result, as a recent study of Wuhan highlights, is that very few enterprises follow the rationale of economic regionalization. Small and medium-sized enterprises have tended to do business (when left free to choose) in exactly the same ways, with the same

29

partners, and using the same channels and mechanisms as they did (when compelled to) under the regime of 'the plan'. It is the administrative path of least resistance. Larger-scale enterprises, for their part, have turned their backs on their local region, and have made national linkages with larger economic concerns with whom they can create common economic interests.[13]

Clearly, the nature of the cadre force is a significant factor encouraging or constraining the emergence of economic regionalization. In a comparative study of contemporary economic reform in the USSR and the PRC, Kaser has suggested that the latter (unlike the former) has basically solved its personnel problem in the localities. He points to the recent leadership changes in the PRC — which have indeed rejuvenated local leadership, and increased its professional and educational competence.[14] Although it may be true, as Kaser indicates, that 'Gorbachev's problem is that he has inherited Party officials in the regions whose perspectives are too narrow to administer the new system',[15] it does not follow that the PRC has solved all its problems. Crucially, there is still (and likely to be for the conceivable future) a severe shortage of technically competent cadres. For example, official sources have estimated that the PRC would be hard-pressed to find half a million of the 8.5 million economic specialists said to be needed by the year 2000.[16] As in the USSR, the dominant administrative ethos remains that from the pre-1978 years, when most of today's cadres received their training and political socialization.

Kaser sees a further impediment to reform in the USSR, in contrast with the PRC, in the continuation of 'ethnic "baronies" with interlocking ties afforced by bribery and mutual understanding'.[17] The strictly ethnic dimension of the USSR's republics may be absent in the PRC, and bribery (as well as other forms of corruption) may be less clearly defined in the political culture. However, there can be little doubt of the importance of special relationships and 'networking' in the workings of the Chinese political system. Moreover, these clearly have a territorial dimension, even if politics is not determined by factions with local bases.

In the Imperial system, government officials were not permitted to serve in their 'native place', or to stay in one place for extended periods. In these ways it was hoped that officials would not develop local ties and remain agents of central control. The administrative experience of the PRC has been somewhat different. In the first place, a certain proportion of 'natives' has always served in local government. One reason for this phenomenon relates to the CCP's history before 1949, when its activities had largely been concentrated in East-Central and North China. Particularly during 1949–56, when the CCP was first consolidating its national position, it was faced by large areas of the country where it previously had little organizational experience. There were, for example, members of the CCP from Guangxi, Guangdong and Sichuan, but for the most part these were people who had joined the CCP when the Long March passed through their home towns, or who had joined elsewhere. Accordingly, the CCP was able to send them back to their home areas in the hope not only that they would be able to relate well to local inhabitants (and at a minimum speak the same language) but also that they would have few remaining particularistic ties and that their prime loyalties would rest with the centralized CCP. A second reason that some 'natives' have been appointed local leaders is a function of the CCP's policy towards the 'united front'. Again before 1957, but also since 1976, local non-CCP 'notables' have been encouraged to play their role in local politics.

However, the main characteristic of the PRC's administrative experience in these terms has not been a 'law of avoidance' but a contrived balance between cadres with local experience and knowledge, and those brought in from outside. Moreover, in most localities for almost every year since 1949, the majority of cadres could be considered 'insiders' rather than 'outsiders'. For example, among provincial-level leaders (the ranking cadre and deputies in each of the CCP, state administration, and People's Liberation Army (PLA) hierarchies, 24 per cent of appointments between October 1949 and September 1985 were of individuals native to the province of appointment; 19 per cent were of people who, as far as can be ascertained, had spent the majority of their working lives in the province of appointment but were not natives of that province; and a further 23 per cent were appointed from positions within the same province.

Even these statistics underestimate the extent of cadres with local experience and knowledge, for it would appear that it has been deliberate practice to appoint cadres within the boundaries created by the six large administrative regions first created during 1949–54. Some 27 per cent of provincial leaders appointed during 1949–85 (and who have not already been counted in the categories outlined in the previous paragraph) came from positions within the same large region, and, of these, 19 per cent had spent the majority of their working lives (again, as far as can be ascertained) within that large region.

The regional basis for the circulation of the provincial elite is quite remarkable. Altogether some 82 per cent of all appointments in every province (using aggregate data for 1949–85) were of individuals from within the large region. With the exception of the Cultural Revolution, there is little significant variation over time or between localities. Even where neighbouring provinces do not share common characteristics and problems (and many do), it suggests a tight administrative identity within bureaucratic politics. This perspective is reinforced by the apparent role of 'feeder provinces' within four of the six large regions for appointments to the other provinces within the region, as well as at the regional level. In the other two large regions, there are two feeder provinces for appointment to other provinces within the region, and at the regional level. Roughly 19–24 per cent of each province's appointments came from its regionally-dominant feeder province(s). These feeder provinces are Liaoning in the North-east; Shandong and Jiangsu in East China; Guangdong and Hubei in Central-South China; Sichuan in the South-west, Shaanxi in the North-west; and Beijing in North China.

Politics and economics in conflict

Although the influence of bureaucratic inertia is uncertain, the potential conflict between economic and political imperatives is probably the most important impediment to regionalization. Despite the CCP's current attempt to differentiate more clearly between economics and politics, the two cannot be completely separated. In terms of regionalization, the contrasting attempts during 1986 and 1987 to create two new provinces — one for the Sanxia project, the other on Hainan Island — provide a useful (if speculative) example of the problems involved.

The project to dam the Yangtze at the Three Gorges (*Sanxia*) (on the Sichuan-Hubei border) has become a political symbol as potent in its own right as was the building of the Chongqing-Chengdu railway from the late Qing dynasty until the early 1950s. Sun Yat-sen put forward a proposal to build a dam at Sanxia in 1921, and various plans have been aired since. A planning group was established in the mid-1950s, though little positive seems to have emerged. Sometime in late 1984 or early 1985 the decision appears to have been taken to push ahead with the project, and to include it as a 'key project' of the Seventh Five-Year Plan then being drafted. In general terms, the project was designed with three main aims in mind: as a source of hydroelectric-power generation, as a means of flood prevention, and as a way of ensuring navigation along the Yangtze to Chongqing. None of those aims is inconsiderable. It has been estimated that the Sanxia project could supply electricity to Beijing, Tianjin and Shanghai, and overcome the electricity shortages of Central and East China. Flood control is a constant preoccupation in the middle Yangtze, to some extent because of the gorges; and navigation to Chongqing is currently hampered by conditions in the gorges. Proponents of the project, of whom perhaps Li Peng (himself once a hydraulic engineer) would appear to be the most famous, envisaged that with a rise in the water level it should be possible for vessels of 10,000 tons to navigate the Yangtze safely to Chongqing.[18]

However, the project was clearly not without its costs. Financially it was expected to pay for itself within its first eight years of operation, even though it would take seventeen years to complete. The most important and immediate problem was that up to a million people (estimates vary from as low as half that figure) would need to be resettled. For that reason, and in order to make technical and logistical preparations for the project, the decision was taken to establish Sanxia province. Later, after the political opposition expressed at the time of the Fourth session of the Sixth NPC in April 1986, Li Peng categorically denied that such a decision had been taken.[19] Previously, however, it had been announced that a Preparatory Group for Sanxia province had been established; that the new province would have a population of 18 million, with its capital at Yichang; and that it had been listed as a provincial-level unit for planning purposes as from 1 January 1986.[20]

Opposition was first openly articulated at the Third session of the Chinese People's Political Consultative Conference (CPPCC) in the spring of 1985, which set up an investigation group. This reported in June 1985 against the project. It claimed that the Sanxia project's capacity for power-generation had been exaggerated, as had the claim of navigation to Chongqing. It argued that there would be aggravated flood damage in the upper reaches of the Yangtze and that Chongqing port would be silted over. It claimed that twelve new towns would have to be built at a cost of 10 billion yuan to resettle the displaced population. Instead of the Sanxia project, the investigation group suggested the construction of twenty large or medium-sized hydroelectric power-stations. Needless to say, the proponents of the project were not slow to respond, and in October 1985 the Sanxia Planning Department restated its case.[21]

It would appear that the decision not to proceed with either the project or the establishment of a new province occurred in late March or early April 1986. Certainly the Sanxia project was not included in the Seventh Five-Year Plan, and in May it was announced that a Sanxia Economic Development Office (under the State Council) had been created to replace the former preparatory group. This Development Office was to establish a study group to report on the project's viability by March 1987, in order that the project could start with the Eighth Five-Year Plan. Reading between the lines of its terms of reference, and between those of the more public debate between the Sanxia Planning Department and the CPPCC investigation group, it would seem that there were additional political complications.[22]

Although there clearly is genuine debate about the technical and logistical aspects of the project, there are also problems about establishing a new political and economic force in Central China. A new Sanxia province would come into economic and political competition with the administrative units within its immediate vicinity — particularly Chongqing, Sichuan, Wuhan and Hubei. It is reasonable to assume it was for that purpose that the first task allotted to the study group was to investigate the economic effects of the project on 'Chongqing, Southwest China, Central China and East China'. Moreover, because the new province would deny resources to currently existing authorities, it is also reasonable to assume that the issue of compensation was raised. This would be difficult enough to resolve were the new province to be contained within existing administrative boundaries. However, in Sanxia's case the issue was further complicated because the new province was to cross existing administrative (particularly provincial) boundaries. As the experience of the Special Economic Zones demonstrates (as discussed in chapter 7), political and administrative interests are substantial and powerful in such circumstances.

In complete contrast, the proposal to establish a new Hainan province appears to have proceeded smoothly, despite the island administration's more recent problems. In May 1984 Hainan became an administrative region and an 'open zone'. The 'trade scandal' soon followed, and in its wake came the reorganization of the local leadership. In November 1986 Gu Mu visited the island on an inspection tour and discussed various ideas for its development. Its economic importance lies in three areas: as a producer of tropical economic crops; its mineral wealth; and its ability (currently more by location than anything else) to service the oilfields not only in the north of Hainan, but also in the South China Sea, Beibuwan, and the Zhujiang (Pearl River) delta. As an 'open zone' for foreign investment and as a port, it would seem ideally situated as a 'key-point' development area.[23]

The ease with which Zhao Ziyang appears to have gained acceptance for the proposal that Hainan should become a province[24] reflects its economic and political position, particularly by comparison with the earlier Sanxia proposal. Hainan was currently an economically undeveloped area, with little more than potential. It seems likely that for the Guangdong authorities it had proved more of a headache than an asset during the previous few years. It has a considerable minority nationality population, and is not really part of mainstream Cantonese culture. It is an island with its own sense of identity and patterns of bureaucratic interaction. Because it was previously subordinated to only one provincial-level authority, it was that much easier to detach administratively. Moreover, its planned economic development is not subject to the same sort of political competition that afflicts the Sanxia scheme. Of course, the paradox of the comparison between the fate of the proposals to establish provinces for Sanxia and Hainan is that for entirely other reasons Sanxia is more likely to be a long-term economic success.

Problems of transition

It would be foolhardy to underestimate the short- and medium-term obstacles to the emergence of new patterns of economic regionalization in the PRC. None the less, there is a need for a long-term perspective. The problems facing regional development are essentially those that result from the transition from an administered economy to one that is more market-oriented. They are not insignificant, but they are also not insurmountable given political will on the part of the leadership and political stability.

A simple example may serve as a useful reminder that the PRC is experiencing more than usually rapid social and political change — despite the absence of the political instability which characterized and accompanied such change in the PRC's past. At first sight it might seem likely that regionalization would be hindered by the potential conflict resulting from the differnt patterns of regionalization. Various concepts of region and ideas about regional development have been aired since 1976. These range from the six large administrative regions resurrected in 1977, through regionalization based on large metropolitan centres or the seventeen 'zones for comprehensive territorial development' announced in January 1987 for creation by the end of the century, to the 'city districts' of Jiangsu and Liaoning provinces.

However, there is no necessary conflict between different patterns of regionalization. Indeed, different economic activities of necessity require different kinds and sizes of region. To give an extreme example, the region of food production for a metropolitan area is likely to be smaller, and closer to the city, than that metropolitan area's region of power-generation. Transport regions will follow the main lines of communication, rail and river in China's case, and avoid hill and mountain ranges. Problems arise in the long term only if different kinds of regions overlap territorially and compete for the same resources. Undoubtedly there is likely to be some confusion in the short term resulting from the proliferation of administrative 'regions'. On the other hand, this is unlikely to be a long-term problem: complex societies need and have complex patterns of regionalization. The PRC may not have had them in the past, but its current policies require them for the future.

Notes

1 NCNA, 19 August 1987.
2 *People's Daily*, 8 May 1977 and 12 September 1977.
3 'Comrade Zhou Lin on Present Rural Work', *Guizhou Daily*, 19 October 1959; Dai Xiaodong, '1959 Agricultural Production Conditions and the Tasks for 1960', ibid., 6 January 1960.
4 *China Daily*, 28 September 1987, p. 2.
5 *Ningxia Daily*, 27 May 1986.
6 Unless otherwise stated, the information presented in this section is derived from interviews undertaken in Beijing during November 1987

under the auspices of the Institute of Political Science of the Chinese Academy of Social Sciences. The research visit was part of the exchange scheme between, on the one hand, the Chinese Academy and, on the other, the British Academy and the Economic and Social Research Council. Grateful acknowledgement is made of the support provided by the exchange scheme as well as the assistance afforded by colleagues in the Institute of Political Studies.

7 *China Daily*, 5 October 1987.

8 van de Ven, H.J. (1987) *The Founding of the CCP and the Search for a New Political Order, 1920–1927*, Harvard PhD, pp. 161ff.

9 Solinger, D.J. (1978) 'Some Speculations on the Return of the Regions: Parallels with the Past', *China Quarterly*, no. 75.

10 Shambaugh, D.L. (1984) *The Making of a Premier: Zhao Ziyang's Provincial Career*, Boulder: Westview.

11 *New China Semi-Monthly*, no. 20 (1956), pp. 52–4.

12 See, for example: Stern, L.M. (1979) 'Politics Without Consensus: Center-Provincial Relations and Political Communication in China, January 1976–January 1977', *Asian Survey*, vol. 19, no. 3 p. 260; Solinger, D.J. (1982) 'Politics in Yunnan Province in the Decade of Disorder: Elite Factional Strategies and Central-local Relations, 1967–1980', *China Quarterly*, no. 92, p. 628; and Goodman, D.S.G. (1986) *Centre and Province in the People's Republic of China: Sichuan and Guizhou 1955–1965*, Cambridge University Press.

13 Solinger, D.J. (1987) 'City, Province and Region: The Case of Wuhan', paper presented to the conference on 'China in a New Era: Continuity and Change', Manila.

14 All information on local leadership presented here is drawn from ESRC Project E0023–2173 on *Provincial Leadership in the People's Republic of China*. A computer database is available at the University of Newcastle upon Tyne.

15 Kaser, M. (1987) '"One economy, two systems": Parallels between Soviet and Chinese Reform', *International Affairs*, vol. 63, no. 3 (Summer), p. 395.

16 Wang Zhaohua (1985) 'Accelerate the tempo of cadre training to meet the needs of the Four Modernizations', Beijing Home Service (radio broadcast), 3 February, translated in SWB, 7 February.

17 Kaser, '"One economy, two systems"', op. cit., p. 402.

18 Mu Fu (1986) 'The Earth-moving Three Gorges Project', *Zheng Ming*, 1 June.

19 'Chinese Leaders' Press Conference: Yao Yilin and Li Peng Answer Questions', *Da Gong Bao*, 4 April 1986, translated in SWB, 8 April 1986.

20 *Ta Kung Pao* (Weekly Supplement), 30 January–5 February 1986.

21 *Wen Wei Po*, 23 December 1985 and March 1986, in SWB, 17 June 1986.

22 *Wen Wei Po*, 29 October 1986, in SWB, 5 November 1986.

23 *Wen Wei Po*, 9 August 1987, Kuang Yu (1987) 'Plan to establish whole

of Hainan as a special zone: Gu Mu comes south to discuss feasibility',
in SWB, 11 August.
24 NCNA, 28 August 1987, at the Twenty-second Session of the NPC
    Standing Committee.

Chapter three

The economic and financial dimension

Peter Ferdinand

In centrally planned economies, or those which are variants of the Soviet-style command economy, the budgetary relationship between central and local government is clearly a crucial determinant of regional development. It has always been an important mechanism whereby the national government controls the regional distribution of wealth, as well as of production, and is becoming increasingly vital with the introduction of market reforms. By 1976 that budgetary relationship in the PRC — particularly as between the centre and the provinces — had become untenable. Central and provincial governments felt both that too much was expected of them, and that they could not (for various reasons) actually meet those expectations.

As this chapter explains, first attempts at reform during the late 1970s rapidly led on to a more substantial and systemic reform in 1982. Though that has been successful in many respects, problems remain, not least because of more recent developments within the Chinese economy of the 1980s. The instability and unpredictability that characterized budgetary relations between central and local governments before 1976 have largely disappeared. However, in their place are new areas of dispute over the allocation of resources.

Provinces have gained an increased room for financial manoeuvre. One cause of that has been the regularization of budgetary relationships between centre and province; another has been the relaxation of other administrative controls that had previously kept economic decentralization in check. One consequence has been an increasing sense of weakness on the part of central government and a nervousness about its ability to pay for all its needs. The corollary has been a growing self-confidence on the part of the provinces about their ability to direct their own economic development.

The need for reform

By 1976 the power of central government had weakened since the heyday of centralization during the First Five-Year Plan (1953–7). An

38

indication of the change can be seen from Table 3.1. In the 1950s almost all of the nation's industrial enterprises were either under the direct control of local governments, or under 'dual subordination' to both central and provincial governments, which meant that local governments could have a significant voice in the development programmes of those enterprises and of their area. Even the massive Anshan steelworks came into this category. Since one of the key principles of the Chinese road to socialism as it had developed both before 1949 and after 1957 had been decentralization, it might be assumed that the tendency away from centralization was greatly appreciated by local leaders. This was not the case.

Table 3.1 Relative shares of state expenditure attributed to central and local government (%)

	1955	1959	1965	1971	1976	1984
Centre	78.1	47.6	62.2	59.5	46.8	46.6
Local	21.9	52.4	37.8	40.5	53.2	53.4

Sources: For 1955 and 1959, Lardy, N. (1978) *Economic Growth and Distribution in China*, Cambridge: Cambridge University Press, p. 38; for 1965, Tian Yinong, Zhu Fulin and Xiang Huaicheng (1985) *Lun Zhongguo caizheng tizhide gaige*, Beijing, p. 56; for 1971 and 1976, Xu Yi and Chen Baosen (1982) *Zhongguode caizheng 1977–80*, Beijing, p. 42; and for 1984, *Caizheng*, 1986(3), p. 2.

The figures in Table 3.1 understate the extent of central government control. Since 1949 local governments could neither levy taxes nor spend revenue simply as they chose. They had to collect all fiscal revenue in their area and then forward a predetermined proportion to Beijing. However, the division of state budget income between the centre and the localities was not based upon any firm set of rules, but rather upon *ad hoc* arrangements which had formed into a pattern over a number of years. The share of total tax revenue allocated to a province was subject to unpredictable variation every year, and no province could have any certainty about future income. Thus the beginning of every year saw a round of intense haggling between the Ministry of Finance and all the provinces. Moreover, even though various types of expenditure were their apparent responsibility, local governments were subject to various administrative checks by central government before they could actually spend the money. Provincial governments were not even allowed to establish a relationship between the overall income and revenue targets which were imposed upon them by central government. Thus they had no direct interest in whether they ran a surplus or a deficit. Balancing fiscal income and expenditure was a matter for the centre alone.

At the same time, the lack of a clear division of responsibilities and powers between central and local government meant that the Ministry of Finance felt itself besieged by what it considered 'irresponsible' provincial governments, whose spendthrift ambitions it had to keep in check. Thus by 1976 neither central government nor the provinces were satisfied with things as they were. Central government still had power and the provinces had autonomy, yet neither could exercise them as they wished.

Although this problem had existed for several years, reform became likely after Mao's death for several reasons. The immediate post-Mao leadership found itself in a particularly acute economic crisis. In 1976 the government had run a deficit of 2.6 billion yuan RMB, one of the largest since 1949, and something had to be done about it. The new leadership after 1978 was committed to reducing state interference in the economy. In practice this was bound to mean a reduction in the leading role of central government. Even though it was also supposed to lead to a reduction in the provinces' control of the economy, central government would be the greater loser, for so much of its control had rested upon its manipulation of the economy. In addition, the poorer areas were openly discontented and felt that central government had not done enough for them. One spokesman for Qinghai, for example, pointedly claimed that there were many similarities between the geography of that province and Saudi Arabia, yet in 1978 Saudi Arabia had an average per capita national income of US $9,000, while in Qinghai it was only US $244.[1]

By the time of Mao's death, therefore, there existed quite broad support for further decentralization. As early as December 1976 the province of Jiangsu — where the leadership had taken a leading role in the struggle against the Gang of Four — was allowed by the State Council to experiment in its economic relations with central government, including its budgetary relations. In particular, the province was allowed to establish its own balance between income and expenditure. Central government fixed a target for budgetary income which was higher than in the previous year, the province being allowed to keep an agreed percentage of any excess. Finally, the province was assured that this system would be in force for three years, which removed some of the uncertainty from the annual round of budgetary negotiations. During 1976–9 a number of other provinces also embarked upon similar experiments. In Sichuan the centre retained greater administrative control over the way in which different categories of income were divided between itself and the provinces, not merely over the overall total of revenue as in the Jiangsu case.

All of those reforms appeared to bring economic improvements, and early in 1980 the State Council directed that most provinces should introduce the Sichuan model of budgetary relations with the centre. Provinces acquired greater responsibility for balancing their income and expenditure, although the centre still attempted to control its share of overall revenue as well as the proportions of different types of income. The only exceptions were to be Jiangsu (which persisted with its own model), Guangdong and Fujian (to be discussed later). Greater stability and predictability was promised by central government's announcement that this new system would last for at least five years.

Fairly quickly, however, it became apparent that the Sichuan model was too inflexible when the rest of the economy was undergoing rapid change. Provinces suddenly found themselves short of funds, and turned to short-term solutions, such as encouraging the production of goods with high profit margins, as for example, electric fans. When the market for such goods became saturated, some of the same local authorities took measures to 'protect' their own enterprises from outside competition. The continuing inflexibility of centre-provincial relations was clearly leading to irrational policies from a macroeconomic perspective, and also to greater volatility rather than greater predictability in provincial economic policies.

The 1982 reform

In 1982 a further phase of decentralization took place, and the system established then has basically applied up to the present. The various relationships that have resulted between central government on the one hand, and the different provincial-level governments on the other, may be viewed as ranging along a spectrum running from maximum centralization to maximum decentralization. At one end there are the provinces of Guangdong and Fujian, with the highest degree of autonomy. Then there are the twelve provinces (most of them net contributors to central government revenue) which practise the Jiangsu system. Next come a further twelve provinces (all net recipients of subsidies from central government) which still practise the Sichuan model of fiscal relations. Finally, at the other pole, there are the three provincial-level cities of Beijing, Shanghai and Tianjin, which have the least autonomy. In general it can be said that all provinces now enjoy greater autonomy than they did, but it is those in surplus which have acquired the greater ability to direct their own economic development.

Since 1979 the two provinces of Guangdong and Fujian have been granted even greater autonomy than other provinces in an effort to attract foreign capital to their Special Economic Zones (see chapter 7). Almost all the tax revenue and profits from state enterprises were assigned in the first instance to the province, and almost all expenditure was to be borne by the provincial government. In the case of Guangdong, a proportion of the planned surplus of income over expenditure was assigned to central government. In the case of Fujian, since expenditure was expected to exceed income, a central government subsidy was determined. Both Guangdong's remittance to, and Fujian's subsidy from, central government were based upon 1979 figures, and they were supposed to be fixed for five years in advance. (For the other provinces, while the system was supposed to last for five years, the actual amounts they were allowed to retain could fluctuate.) After that, any extra income would go entirely to these two provinces.[2] This was the largest degree of financial autonomy which any province in China had enjoyed since 1949. It is likely that the new province of Hainan Island, created in 1988, will also come into this category, since it too is expected to play a major role in promoting investment from abroad.

Twelve provinces have adopted the Jiangsu pattern of relations with the centre. These are all relatively prosperous provinces and are mostly net contributors to central government revenue. They have great freedom to vary the sources of local revenue without interference from the centre, provided they meet their revenue target. Thus they acquired greater autonomy than before, but central government could accept this, since it too gained something — a reduction in its workload, and in the uncertainties that could creep into its dealings with provinces, as well as increased flexibility of operation.[3]

Some provinces continue to receive subsidies from the centre because they are relatively underdeveloped. In those cases the centre continues to exercise greater detailed supervision along the lines of the Sichuan model. These are the eight provinces or autonomous regions with a significant ethnic minority population (Mongolia, Xinjiang, Ningxia, Guangxi, Yunnan, Qinghai, Guizhou and Tibet), as well as four others (Gansu, Jilin, Heilongjiang and Jiangxi). They were assigned an income target and allowed to retain the whole of any extra revenue which they managed to raise. In addition, the minority areas were guaranteed that their subsidy from central government would increase by 10 per cent annually over the five-year period.

The three major cities with the status of province (Beijing, Tianjin and Shanghai) remain the provincial-level units of government that are the most tightly controlled from above. With their large industrial might, they raise the core of central government finance — 25 per cent in all. The centre attempted to guard against the possibility of conceding too much revenue to the provinces by retaining tighter control over the income which could be extracted from these three major cities. So the latter were allowed to retain a smaller proportion of revenue than other provinces. In the early 1980s Shanghai, for example, was allowed to retain only 10 per cent, while the neighbouring province of Jiangsu was allowed 38 per cent. Although other provinces were allowed to retain a higher proportion of the revenue which they raised over and above their targets, if these three major cities raised extra income, they were allowed to retain only the same proportion as the share that they could retain within the income target. Moreover, the amounts which the three cities could retain had to be renegotiated each year, so relations continued to be liable to annual fluctuation.

It has been suggested that in many ways the authorities in cities and county-towns below the provincial-level enjoyed an even greater increase in their effective financial powers than did provincial leaders in the 1980s.[4] Some of the largest cities now draw up their own budget and attempt to balance their own income and expenditure. Yet, on a purely budgetary level, there is also evidence suggesting that most counties have actually experienced greater control by the provinces. Certainly the Director of the Central Committee Party School recently claimed this in a speech.[5] There is other evidence to support his view. Two-thirds of all China's counties run a budgetary loss.[6] It would not be surprising if, just as loss-making provinces have to accept greater supervision of their finances from Beijing as the price for subsidy, so loss-making counties have to accept greater supervision from the provincial capital.

It is true that official policy is currently being directed towards the strengthening of county-level government and finances. If it is successful, it will no doubt lead to greater autonomy for counties. For the moment, however, it seems as though, with the exception of prosperous counties and cities, it is still the provinces which have benefited from the budgetary reforms of the 1980s. They have gained power at the expense of authorities both above and below them in the administrative hierarchy.

Problems of central control

All this has posed problems for central government, not least since it is still dependent upon the provincial authorities for collecting most of the tax revenue and enterprise profits to which it is entitled. Relatively little goes directly to the centre. Partly this reflects the practical problems of collecting central taxes in a country as big as China. Equally, however, it resonates with a centuries-old Chinese tradition, from which present-day leaders are not immune, whereby provincial authorities try to hamstring central government by preventing it from collecting taxes locally.

The point can be illustrated clearly by a comparison of central and local shares of state budgetary income with the figures on their relative shares of expenditure which were listed in Table 3.1. In 1976, for example, central government was responsible for spending 53.2 per cent of the total state budget, but it received directly only 16 per cent of the total state income.[7] Under the old system this disparity was less important because the centre had other devices at its disposal for regulating the economy, but as they declined in importance, so the shortage of funds directly at the disposal of the centre was felt more keenly.

The problem was exacerbated by a number of miscalculations which were made at the time of the first reforms in 1980. For example, many large-scale enterprises were supposed to change from dual subordination to central control. In this way the centre would be assured of more ample funds directly at its disposal.[8] But this never took place — perhaps because of resistance from the now more powerful provinces. The calculation of future revenue targets was carried out in 1979 at a time of over-optimistic revenue projections.[9] Moreover, the overall state budget has been in deficit for most of the 1980s, at least in part because of the unpredictable effects of trying to change the tax and price systems simultaneously. Consequently, although there are repeated calls for the central government's direct share of budgetary income to increase, not much progress has been made. By 1982 the figure was 20 per cent, only marginally larger than in 1976.[10]

To make matters worse, the financial obligations of central government actually increased in the early 1980s. The enormous cost of food subsidies was borne by central government, and by the early 1980s was equal to almost one-third of total budgetary expenditure.[11] In addition, more provinces now required subsidies than in the 1950s. Whereas in 1956 basically four provinces were net recipients of aid, by the 1980s fifteen provinces came into that category. This can be seen from Table 3.2. These figures are admittedly incomplete. Most importantly they do not include information on the revenue-sharing agreements in 1956 between central government on the one hand, and Shanghai, Beijing and Tianjin, not to mention the key province of Liaoning, on the other. Nevertheless, they suggest that only two provinces — Hebei and Anhui — were paying a higher proportion of their income to the centre in 1982 than in 1956. Most were paying less. By 1985 the number of provinces running deficits had risen to eighteen. Consequently, whereas in 1978 central government had been able to draw upon provincial surpluses of approximately 32.1 billion yuan RMB, by 1985 those surpluses had roughly halved. Shanghai now contributes almost all the surplus enjoyed by central government: otherwise on a national level, provincial surpluses and deficits largely cancel each other out.

The extent of overall change is graphically illustrated by the case of Heilongjiang, which in 1956 was contributing 32 per cent of its revenue to the centre, and in 1978 50 per cent, but by 1982 was receiving the second highest subsidy from central government. A whole combination of circumstances had combined to depress its economic development: declining soil fertility, a number of natural disasters and 'seriously unbalanced' development in mineral extraction industries. Nevertheless, a report in 1979 concluded that the basic problem was that the various ministries and departments had paid too much attention to taking things out of Heilongjiang and not enough to putting resources in.[12] Thus central government is now having to pay the price for the mistakes of regional development policy in the years since the Great Leap Forward.

Table 3.2 Revenue-sharing arrangements between the central government and individual provinces (%)

Province	1956	1978	1982	1983	1984	1985
North						
Beijing	—	59.6	64.5	50.8	40.4	37.0
Tianjin	—	—	64.2[1]	—	55.1	44.1
Hebei	5.1	28.1	18.4	22.3	6.8	33.2
Shanxi	11.9	−7.0	−2.7	0.6	−25.1	−30.6
Inner Mongolia	0.0	−63.1	−74.4	−69.4	−72.6	—
North-east						
Liaoning	—	68.0	59.0	56.5	44.4	28.3
Jilin	—	3.4	−30.8	−27.3	−26.2	−32.7
Heilongjiang	32.7	50.0	−44.3	−41.3	−41.2	−16.1
East						
Shanghai	—	84.6	87.7	85.7	81.1	76.9
Jiangsu	63.4	53.5	63.0	56.0	47.3	42.5
Zhejiang	61.1	35.4	49.3	46.1	37.5	38.4
Anhui	10.5	19.1	23.2	8.8	3.7	−4.1
Fujian	—	−0.1	−16.7	−28.3	−18.2	−18.1
Jiangxi	34.0	−24.5	−20.6	−22.9	−31.6	−30.4
Shandong	59.2	10.5	9.9	15.7	27.3	23.7
Central-South						
Henan	40.2	—	—	17.8	6.3	−1.3
Hubei	35.5	4.4	30.1	30.0	24.7	13.3
Hunan	41.0	12.6	23.3	22.1	8.6	−2.3
Guangdong	59.6	31.3	20.2	16.8	3.0	3.7
Guangxi	18.5	−28.3	−23.6	−27.9	−41.6	−32.2
South-west						
Sichuan	62.5	4.3	10.0	9.1	−3.2	−8.9
Guizhou	30.3	−49.2	−54.0	−45.0	−48.8	−39.3
Yunnan	18.7	−35.7	−16.7	−29.1	−37.5	−25.3
Tibet	—	—	—	—	—	—
North-west						
Shaanxi	23.5	7.4	−21.6	−22.7	−33.0	−26.5
Gansu	−11.0	30.2	−2.4	−9.7	−37.7	−31.8
Qinghai	−61.5	−60.1	−79.2	−79.2	−81.8	−76.1
Ningxia	—	−45.2	−74.9	−74.5	−74.9	−69.6
Xinjiang	−5.2	—	—	−68.7	−69.0	−70.4

Note: 1. Figure for 1980.
Positive numbers show (for 1956) provincial net remittances to the centre, or (for later years) the surplus of income over expenditure, as a percentage of total revenues collected by the provincial-level units. Negative numbers indicate (for 1956) net subsidies from the centre, or (for later years) the deficit between provincial income and expenditure, as a percentage of total expenditure.
Sources: Lardy, N. (1978) *Economic Growth and Distribution in China*, Cambridge: Cambridge University Press, p. 76; *Zhongguo jingji nianjian 1984*; and *Zhongguo jingji nianjian 1986*.

The very size of this problem means that central government will find it extremely difficult to achieve through its own efforts a major transfer of resources from richer areas to poorer ones. Since 1980 there has been an official Fund to Aid the Development of Underdeveloped Regions, but its effectiveness is obviously limited by the size of the central government budget. That lesson had already been brought home in the early 1980s. Between 1980 and 1982 the Fund was allocated 1.5 billion yuan RMB. Between 1981 and 1982, however, central government itself had to borrow over five times as much, that is 11 billion yuan, from provincial governments so as to make good a short-term deficit. Overall between 1980 and 1986 the fund allocated about 4 billion yuan RMB.[13] In absolute terms this is a large sum, but it represented only approximately 0.38 per cent of total state budgetary expenditure over the same period. Indeed, the figure for 1986 (0.31 per cent) was actually lower than the average for 1980–2 (0.43 per cent). Yet a spokesman for the western province of Qinghai had called for the Fund to be rapidly increased to 5 per cent of the state budget.[14]

This can be contrasted with the experience of Yugoslavia, where two separate funds for aiding underdeveloped regions have been in existence since 1965 (and there had been policies for such aid even before that). By the early 1980s these funds were supposed to be running at an annual rate of about 2.7 per cent of Yugoslavia's Gross Material Product. Yet, despite that, on many indicators it was calculated that regional inequality in Yugoslavia had actually increased since 1945.[15]

In China, however, the Fund to Aid Underdeveloped Regions was equal to only about 0.1 per cent of national income. Moreover, it was spread thinly: by 1986 roughly 60 per cent of all China's counties were receiving some money from it, roughly double the percentage when the Fund was first established in 1980. Apart from indicating the degree of poverty still to be found in the Chinese countryside, this increase also demonstrates once again the power of regional and provincial lobbies. Since almost all provinces have some poor counties, they all begin to demand aid once they see that other areas are receiving it. The scale of the overall problem of subsidies and aid can be seen from the estimate that, whereas between 1980 and 1983 the income of central government grew by 0.9 per cent, its expenditure grew by 8.7 per cent.[16] By 1988 the centre's revenue from local government was insufficient to cover the subsidies which it had to pay out.[17]

For all these reasons, then, central government has felt under intense pressure. In addition, there are demands made upon it for large-scale infrastructural projects (described in chapters 5 and 6) which are essential for future economic growth. In 1981 matters came to such a pass that, notwithstanding its commitment to leave provinces with stable revenue for three years, central government had, at short notice, to

extract from them loans of 7 billion yuan RMB to meet its obligations, and in 1982 it borrowed a further 4 billion. Later years have
seen further calls on the provinces for funds to bail out central
government.

Not surprisingly, there have been demands for central government's
share of state budget expenditure to be raised to 60–70 per cent. The
Minister of Finance, for example, has been calling for this since at least
1984.[18] Envious comparisons have been drawn with Japan, where
central government does receive and spend two-thirds of all fiscal
revenue.[19] Nevertheless, nothing much has been achieved in this
respect, and there seems little likelihood that it will be, for the centre
no longer has the power to impose it. Indeed, the major change in centre-
province budgetary relations for 1988 was the acquisition by the provinces
of the right to retain all of their income from a number of minor taxes
instead of revenue-sharing with the centre.[20]

Instead, the most that can be expected is that central and local
governments should have their own separate taxes. As a result, central
government could be more confident about its future income and less
dependent upon the honesty of provincial governments in declaring
all the income which they have collected. In the meantime it was
proposed that central government should be entitled to most of the revenue
from specific categories of enterprise — a concession designed to stabilize
its income. So in 1985 four central economic agencies, and the enterprises which were directly subordinated to them, began to pay most of
their taxes to central government. These were the Ministry of Petroleum,
the Ministry of Electric Power, the General Petroleum Company and
the General Non-Ferrous Metallurgical Company. It was laid down that
70 per cent of the revenue from the product tax, value-added tax,
and turnover taxes paid by these bodies, would be certain to go to
central government, while 30 per cent went into the general revenue
pool to be divided between the centre and individual provincial governments.[21] No doubt this process of differentiation of revenue will be
taken further.

Financial regulation

Central government is consequently less able to ensure a regionally
co-ordinated programme of economic development. Many provinces have
gained from the change and have become more assertive. For example,
even Shanghai, one of the three provincial-level cities whose revenue
and expenditure are most tightly controlled from the centre, has managed
to increase its share of income from 10 per cent to 25 per cent during
the 1980s.

Nevertheless, national economic life will not necessarily disintegrate as a consequence. One of the key elements of economic reform since 1978 has been the change to less direct economic control by the state, and in particular greater use of market methods and financial levers, than administrative measures. The financial sector has acquired greater powers and responsibilities than ever before, so that if a unified national market could be created, it would represent as powerful a force for national integration as anything central government had been able to do in the past. In 1984 the state established four 'specialized' banks to perform normal commercial banking operations — the People's Construction Bank, the Industrial and Commercial Bank, the Agricultural Bank and the Bank of China (to handle foreign exchange transactions). These were to be supervised by the People's Bank of China as a kind of central bank both nationally and regionally. These four commercial banks were intended to operate with uniform policies throughout the country. They all had provincial and lower-level branches, which were allocated funds from their head offices in Beijing. Initially, therefore, the aim was to create a co-ordinated and fairly centralized banking sector, which would integrate the national economy.

A major problem emerged fairly quickly: the ability of bank branches to operate commercially, in the normal sense of the term. If they were tightly controlled by their own headquarters, then lower-level bank officials would not learn how to allocate credit on a commercial basis, and they would learn little about the means of stimulating enterprises to produce more while minimizing risks. Unless they could be brought to do this, the underlying intention of the reform, namely to introduce commercial and market discipline into the use of resources, would continue to be frustrated. In other words, bank branches had themselves to become more commercial in their orientation and operations.

To overcome these difficulties, in 1985 five major cities were designated experimental financial centres. Among other things this meant that the banks there began to operate as enterprises in their own right on a self-financing basis. They would be allocated a certain share of their parent bank's resources, and then would be responsible for their own profits and losses. The experiment was judged a success, and by mid-1987 the reform had been extended to a further twenty-two cities. A key feature was that it tended to strengthen financial co-ordination at a level below that of the province. These cities were all expected to play a central role in the integration of national development (mentioned in chapter 1). By doing so they could, among other things, mitigate the effects of the provinces' enhanced budgetary autonomy and help shore up central control.

As market reforms have gradually developed, bank officials in the major cities have begun to set up regional networks for exchanging short-term credit and information, and these networks cut across provincial boundaries. One, for example, is centred on Shanghai and links fifteen cities in the Central-South region.[22] Thus there is no doubt that these central cities are indeed beginning to establish 'horizontal links' across the country (chapters 1 and 2).

The more management of the banking system comes to resemble that of other sectors of the economy, the more it is likely to encounter the same sorts of problems which have bedevilled management elsewhere, in particular the danger of administrative interference by local officials. The relaxation of central controls has given the latter greater latitude to pursue their own priorities. For example, urban officials have demanded extra 'contributions' from local enterprises towards the enormous costs of urban development. They have used unofficial methods to protect local industries and even prevent the closure of loss-making enterprises, provided their officials have been 'co-operative'. Thus local party officials have acquired an incentive to obstruct both the simplification of the management of the economy and also the greater reliance upon market forces, for thorough-going reform would weaken their power and patronage.

Bank officials can suffer from the same kind of administrative interference as factory officials. Prybyla, for instance, notes the example of a county-level party committee in Guangxi province which told local bank officials who were reluctant to lend money for building questionable town and township enterprises: 'We are not in charge of personnel administration, but your "party tickets" are in our hands . . . You don't have to follow the leadership of the county government . . . [But] if you refuse to give help, don't call us when you have a problem'.[23] The suicide in 1985 of a Sichuan bank official caught between local party officials who wanted him to make more credit available for local enterprises, and his banking superiors who wanted him to keep credit steady, provides an even more piquant example.

It is true that a number of Chinese bank officials claimed in interviews in 1987 that there were no such problems because local governments had no legal right to interfere, and because both county- and provincial-level authorities were basically rational.[24] It is also the case that the former head of the People's Bank, Chen Muhua, recently claimed that the co-ordination of the work in the specialized banks has now improved, with the old principle of horizontal subordination to local control better integrated with vertical subordination to the banks' own leaders. Increased training of bank officials should also contribute to this integration.[25] Yet it is still the case that provincial governments have a major say in the appointment of provincial-level officials in the specialized banks, and the provincial party committee claims the right to oversee such appointments. Since such bank officials are likely to be party members, the authority of the party committee is no doubt great. This is yet another dimension of the thorny and complex question of defining the appropriate role for the party in an increasingly market-oriented economy. In any case the local authority, whether county or province, can choose whether to 'help' with problems of family accommodation and social welfare according to the extent of co-operation received from banking officials.

Even though the reforms may indeed bring greater market discipline to financial operations, the gradual transformation of lower-level branches of banks into distinct profit centres will also increase the potential leverage of local political officials over sources of credit, and limit the ability of central bank officials to stem the tide of excessive credit expansion. Factories may find that their budgetary constraints are as soft as they were before, provided their management stays on good terms with local party and state officials. In turn this will restrict the effectiveness with which national leaders can use indirect levers such as credit policy to regulate the economy and to control problems such as inflation.

Regional governments have themselves begun to set up financial agencies to compete with banks. For example, trust companies and funds with resources drawn from local fiscal revenue have been established with the intention that they should be (at least ideally) self-financing and offer loans to local enterprises for specific projects. This has occurred both at provincial and lower levels. Since 1982 the city of Chongqing has established funds for capital investment, for developing the circulating capital of agricultural enterprises, for preserving the environment, for developing urban services, for developing science and technology, for the technical re-equipping of enterprises, for export promotion and for creating vegetable plots. By the end of August 1987 the city had over 300 million yuan RMB capital in those funds.[26] It is no wonder that in 1986 a spokesman claimed that the city now enjoyed a 'balanced dialogue' with the authorities in Beijing.[27]

One key feature of this change is that there is as yet no national legal framework to regulate the operation of such funds, and presumably this means that local authorities are fairly free to set their own conditions to loans, including interest rates. Presumably, too, they are to some extent competitors of the specialized banks and this is yet one more way in which they can exert pressure on those banks.

Financial developments thus seem unlikely to reduce the decentralizing tendencies in the economy. In one respect more general economic developments may mitigate the effects of the increasing fiscal autonomy of the provincial level of government. Indeed Unger has suggested that a main reason counties set up new corporations to manage local enterprises was to prevent tax revenue from flowing out of their area.[28] If large cities, as well as provinces, can now effectively co-ordinate their local development, this will mean that central government may be able to manipulate the divisions between the interests of provinces and cities in such a way as to maintain a large degree of control. On the other hand, the prospect of major cities such as Chongqing, as well as provinces, now enjoying a 'balanced dialogue' with Beijing is unlikely to be relished by many officials in the capital. The demands made upon them are likely to increase, and resources will be even more tightly stretched.

One other development seems particularly significant. The financial experiments have now been officially extended to the provincial as well as to the subprovincial level. The province which since 1986 has been designated as the one to lead the way is Guangdong, the province which already has maximum budgetary autonomy. An official in the reform office of the Guangdong provincial government has come out strongly in favour of a proliferation of financial institutions (for example, credit co-operatives, or local credit markets) as well as greater business autonomy for provincial and city branches of the specialized banks.[29] Within a few years, then, there is the prospect of major financial as well as budgetary autonomy for Guangdong. If Guangdong is successful, then no doubt other provinces will be tempted to follow suit.

Conclusion

It has been argued that central government in China is now financially weaker than at any time since 1949, while local authorities, especially those at provincial level, have become more assertive. Nevertheless, this should not be taken to imply that central government is weak and helpless, nor that provincial governments are all-powerful. After all, one of the reasons why the reforms have gone so far has been the ability of central government to push them through despite the opposition of some conservative provincial leaders. In moments of real economic crisis, as in 1985 when inflation threatened to get out of hand, central government can force through contractionary policies despite local opposition.

What is emerging is moderated central leadership, and more genuine partnership, though not everyone in Beijing has fully come to terms with it. The continued existence of dual subordination, where departments in provincial governments are subordinated both to their own provincial leaders and also to the corresponding sectoral ministry in Beijing, means that central government is still expected to play a leading role in formulating and co-ordinating national policy, for example, through national work conferences, as well as stacks of documents and directives. Local government has to pay attention to all of that.

Obviously local departments often use local circumstances to obtain help from their corresponding ministry in Beijing, or to resist central decisions which are thought likely to harm local interests. On the other hand, it is also regularly the case that a local department, in order to reach its own goal, will cite the opinions of its ministry to persuade the local authority. In this way ministries can encourage nationwide co-ordination of policies without having to impose their will. In addition, ministries may have economic inducements at their disposal. For example, every year the state allocates a large amount of foreign currency to the Ministry of Commerce to pay for the import of consumer goods such as colour televisions and refrigerators, as well as chemical fertilizers and pesticides, which will give peasants an incentive to make large deliveries of agricultural produce to the state. Since this can have a major impact on the fulfilment of a province's agricultural output target, local governments and organizations try their hardest to obtain a large share of these goods.

Alternatively, ministries can allocate resources for development projects where local officials are prepared to be co-operative, as is the case in Shanxi and Shandong (see chapters 8 and 9 respectively). Even though central government may feel itself increasingly impoverished, it has still launched new projects to develop backward areas in collaboration with local authorities, as well as channelling foreign aid in their direction (see chapter 1).

In another respect, too, the government can view with some satisfaction the course of recent social and economic trends. During 1979–84 there was an apparent reduction in inequality between the provinces when viewed as economic units, as Table 3.3 demonstrates. Even though the central leadership has since 1978 declared itself ready to tolerate, if necessary, increased regional inequality as the price for more rapid economic development, the evidence suggests that this has not occurred, at least not as far as industrial production is concerned. Of course, the range between the provinces with the highest and lowest per capita output has been reduced simply because Shanghai has been held back by comparison with the rest of the country. It is certainly not because of any accelerated growth in the provinces with the lowest per capita output, Tibet and Guizhou. Yet the coefficient of relative variation shows greater evenness of development, with some of the other provinces that had been markedly strong in industrial production falling back towards the national average (for example, Liaoning, Beijing and Tianjin), while others have begun to outperform the national average for the first time (for example, Zhejiang and Hubei). Thus the overall level of per capita industrial development does seem to be becoming more homogenous.

Admittedly, in the case of agriculture, as can be seen from Table 3.4, there seems to have been a slight increase in inter-provincial inequality. On the other hand, it must be stressed that this started from a base of very low inequality, certainly by international standards. One conclusion

Table 3.3 Provincial distribution of per capita industrial output — 1957, 1965, 1974, 1979 and 1984 (% of national average)

Province	1957	1965	1974	1979	1984
North					
Beijing	481	385	617	513	437
Tianjin	1,112	572	663	498	463
Hebei	55	86	122	84	78
Shanxi	92	n.a	72	91	97
Inner Mongolia	60	251	187	63	61
North-east					
Liaoning	385	334	300	257	232
Jilin	161	148	109	120	121
Heilongjiang	222	195	127	141	141
East					
Shanghai	1,517	1,165	1,404	1,106	908
Jiangsu	84	93	113	138	162
Zhejiang	76	72	58	85	123
Anhui	36	40	36	51	48
Fujian	69	56	48	59	62
Jiangxi	54	n.a.	49	51	52
Shandong	62	58	77	87	88
Central-South					
Henan	30	41	43	50	51
Hubei	74	64	58	86	108
Hunan	40	41	44	63	61
Guangxi	33	32	37	57	40
Guangdong	84	94	85	79	87
South-west					
Sichuan	55	53	41	54	57
Yunnan	48	38	32	40	46
Guizhou	33	48	34	36	37
Tibet	7	13	14	11	10
North-west					
Shaanxi	56	73	64	80	72
Gansu	51	87	100	92	71
Qinghai	45	73	99	78	59
Ningxia	10	24	35	80	66
Xinjiang	82	86	46	54	65
Range (exc Tibet)	152:1	49:1	44:1	31:1	25:1
Coefficient of variation	1.87	1.5	1.72	1.49	1.32

Sources: For 1957–9, cited or calculated in Riskin, C. (1987) *China's Political Economy*, Oxford and New York: Oxford University Press, p. 226; for 1984, calculated from data in *Zhongguo tongji nianjian 1985*, Beijing, 1985.

that emerges from these agricultural figures is the increasing importance of the Eastern region for agricultural output. Of the provinces in that

Table 3.4 Agricultural output per capita, 1957, 1979 and 1984, by province (% of national average)

Province	1957	1979	1984
North			
Beijing	—	—	—
Tianjin	101	109	101
Hebei	—	—	—
Shanxi	98	98	94
Inner Mongolia	143	94	88
North-east			
Liaoning	81	99	113
Jilin	117	104	119
Heilongjiang	166	115	109
East			
Shanghai	—	—	—
Jiangsu	78	142	150
Zhejiang	103	133	142
Anhui	97	87	98
Fujian	85	94	101
Jiangxi	111	101	88
Shandong	82	133	130
Central-South			
Henan	95	88	87
Hubei	122	125	109
Hunan	103	111	95
Guangdong	102	88	95
Guangxi	97	85	71
South-west			
Sichuan	90	83	83
Guizhou	102	64	65
Yunnan	103	75	68
Tibet	—	139	116
North-west			
Shaanxi	135	87	77
Gansu	119	71	59
Qinghai	119	92	76
Ningxia	—	79	78
Xinjiang	171	104	106

Sources: For 1957–79, calculated or cited in Riskin, C. (1987) *China's Political Economy*, Oxford and New York: Oxford University Press, p. 230; for 1984, calculated from data in *Zhongguo tongji nianjian 1985*, Beijing, 1985

region, only Jiangxi shows a relative decline. In Anhui, agricultural output has remained roughly static, while all the others have shown a significant improvement. By contrast, there has been a dramatic decline in the relative performance of the provinces in the South-west and the North-west. In those regions many provinces that were well above the average level of per capita output in 1957 had by 1984 fallen to a level well below the national average: as, for example, Gansu, Qinghai and above all Shaanxi. Even in the Central-South region, output has regressed much closer to the national average. Nevertheless, agricultural production remains relatively even. Although the coefficient of relative variation for 1984 was 0.31, and therefore two-thirds higher than the figure for 1979 (0.19), it was still slightly less than a quarter of that for industry.

The evidence on regional development since 1978 is mixed. At the very least, however, it suggests that if this performance can be maintained, it will assuage some of the anxieties about growing regional inequality. On the other hand, it is doubtful if that will mollify less developed regions who want a clear reduction in their relative backwardness. The National People's Congress in April 1988 heard vociferous complaints about this from delegates from poorer areas, and as the NPC comes to occupy a more prominent place in national life, it is likely that public opinion in those areas will become more vocal on the issue. Nor will the apparent success in containing regional inequality be of much consolation to the Ministry of Finance, which will continue to lament the shortage of funds at its disposal and the many urgent projects which it cannot finance. The way seems set for more heated exchanges between the centre and the provinces over the allocation of resources in the future.

Notes

1 Yu Ruihou (1981) 'Finance should energetically support the development of underdeveloped regions', in *Lun caizheng zhidu gaige, di si ci quanguo caizheng lilun taolunhui wenxuan (On Reform of the Financial System: a selection of papers from the fourth national conference on financial theory)*, Beijing, p. 158.
2 *Guojia yusuan (The State Budget)*, Beijing: 1982, p. 53.
3 Tian Yinong, Zhu Fulin and Xiang Huaicheng (1985) *Lun Zhongguo caizheng guanli tizhide gaige (On Reform of the Chinese Financial Management System)*, Beijing, p. 76.
4 Unger, J. (1987) 'The struggle to dictate China's administration: the conflict of branches vs areas vs reform', mimeo, Australian National University.
5 Gao Yang, 'On the problems of raising the leadership level of leading cadres', *Hongqi*, (1987) 16, p. 3.
6 Dai Yuanchen and He Suoheng, 'Macro-economic policy choices to be faced in a time of financial difficulties', *Jingji Yanjiu*, (1987) 6, p. 29.
7 Hu Yueting, (1984) 'A discussion of problems in local government finance', in *Di liu ci quanguo caizheng lilun taolunhui wenxuan (Selection of papers from the sixth national conference on financial theory)*, Beijing, p. 261.

8 Zhu Fulin, 'Some views on the reform of our financial system in recent years', *Caizheng*, 1983 (3), p. 17.

9 Tian Yinong *et al.*, op. cit., p. 76.

10 Ibid., p. 90.

11 Liu Suinian, 'The necessity of upholding the policy of a slight surplus in balancing income and expenditure', *Caizheng*, 1982 (8), p. 6.

12 Chen Jiyuan (1981) 'Regional Economic Structure', in Ma Hong and Sun Shangqing (eds), *Zhongguo jingji jiegou wenti yanjiu (Research on China's Economic Structure)*, Beijing, vol. 2, pp. 680–1.

13 *Caizheng*, 1981 (1), p. 1.

14 Yu Ruihou (1981) op. cit., p. 165.

15 Schrenk, M., Ardalan, C. and Tatawy, E. (1979) *Yugoslavia — Self-Management Socialism: Challenges of Development*, Baltimore: The Johns Hopkins University Press and the World Bank, pp. 286–308; Berković, E. (1986) *Socijalne nejednakosti u Jugoslaviji*, Belgrade: Ekonomika, pp. 140–60.

16 Wang Zuyao and Fan Yong, 'Enquiry into reform of the financial system and strengthening the financial resources of the central government', *Caizheng*, (12), p. 20.

17 Yao Dechao, 'The necessity of increasing two proportions', *Caizheng*, 1988 (3), p. 35.

18 Wang Bingqian, 'New problems in financial work', *Hongqi*, 1984 (7), p. 4.

19 Xiang Wenqiao, 'The key lies in rationally dividing the fiscal powers of central and local government', *Caizheng*, 1988 (3), p. 36.

20 Huang Daxiao and Xu Yonghua, 'An explanation of the changed situation in the division of budgetary revenue between centre and province for 1988', *Caizheng*, 1988 (4), p. 17–19.

21 *Caizheng*, 1985 (4), p. 23.

22 Zhou Zhishi and Wu Yalun, 'The capital market and liaison network of 15 cities is opening up and developing', *Zhongguo Jinrong*, 1988 (1), p. 59.

23 Prybyla, J.S. (1986) 'China's Economic Experiment: from Mao to Market', *Problems of Communism*, January-February, p. 31.

24 White, G. and Bowles, P. (1987) 'Towards a Capital Market? Reforms in the Chinese Banking System', China Research Report no. 6, Institute for Development Studies, University of Sussex.

25 'Main achievements in reform of the financial system and a few thoughts on personal experience', *Zhongguo Jinrong*, 1988 (3), p. 14.

26 Guo Daimo, 'Develop fiscal credit, open up financial management', *Caizheng*, 1988 (3), p. 37.

27 *Far Eastern Economic Review*, 3 July 1986.

28 Unger (1987) op. cit.

29 Liao Shuhui, 'On our current financial reform', *Lilun Yuekan*, 1987 (9), pp. 17–18.

Chapter four

Foreign trade

Martin Lockett

For almost a decade the 'opening up' of the Chinese economy to the outside world has been a key part of China's reforms. This chapter analyses the uneven impact of that policy on China's regions and its implications for the future. Greatly increased foreign economic relations have reinforced existing differences among regions of China, in particular the predominance of eastern and southern coastal regions. It is argued that regional inequalities have led to differing patterns of development, accompanied by distinct regional economic and political interests regarding foreign economic relations. In particular, some coastal areas are moving towards a form of export-oriented development which is in certain respects similar to that of the newly-industrializing countries (NICs) of East Asia.

In examining regional aspects of Chinese development, one must remember that China's provinces are not small if judged by international standards. Sichuan, for example, has a population which, if it were independent, would make it the eighth largest country in the world. The existence of substantial regional diversity should therefore not be surprising. Detailed analysis, however, is difficult, since the statistical and other data necessary for examining differences in foreign economic relations among China's regions is hard to come by.

The 'open-door' policy

Since 1979 China's foreign economic relations have been based on the principle of the 'open door' to promote foreign trade and investment. In contrast to past policies stressing 'self-reliance', the Chinese leadership now sees major benefits from international specialization and trade. This includes some acceptance of the principle of comparative advantage as well as the benefits of international competition. However, economic policies generally support protection of the domestic market in sectors where domestic producers exist. Administrative controls persist, limiting many types of import and some exports.

China's exports to the rest of the world increased rapidly during the 1970s and especially the 1980s. By the mid-1980s exports were over ten times their 1970 level. Over time, China's imports have risen roughly in balance with exports as China has tended to pursue a goal of trade balance. In practice the growth of exports usually limits imports. However, in the mid-1980s a major trade deficit emerged as a result of stagnating exports and rising imports. In 1987, export growth, combined with limits on imports, had again balanced foreign trade, leaving a small surplus of US $1.9 billion.[1]

China has also sought to diversify its trading links, perhaps still mindful of the problems of dependence on the Soviet Union during the 1950s, and its subsequent international isolation. China's biggest trade partner is Japan, with which 30 per cent of total trade was conducted in 1985. Next come Hong Kong with 17 per cent, and the USA with 11 per cent. Trade with European countries constituted 21 per cent of the total. China's trade is therefore centred on its neighbours, and on the more advanced industrial countries, rather than on the Third World or other socialist countries — though 3 per cent of trade was with the Soviet Union.

Authority to conduct foreign trade has been substantially decentralized. As with many of China's reforms, the progress has been uneven, and details are often uncertain. Two main forms of decentralization can be seen. The first is 'geographical' decentralization, whereby provinces (and in some cases cities) have set up trading corporations for their own area. The second is enterprise decentralization, with some enterprises being given rights to conduct foreign trade negotiations independently. In addition, rights to borrow from foreign sources and to invest in joint ventures have been given to national bodies, including the Bank of China and the China International Trust and Investment Corporation (CITIC).

In line with other economic reforms, there have been moves towards using indirect economic, rather than direct administrative, levers to control foreign trade. Provinces and enterprises have in theory been given the right to retain part of their foreign currency earnings, though in practice the extent to which this happens varies substantially. Further, the trade deficit in the mid-1980s led to a reimposition of many administrative controls. At that time, many enterprises saw domestic sales as both easier and more profitable than exports, while imports were relatively cheap. However, the subsequent devaluation of the Chinese yuan against the US dollar and other currencies has corrected this situation, at least in part. From 1988 further reforms in the foreign trade system will increase the autonomy of local foreign trade bodies and certain enterprises, so that they will be more responsible for their foreign-exchange transactions.

Reversing previous policies, China now encourages foreign investment, mainly through establishing joint ventures, but also by permitting wholly-owned subsidiaries of foreign firms. A number of laws have been passed concerning joint ventures, and in the mid-1980s further measures were put forward to boost foreign investment. Of the two types of investment open to foreign companies — joint ventures with Chinese partners or wholly-owned subsidiaries in China — the central authorities generally prefer joint ventures, of which there are two types, equity and contractual. They have tried to encourage, in particular, equity joint ventures, which involve establishing a completely new company with shareholdings from China and abroad. Contractual joint ventures are preferred by many foreign investors, and have a legal contract specifying the contributions and benefits on both sides.

China has been successful in starting to attract foreign investment, especially from Hong Kong. Much has gone to the Special Economic Zones (originally four, but five since Hainan was accredited in 1988); the fourteen 'open' coastal cities; and the three 'open economic zones' the Zhujiang (Pearl River delta in Guangdong, the southern Fujian delta area of South-east China, and the Yangtze delta centred in Shanghai). By September 1987 there were 8,943 enterprises with foreign investment. Although US $21 billion of investment had been agreed, only US $7.6 billion of this had actually been utilized.[2] At the end of 1986, 46 per cent of such enterprises were equity joint ventures, 51 per cent contractual joint ventures and 2 per cent wholly foreign-owned. China had also set up 385 enterprises abroad (including Hong Kong and Macao) with a US $0.6 billion investment, [3] many as joint ventures with foreign partners.

Although most joint ventures are claimed by China to be operating well, there are many problems for foreign investors, including, in particular, weak infrastructure, administrative bureaucracy, foreign-exchange constraints and the quality of the labour force. There have been conflicts related to objectives: China wants to increase exports and absorb advanced technology, whereas some foreign investors are looking for a means of entry into China's domestic market. Currently such access is limited, although recent regulations have extended preferential treatment to import-substitution as well as exports. The management rights of foreigners are being extended, for example through proposals by Communist Party general secretary Zhao Ziyang for foreign managers to bid to run Chinese enterprises under contract.[4]

The regional pattern

As indicated in chapter 1, the Seventh Five-Year Plan embodies the official promotion of regional differentiation in development, and this is reflected in the pattern of China's trade during the 1980s. The policy of the 'open door' has been limited in its impact largely to the coastal areas, particularly the SEZs and coastal cities. In addition, the expansion of foreign trade implies a greater role for ports and other transport centres. Generally, the coastal areas of China are seen as the leaders in both 'opening up' and overall economic reform.[5]

However, an examination of the three regions specified in the Seventh FYP indicates that the Eastern Coastal Region is even more dominant in foreign trade than in production, as shown in the figures in Table 4.1. Over three-quarters of China's exports come from the Eastern Coastal Region, compared with about half of national income and 40 per cent of the population. Thus the position at the start of the Seventh FYP is one of major regional differences between a more prosperous Eastern Coastal Region and less prosperous Central and Western ones, with the latter much less involved in foreign trade.

Table 4.1 Population, income and trade by Seventh FYP region, 1986

Region	Popu- lation (1985, m)	National income (¥bn)	Exports (US $ bn)	% Popu- lation	% of national income	% of exports	Exports/ national income (%)
Eastern Coastal	430	405	17.7	41	52	77	13
Central	371	247	3.9	36	32	17	5
Western	240	127	1.2	23	16	5	3
		(GNP, US$bn)					
Taiwan	20	73	39.8	n.a	n.a	n.a	55

Source: See Table 4.2.

An index of the importance of foreign trade to each region can be derived from the export statistics. This shows that the Eastern Coastal Region is much more involved in foreign trade relative to its overall level of national income than either the Central or the Western Regions. In fact, the main gap is between the Eastern Coastal Region and the rest of China. However, even in the Eastern Coastal Region the involvement in foreign trade is still low in world terms — with an average of around US $40 exports per person. A comparable (1985) figure for Taiwan was US $2,000 exports per person. In the Central Region, exports were only US $11 per person and even lower — at US $5 per person — in the Western Region.

While these figures show major differences, further subdivision down to the provincial level indicates a more complex pattern, as shown in Table 4.2. The provincial-level cities of Shanghai, Tianjin and Beijing have both higher national income and higher exports per person than

Table 4.2 Population, national income* and exports by Seventh FYP region and province

Region/ province	Population (1985, m)[b]	National income[c] (¥bn)	Exports (US $m)[d]	National income/ person (¥)	Exports/ person (US $)	Exports/ national income (%)
Eastern Coastal						
Beijing	9.60	21.00	720	2,188	75	10.1
Fujian	27.13	17.81[e]	579	657	21	9.6
Guangdong[a]	62.53	56.10	4,290	897	69	22.5
Guangxi	38.73	17.74	431	458	11	7.1
Hebei	55.48	37.50	1,050	676	19	8.2
Jiangsu	62.13	63.10	1,720	1,016	28	8.0
Liaoning	36.86	48.00	1,170	1,302	32	7.2
Shandong	76.95	49.50	2,140	643	28	12.7
Shanghai	12.17	35.70[e]	3,550	2,933	292	29.2
Tianjin	8.08	16.84[e]	847	2,084	105	14.8
Zhejiang	40.30	42.00	1,156	1,042	29	8.1
TOTAL	429.96	405.29	17,653	943	41	12.8
Central						
Anhui	51.56	31.40	370	609	7	3.5
Heilongjiang	33.11	32.75	605	989	18	5.4
Henan	77.13	42.37[e]	442[e]	549	6	3.1
Hubei	49.31	38.30	720	777	15	5.5
Hunan	56.22	33.70	500	599	9	4.4
Inner Mongolia	20.07	12.70	147	633	7	3.4
Jiangxi	34.60	18.91	300	547	9	4.7
Jilin	22.98	18.88	525	822	23	8.2
Shanxi	26.27	18.00	302	685	11	4.9
TOTAL	371.25	247.01	3,911	665	11	4.7
Western						
Gansu	20.41	11.50[e]	100	563	5	2.6
Guizhou	29.68	13.08[e]	6	441	0	0.1
Ningxia	4.15	2.60	75	627	18	8.4
Qinghai	4.07	2.70[e]	25	663	6	2.7
Shaanxi	30.02	15.90	170	530	6	3.1
Sichuan	101.88	53.70	489	527	5	2.7
Tibet	1.99	1.26[e]	5	633	3	1.2
Xinjiang	13.61	10.28[e]	203	755	15	5.8
Yunnan	34.06	15.53	169	456	5	3.2
TOTAL	239.87	126.55	1,242	528	5	2.9

Notes:
(a) the figures for Guangdong province include Hainan Island. Hainan was established as a separate province in 1988.
(b) population figures are from *Zhongguo tongji nianjian 1986.*
(c) figures for national income and exports are taken from provincial annual statistical communiqués, where available, or from other sources reported in SWB during 1987. Where figures are not available, national income was estimated on the basis of 1984 figures multiplied by the national growth rate of national income between 1984 and 1986. The figure for Henan's exports were estimated from figures for the first part of 1987.
(d) the average 1986 RMB/US$ exchange rate of 2.96/$ is used to calculate the proportion of exports in national income.
(e) when these provincial figures are compared with the national ones from the State Statistical Bureau, some discrepancies emerge. A difference between provincial and national total population figures was due to non-counting of PLA personnel. In the case of national income, there was a small difference between the provincial figures and the 1986 national total, which can be accounted for by the need to estimate the figure for some provinces. In the case of export figures, the difference was larger, with 11.5 per cent of total exports not in the total of provincial figures. This may be due to some exports not being recorded under provincial totals, differences in calculations or other errors and omissions.
* National income is a measure of economic development based on the net output of industry, agriculture, construction, posts and communications, and commerce. It has been used in this chapter as it is the most widely available figure related to net as opposed to gross output. However, it does exclude various economic activities which would be included in GNP or GDP calculations.

any other province. But more striking is the high level of foreign trade in Guangdong, which is now the province with highest exports, displacing Shanghai from its previous top position. This reflects major changes in the economy of Guangdong and other coastal provinces as a result of the policies of the 'open door'.

The southern coastal provinces

Reforms in foreign economc relations have developed furthest in Guangdong and Fujian. In the future, Hainan Island is likely to go further still. All three provinces have been given special powers in dealing with foreign exchange, and encompass all China's SEZs. At provincial level, Guangdong and Fujian both have the right to decide on, and use, foreign loans subject to a centrally-set ceiling,[6] as well as greater autonomy in overall provincial finances.[7]

This is essentially 'geographical' decentralization to local government rather than to individual enterprises. In principle, state enterprises should go through provincial or national trade organizations for foreign trade. However, some state and all collective-sector enterprises — notably rural industries — may also deal directly with foreign customers. But there are limits: rural entrepreneurs, for example, found themselves forbidden by regulations to export canned mushrooms.[8] While this means a complex set of relationships for foreign investors, the overall effect is to create a more receptive environment for foreign trade and investment compared with most of the rest of China.

Guangdong and Hainan are also going faster than other regions in implementing a wider set of economic reforms. The Chinese government has approved a ten-point reform plan put forward by Guangdong, which includes liberalization of foreign-exchange controls, and the setting of prices through market forces within five years, except for energy, grain, transport and communications.[9]

As detailed in chapter 7, there are signs that the disappointing export performance of the SEZs is improving. In the first half of 1987, exports increased by 127 per cent over 1986. Moreover, Hainan Island, established as a new province and area for development in 1988 is intended to be 'more special' than the other SEZs, not least because it is seen as 'an advanced experimental area for overall economic reform'.[10] The state sector will not be as dominant as in the rest of China, with foreign investment playing a leading role. Tariffs will be lower than elsewhere, with restrictions being put on domestic trade so as to avoid a repetition of a previous scandal involving the selling of imported cars to the mainland. Already many qualified people are coming to Hainan seeking the jobs which should be created by the new policies — one report talks of 150,000 such job-seekers.[11]

Throughout the southern coastal provinces the expansion of processing and export production has led to much greater imports. Part of this has been in upgrading production facilities to increase capacity and improve quality. In 1986, equipment imports into Guangdong were US $500 million.[12] Imports of raw materials are likely to rise significantly as a result of the shift in policy towards obtaining imported materials for export-processing industries. There has also been a growth in consumer product imports, especially in the SEZs, but also more generally in Guangdong and Fujian. It has been financed by local retention of foreign-exchange earnings. Recent import curbs have reduced this to some extent, but the exact picture is unclear owing to a lack of systematic information. Both wages and prices have risen as a result of these policies, especially in the SEZs. In Shenzhen, prices now reflect those in Hong Kong more than the rest of China, while wages are much higher.

The other southern coastal province, Guangxi, has changed less, though it has direct access to the outside world through its ports, in particular Beihai — designated an open coastal city. However, Beihai has been seen as the weakest of the fourteen coastal cities. By 1987, it had only attracted about US $20 million in foreign investment.[13] Potentially, Guangxi could emulate Guangdong — and this is now being recognized. Guangxi claims to have moved away from defensiveness towards Guangdong, and is now advocating increased links.[14] Guangdong's advanced level of economic development and exports, and Guangxi's resources and energy could be complementary. If such links do develop, then Guangxi could become the link between Guangdong and the outside world on the one hand, and much of south-west China on the other. Guangxi has also been pushing ideas of co-operation with east China, including joint ventures. For example, Guangxi has been offering half-rate corporate taxes for Jiangsu investors.[15]

The pattern of development in Guangdong, and to some extent Fujian, is moving towards export-orientated industrialization — as is intended for Hainan, and potentially Guangxi, in the future. The main exports are in light industry, especially processing contracts, textiles products and electronics, as well as agricultural and processed food products. This is similar to the form of development in other rapid-growth East Asian economies, except that much of the trade is through Hong Kong rather than directly with other countries. 1987's export growth in Guangdong and Fujian is comparable with that of other East Asian economies in the past: Fujian's exports rose by 49 per cent and Hainan's by 110 per cent in the first nine months of the year,[16] while in the first half of 1987 Guangdong's were 53 per cent higher than in 1986.[17] The parallel with the 'four little dragons' of East Asia — Hong Kong, South Korea, Singapore, Taiwan — at the beginning of the 1980s has been explicitly recognized by the CCP.

The shift to export-oriented industrialization is inhibited by a weak economic base and infrastructure, particularly in Hainan, but also more generally in much of Guangdong and Fujian. Except in some areas like Guangzhou and Xiamen, the skills of the labour force are often quite low, and many are first-generation workers. The supply of energy and other raw materials is a continuing and serious problem. Yet the combination of a favourable regulatory environment and other factors has led to rapid expansion of trade and investment, especially in Guangdong. Particularly important factors are the cultural, linguistic and family connections between Guangdong, Hong Kong and Macao, as well as those between Fujian and Taiwan. More generally, most of the overseas Chinese in South-East Asia and other areas come from Guangdong or Fujian. These family connections mean both financial transfers from overseas relatives and a propensity to invest in 'home towns', even when economically this may not be optimal. As a result the connections of Guangdong and Fujian with Hong Kong and Taiwan are of substantial importance.

Hong Kong companies have been increasing their contacts with China by both direct investment and contracts with Chinese enterprises. By 1987, Hong Kong and Macao firms were contracting processing and assembly work to some 10,000 factories employing almost one million workers in neighbouring Guangdong province. China has also been increasing its direct and indirect investment in Hong Kong, as well as through direct trading links. By mid-1986, it was estimated that PRC-based companies had over HK \$1 billion invested in Hong Kong.[18]

Fujian's greatest potential is in links with Taiwan. These are restrained by political rather than economic factors, as a result of the adherence of the Taiwan authorities to the 'three no's' of 'no compromise, no contacts and no negotiations'. Meanwhile the PRC is pushing for the 'three links' of posts, transport and trade. The prospects for a change in Taiwan's attitude in the short term are not good. In October 1987, Taiwan Premier Yu Guohua saw trade with the PRC as essentially a political issue, arguing that 'not only will the Republic of China's free economic system suffer from direct trade with Chinese communists, but national security will also be endangered'.[19] Yet the gaps in the policy are significant. Just as thousands of Taiwan residents 'illegally' visited the mainland before 1987, there is already significant indirect trade and some Taiwan investment in the PRC. Indirect trade was around US \$1 billion according to estimates for the first half of 1988, 66 per cent higher than the previous year.

There are signs of significant changes in Taiwan's attitudes. Yu Guohua explicitly stated that indirect trade would not be banned — though the Taiwan media from time to time tell cautionary tales of troubled businessmen who had such dealings with the PRC. In addition, Taiwan has liberalized trade arrangements with Eastern Europe. Trade has been growing dramatically during 1987 and early 1988, but is still at a low level compared with other trading partners.

Investment is even more controversial for Taiwan. Fujian has offered especially favourable terms to Taiwan-based investors, including the facility to appoint relatives as agents, and simplified investment approval procedures. In Fujian there are already forty-six enterprises with Taiwanese investment, of which ten are wholly owned by Taiwan investors.[20] It is reported that 70 per cent of Taiwan-financed enterprises are profitable, 20 per cent are breaking even, and only 10 per cent 'have problems'.[21] Unless Taiwan relaxes restrictions, such investment is likely to remain small. However, the economic advantages to Taiwan could be substantial — and in the longer run this economic logic may prevail, especially if South Korean business is seen to be entering the PRC. There are indications that a reappraisal is under way, including a study of importing raw materials from the mainland and proposals for the formalization of indirect trade links. The PRC's possible entry into GATT would also force Taiwan to reassess its position, since GATT rules imply direct trade if Taiwan wishes to be associated.

Eastern and northern coastal provinces

The growth of south China's foreign trade has reduced the previous dominance of east China, in particular that of Shanghai. Guangdong has overtaken Shanghai as the province with highest exports.[22] The coastal provinces of Jiangsu, Zhejiang and Shandong have expanded their economic role dramatically relative to Shanghai. As a result, Shanghai has been told it should learn from Guangdong in 'deepening reforms and in pursuing [an] open policy'.[23]

Shanghai's previous reputation for relative flexibility was tarnished by the mid-1980s, probably as a result of the speed of change elsewhere in China. Increasing exports is now seen as a policy goal, and machine tools in particular is a target sector for expanding exports. Aims for the future imply lower export growth rates than in the south, with a 1990 target of US $4.5 billion[24] and a Seventh FYP target of 8.4 per cent a year[25] — little more than overall economic growth.

In contrast to Shanghai, other provinces on the east coast have been expanding their involvement in foreign trade rapidly (chapter 9). Part of this has been based on agricultural products and food-processing. Shandong's 1986 grain exports, mainly of maize and sweet potatoes, have increased to six times the 1984 figure.[26] One in every three farmers in Shandong is producing some export products, making a total of around US $1 billion a year.[27] In the future, the potential of Shandong for links with South Korea is substantial, assuming that current moves to improve political and economic relations with China continue.

East China's manufacturing industry has seen problems in boosting exports despite rapid economic growth, notably in the rural areas. Much of that industrial development has been oriented to the domestic market, while foreign trade links have been through Shanghai. Given profitable opportunities for domestic trade, foreign trade was seen as difficult. According to Suzhou's deputy mayor, a combination of lack of understanding of international markets, demanding quality requirements, and over-complex administrative procedures, has retarded export growth. There has been a shift of view, with Jiangsu's governor arguing that 'we have to test our products in the international market in order to protect our position in the domestic market. If we can export, there will be no problem competing in the domestic market.'[28]

A centre for these plans is the area around Suzhou, Wuxi and Changzhou, part of the Yangtze open economic zone, which expects to double its exports to US $2 billion, accounting for 20 per cent of the area's GNP figure. However, there are still problems of co-ordination between the three municipalities involved.[29] A related problem is the weak link between production enterprises and foreign trade corporations. Zhao Ziyang saw this as a particular problem in the textile and garment industry in a 1986 speech, arguing that enterprises and trade corporations 'tend to counteract each other's efforts by endless wrangling'.[30] Some moves to solve this have been made in Jiangsu, where officials from import-export corporations are being attached to individual enterprises, effectively as international marketing managers.[31] Initial results seem to be positive, since exports grew at around 30 per cent during the first part of 1987.[32]

The coastal areas of north and north-east China are also increasingly involved in foreign economic relations, but to a lesser degree than most of the southern or eastern provinces. Tianjin plays the most prominent role in foreign economic relations of those areas of China. It is one of the fourteen coastal cities and has been given special rights to use up to US $1 billion of foreign investment by 1990, mainly in export-oriented industries, including textiles, food-processing, light engineering and computing software. The exact level of autonomy which the city will have is unclear, but reports indicate local autonomy up to 200 million yuan RMB.[33] Tianjin's reputation as a port has been growing, partly as a consequence of its autonomy, for example in importing needed equipment from abroad.[34] It is also attempting to ease the problems of foreign investors by setting up a centre to manage some of the necessary contacts with local government departments.[35] Beijing and surrounding Hebei province also have significant exports and have attracted foreign investment. For example, Beijing has agreed around US $3 billion in investment.[36] Textiles are a major part of exports, forming over a quarter of Beijing's 1986 exports.[37]

Liaoning, the most northerly coastal province, has been active in moving towards the world market as well as being a leader in some aspects of economic reform, as for example, the new procedures for bankruptcy. Dalian (Luda) has been particularly active in making use of its status as a coastal city, with fifty-four foreign investors already in place.[38] More generally, Liaoning aims to build 200 export-orientated bases and enterprises, aiming at US $5 million exports each, as part of its effort to increase exports faster than the economy as a whole.[39] Liaoning intends to create fifty export-orientated agricultural bases,[40] with foreign investment being sought in food production. Further moves include opening one hundred of the province's major enterprises to joint-venture operation or management under contract by foreigners; substantially extending its 'open areas' with special terms for foreign investment; and advocacy by the provincial Communist Party secretary that South Korea should be studied.[41] Liaoning also has some relations with neighbouring North Korea, including a joint-venture power station.

The Central Region

Where the Eastern Coastal Region has moved rapidly towards strong involvement in foreign economic relations, such moves have been more restricted in the Central Region. Except in the northern and north-eastern provinces of Inner Mongolia, Jilin and Heilongjiang, there are no land borders or coastal ports to act as channels for foreign trade.

China's north-east has historically been its heavy industrial base, as well as having had some of the closest links with Japan in the 1930s and the USSR in the 1950s. Much of its production is still oriented towards the domestic market. However, trade is being expanded with the USSR, which equipped much of the region's industry in the past. Increasing links with the USSR could facilitate the re-equipment of existing enterprises as well as provide export opportunities. In addition there is the potential for more local links. Heilongjiang and Inner Mongolia are allowed to undertake cross-border trade outside the state plan.[42] This trade is still at a low level but is expanding fast — that between the USSR and Heilongjiang, by 80 per cent in 1987 according to a Soviet report.[43] Inner Mongolia has also been increasing cross-border trade with the Mongolian People's Republic since 1985.

The rest of the Central Region has been less directly involved in foreign trade, not least because its provinces have no direct trade outlets either to the sea or across land borders. The effects of the 'open door' come more from the changing role of the coastal regions and lateral relationships between these and the Central Region. Broader economic reforms allowing joint ventures between regions through new forms of ownership could be expected to provide further links which previously were impossible. However, such links undermine provincial and local government control, and are impeded by widespread local protectionism which seeks to benefit local producers.

Although current policy for the Central Region is more concerned with the domestic market, efforts are being made to increase trade and investment. For example, Hunan has been taking a range of measures above those decreed nationally to boost exports. Enterprises are allowed to retain extra profits if they expand exports above their quota. Tax-free bonuses can be given to workers in enterprises which increase their foreign-exchange earnings by more than 10 per cent over the previous year.[44] However, the bulk of such exports are sent through overloaded and often inefficient ports in coastal provinces, and are frequently sold by national corporations.

Henan has been looking to increase exports by dealing directly with foreign customers. It has targeted the USSR and Eastern Europe, which are its largest customers after Hong Kong, accounting for 21 per cent of exports in 1986 compared with only 4 per cent in 1984. It set up a container station in Zhengzhou, and is using this to send containers on the trans-Siberian railway to speed up transport times — by 40 days compared with the time taken if goods are sent by sea through China's ports.[45] In 1988 parts of the Central Region were allowed to create zones for foreign investment with preferential treatment for foreign investors, though on a much smaller scale than in the Eastern Coastal Region.

The other major potential for foreign trade in the Central Region is energy and materials exports. Shanxi is seen very much as an energy production centre in the Seventh Five-Year Plan. Its coal output is planned to increase by 90 per cent, and electric power generation by a factor of five (chapter 8).[46] However, the potential for development of foreign (as well as internal) trade, is hampered by transport bottlenecks. Shanxi, in particular, could export more coal if transport were available (see chapter 5).

The Western Region

The Western Region's involvement in foreign trade is less still than that of the Central Region. The most populous province in China, Sichuan, was a leader in economic reform during the late 1970s and early 1980s, but its involvement in foreign trade and related reforms is still low. There appears to have been some success in developing co-operation within this region,[47] but much less success in developing foreign trade and attracting investment. In fact, Sichuan's economic strategy is to concentrate on the domestic market, accepting a subordinate role relative to coastal areas in foreign economic relations.

However, it is misleading to regard the Western Region as completely uninfluenced by the 'open door' policy. To take but one example, in Tibet the Zhaxi Lhunbo monastery set up the Tibetan Gangjian Development Corporation, with an investment of 3 million yuan RMB, which has signed export contracts with the United States, United Kingdom, Italy, Switzerland and Hong Kong.[48] None the less, the Western Region's involvement in foreign trade remains low.

One potential for foreign investment is that from Islamic countries and businessmen. Ningxia claims to have the highest concentration of Muslims in China, mainly the Hui minority. Its Vice-Chairman has strongly supported ideas of an 'interior Special Economic Zone at Yinchuan' in Ningxia to attract such Islamic investment. Initial links have been formed with businesses from Pakistan, Yemen and Egypt. A reported US $56 million has been invested in Ningxia from Islamic countries.

Animal products are certainly potential export earners. Xinjiang's first joint venture is a cashmere sweater factory which exported goods to the value of more than US $12 million in the first eight months of 1988. Another opportunity is to be found in trade with neighbouring countries. For example, Xinjiang's border trade with the Soviet Union was about 5 per cent of the province's total exports (at SFr17 million) in 1986.[49] This may well increase when a new rail route is opened.[50] Xinjiang also has a small amount of border trade with Pakistan, a total of US $0.6 million in 1986. In the longer term, there is the potential for mineral exports of various types.

Overcoming the problems of a relatively backward economic base and transport system will not be easy. On the other hand, mineral resources and subtropical cash crops could form a basis of future development for exports in the south-west, with Guangxi as the outlet to the world market. There is also potential for growth in trade with neighbouring countries, though Burma's isolationism and Chinese hostility to Vietnam limit this at present.

Regional differentiation

Although manufactured goods now form the majority of China's exports, primary products are still of major importance. China is rich in many natural resources, with noteworthy reserves of many non-ferrous metals such as tungsten. It also has the largest coal reserves in the world and substantial amounts of oil. Domestic demand, especially for energy, will remain high, but there is still potential for substantial increases in exports, especially of minerals and non-ferrous metals. Agricultural products are a source of export growth, while their value could be increased by processing. In regional terms, mineral and related exports would benefit the Western and Central Regions, and agricultural exports could be expected to come mainly from the Eastern Coastal Region. Given the shortages of raw materials and energy in China's domestic market, it is likely that government policies will continue to encourage the Western and Central Regions to serve the Eastern Coastal Region's needs.

The greatest potential growth is in manufacturing. Currently China's main source of advantage in manufactured exports is labour costs, and in some cases cheap raw materials. However, many foreign investors have found that other aspects of Chinese operations are expensive. Office and other overhead costs in cities are high, while labour productivity is often low. The level of management skills and understanding of international market requirements are often low, implying a need for more expatriate managers than would be the case elsewhere, thereby increasing total costs and making China less competitive than some countries with higher labour costs.

The result is that China is often a low-wage but not a low-cost location for foreign investment. It therefore needs to increase productivity and decrease management costs for foreign investors, while also increasing the value of its own exports. This is recognized by top leaders, notably Zhao Ziyang, who argued in September 1987 that textile exports were too often of low quality, while the proportion of raw and semi-processed products was too high.

It has been announced that new policies to increase export incentives will be introduced in 1988, at first in the garments, handicraft and daily necessities sectors. More generally, increased enterprise-level power in foreign trade is to be introduced, with enterprises able to link pay to export earnings.[51] In addition, it has been suggested that enterprises meeting international quality standards should retain a greater proportion of profits — part of which will go to workers.[52] Zhao Ziyang has indicated that greater decentralization in decision-making on foreign investment to city governments is likely.[53]

There are plans to create export bases with priority in access to materials, power and transport. Most of these are in coastal areas, though some are to be inland. Such preferential treatment implies a continuing administrative control over the economy. This tension between reform and export promotion is likely to continue until the economic incentives to export are sufficient, and the administrative problems are reduced.

Imports are likely to produce conflicting demands, while exports continue to limit import growth unless there is further devaluation of the Chinese yuan together with changes in import control from administrative to economic levers. An indication of the problems involved has been provided by Ferdinand and Wang: 'In the early 1980s . . . , in arranging the import of foreign goods, many localities and enterprises calculated the cost at low domestic prices, whilst the difference between those costs and the actual price at the official exchange rate was borne by the central government.'[54]

In the Eastern Coastal Region there will be demand for imported consumer goods (and not only materials and equipment) as the economy looks more to the world market. Regional autonomy and foreign-exchange retention will make it more difficult for the central state to exert control than in the past. In contrast, central and western areas are likely to seek a redistribution of foreign exchange to allow upgrading of their equipment. Some of the same problems may arise at enterprise level. In the longer term, the logical solution is to increase the convertibility of the Chinese yuan so that administrative boundaries and decisions play less of a role in allocating foreign exchange to imports.

If the more export-oriented policies for coastal regions are successful, the likely outcome is that those areas develop higher wages, and lose some of their cost advantage in labour-intensive products. This will create regional differentiation in living standards, while creating incentives for labour-intensive operations to be shifted further inland. Elsewhere, this would often mean an international move and its consequent costs. China's size makes an internal transfer less costly and hence more likely. China's regional development strategy may therefore move away from development of the Central and Western Regions, through central state investment in industry, towards development on the basis of comparative regional cost.

In terms of the categorization of the Seventh FYP, there is evidence to date of some widening of regional differences in both industry and agriculture. The changes in gross output value during 1980 to 1985 are shown in Table 4.3. In contrast to the evidence at the provincial level (discussed in chapter 3), it indicates a clear growth in regional inequalities. Important influences have been the role of foreign trade and investment, as well as the more rapid growth in rural industry and non-farm employment in the more eastern areas. The implication is therefore of a more dynamic and open Eastern Region, using the Central and Western Regions as sources of materials, energy and cheaper labour. Although foreign trade is by no means the only reason for that increased differentiation, its role will not be insignificant, especially in the more export-oriented areas like Guangdong.

Table 4.3 Growth in output value by region, 1980–1985 (%)

Region	Industry	Agriculture
Eastern Coastal	+80%	+52%
Central	+72%	+50%
Western	+71%	+46%

Source: 'Economic growth in different areas', *Beijing Review*, 8 December 1987, pp. 21–4.

Conclusion

China's 'opening up' and regional differentiation are giving rise to divergent political interests over economic and foreign policies. The uneven impact of overall regional development policies, of which foreign trade and investment policies are part, is obviously an important issue.

In March 1987 one NPC deputy from Gansu argued:

> If we continue to advocate the staircase theory of uneven economic growth in different regions, we shall have to bear the consequences of still wider gaps between the developed and less-developed regions, and it will require double the amount of investment when it is time for these regions to develop in the future.[55]

Such calls were greater at the April 1988 NPC, when delegates from Western Region provinces called for greater redistribution of resources by the state to offset the effects of policies concentrating on export-oriented coastal development.

At the same time, those benefiting from the open policies are likely to exert pressure for reform to go further and faster. The Guangdong provincial leadership has actively pressed for extension of the province's powers by expanding the Zhujiang (Pearl River) open economic zone and increasing the province's decision-making powers over foreign investment projects.[56] In 1987 a lobby rapidly emerged to expand Hainan's powers over foreign trade and investment, as part of its transition to provincial status.[57]

Differing regional patterns of trade and trading partners will shape interests with respect to trade, investment and overall foreign policies. One example is obviously the economic interests of border areas in good relationships with neighbouring countries, many of which have been hostile to China in the past, for example the USSR. One could therefore expect northern and western provinces to be most concerned about improving relations with the Soviet Union and Mongolia, while south-western ones might have similar concerns over Vietnam. In contrast, coastal provinces will be more concerned about relationships with capitalist economies, including Japan and the USA, as well as with Hong Kong and Taiwan.

Regions will have different interests in central government policies towards foreign exchange and related issues. For example, the energy-producing regions of the north-west would dislike certain foreign-exchange retention policies when much of their export potential is under central government control. Coastal areas will probably seek to use the foreign exchange they have generated for consumer goods imports, while inland provinces would prefer it to be used for re-equipment of their industrial plant (chapter 8). Inland provinces may also be more inclined towards policies of local and national protectionism as the coastal areas become more competitive under greater exposure to international competition.

This chapter has outlined the emerging regional pattern of foreign economic relations which has arisen from China's reforms and 'opening up' to the world economy. The picture is one of greater regional differentiation, with the coastal region moving towards export-orientated industrialization, notably in Guangdong, while other regions are still based essentially on their local economy. The emerging pattern is one in which coastal areas act as channels for inland ones, developing faster but relying to a large degree on inland provinces for energy and materials.

Notes

1 Wang Pingqing (1988) '1987: Basic balance in foreign trade', *Beijing Review*, 1 February, 31 (5): 18–19. Other figures on foreign trade are taken from *Zhongguo Tongji Nianjian 1986*, Beijing: Zhongguo Tongji Chubanshe, 1987, part 10.
2 'Foreign Investment in China', NCNA, 11 November 1987, in SWB, 25 November 1987.

3 'Chinese joint ventures abroad', NCNA, 13 January 1988, in SWB, 15 January 1988.

4 'Zhao Ziyang urges further opening of coastal areas', *Renmin Ribao*, 23 January 1988, in SWB, 28 January 1988; 'Zhao on coastal areas development strategy', *Beijing Review*, vol. 31, part 6, 14–19.

5 'Reform is key to coastal development', NCNA, 1 April 1988, in SWB, 3 April 1988.

6 'News conference by Gu Mu and others on Hong Kong, Macao and economic matters', *Wen Wei Po*, 2 April 1987, in SWB, 3 April 1987.

7 Ferdinand, P. and Wang Yongjiang (1989) 'Centre-Provincial Financial Relations in the PRC and the Role of the Ministry of Commerce', in Lockett, M. and Child, J. (eds) *Economic Reform and the Chinese Enterprise*, JAI Press.

8 'Fujian entrepreneurs oppose restrictions', NCNA, 3 February 1988, in SWB, 12 February 1988.

9 'Guangdong: ten measures to expedite reform', NCNA, 27 March 1988, in SWB, 28 March 1988.

10 'Press conference by Guangdong and Hainan leaders', Beijing TV, 12 April 1988, in SWB, 13 April 1988.

11 'Hainan officials sent to seek out qualified labour from mainland', NCNA, 30 April 1988, in SWB, 2 May 1988.

12 'Guangdong processes Hong Kong and Macao goods', NCNA, 28 April 1987, in SWB, 6 May 1987.

13 'Development of Beihai', NCNA, 19 August 1987, in SWB, 26 August 1987.

14 'Guangxi to draw support from Guangdong for invigoration', Guangxi Radio, 24 September 1986, in SWB, 6 October 1986.

15 '"Brilliant prospects" for lateral economic ties between Guangxi and Jiangsu', Guangxi Radio, 8 May 1986, in SWB, 15 May 1986.

16 'Fujian's foreign trade in 1987', NCNA, 12 February 1988, in SWB, 15 February 1988.

17 'Substantial rise in value of Guangdong's exports', Guangdong Radio, 4 December 1987, in SWB, 16 December 1987.

18 'Chinese companies invest one billion HK dollars in Hong Kong', NCNA, 27 June 1986, in SWB, 16 July 1986.

19 'Taiwan "will not allow direct trade with the mainland"', NCNA, 14 October 1987, in SWB, 15 October 1987.

20 'Taiwan — capital invested in Fujian', NCNA, 28 February 1988, in SWB, 7 March 1988.

21 'Taiwan delegate discusses relations, exchanges and business', AFP, 30 October 1987, in SWB, 7 November 1987.

22 'Guangdong exports', NCNA, 27 September 1987, SWB, 7 October 1987.

23 'Shanghai mayor calls for expanding exports', NCNA, 24 January 1988, in SWB, 3 February 1988.

24 'Shanghai recovers from slump in export volume', NCNA, 31 December 1987, in SWB, 14 January 1988.

25 'Leaders of Shanghai, Jiangsu, Shanxi and Xinjiang on 1986–90 Plan',

NCNA, 10 May 1986, in SWB, 15 May 1986.

26 'Increased grain output in Shandong', *Dazhong Ribao*, 8 September 1987, in SWB, 7 October 1987.

27 'Shandong farm products lead exports', NCNA, 8 September 1987, in SWB, 16 September 1987.

28 Quoted in Dodwell, D., 'Boost for foreign deals', *The Financial Times*, 8 September 1987, p. 17.

29 Ibid.

30 'Zhao Ziyang's ideas for invigorating the economies of coastal cities', NCNA, 11 September 1986, in SWB, 17 September 1986.

31 *The Financial Times*, 8 September 1987, p. 17.

32 'Growth of Suzhou and Wuxi', NCNA, 17 July 1987, in SWB, 21 July 1987.

33 'Tianjin to get more capital to improve product quality', NCNA, 26 April 1987, in SWB, 13 May 1987.

34 See *Far Eastern Economic Review*, 19 November 1987, p. 98.

35 'Tianjin to open special office to assist foreign investors', NCNA, 4 December 1986, in SWB, 10 December 1986.

36 'Peking's foreign economic relations' NCNA, 17 February 1988, in SWB, 21 February 1988.

37 'Local foreign trade: Peking', NCNA, 11 October 1987, in SWB, 21 October 1987.

38 'Development of Dalian', NCNA, 29 July 1987, in SWB, 12 August 1987.

39 'Liaodong peninsula development', NCNA, 25 May 1987, in SWB, 3 June 1987.

40 Ibid.

41 'Liaoning told to study South Korea', *Liaoning Ribao*, 2 April 1988, in SWB, 4 April 1988.

42 See *The Economist*, 24 October 1987, p. 54.

43 'Heilongjiang's export trade: Soviet report', Moscow Radio in Chinese, 11 December 1987, in SWB, 23 December 1987.

44 'Hunan: incentives for exporting companies and their workforces', Hunan Radio, 5 May 1986, in SWB, 9 May 1986.

45 'Henan organises own exports', NCNA, 7 August 1987, in SWB, 19 August 1987.

46 'Leaders of Shanghai, Jiangsu, Shanxi and Xinjiang on 1986–90 Plan', NCNA, 10 May 1986, in SWB, 15 May 1986.

47 'State Council has listed the SW as a major economic zone', Sichuan Radio, 11 May 1986, in SWB, 14 May 1986.

48 'Tibet: monasteries set up a business conglomerate', NCNA, 19 May 1987, in SWB, 21 May 1987.

49 See *The Economist*, 24 October 1987.

50 'Xinjiang opens up', NCNA, 31 May 1987, in SWB, 10 June 1987.

51 'Experimental export policies', NCNA, 15 October 1987, in SWB, 28 October 1987.

52 'Reforms to bring the quality of products up to international standards', NCNA, 5 June 1986, in SWB, 10 June 1986.

53 'Zhao Ziyang's ideas for invigorating the economies of coastal cities', NCNA, 11 September 1986, in SWB, 17 September 1986.
54 Ferdinand, P. and Wang Yongjiang (1989) 'Centre-Provincial Financial Relations in the PRC and the Role of the Ministry of Commerce', in Lockett, M. and Child, J. (eds) *Economic Reform and Chinese Enterprise,* JAI Press.
55 'Call for more investment in and help for less-developed regions', NCNA, 31 March 1987, in SWB, 4 April 1987.
56 'Guangdong Open Zone to expand, decision-making powers to increase', Guangdong Radio, 15 November 1987, in SWB, 20 November 1987.
57 See *Far Eastern Economic Review*, 15 October 1987, p. 82.

Chapter five

Transport and communications
Maurice Howard

China's economic geography places particularly high demands on
transport. Most of China's natural resources are located either in the
west and centre of the country (for example, metal ores and cement)
or in the north and north-east (notably coal), whereas the overwhelming
majority of industry and population are located along, or relatively near
to, the coast. There is thus a need for long-distance transport of bulk
goods. In addition, there are regional specializations in industry, with
heavy industry notably concentrated in the north-east (for example,
power-plant boilermaking, and the heavy electrical industry), and textiles
in East China. Furthermore, agricultural variations across the climatic
zones from north to south, and from the coastal irrigated areas to the
arid interior, emphasize the need for the transport of produce.

Moreover, the structural characteristics of China's economy contribute
to an exceptionally heavy demand for transport. Heavy industry, which
is particularly transport-intensive, forms a larger part of the economy
than in most developing countries. Freight intensity (tonne-kilometres
transported per unit of GDP) is around 60 per cent higher in China than
in the USA, and considerably higher than in Japan or the Republic
of Korea. Even if the service sector is excluded from the calculations,
freight intensity in China still remains higher than in other developing
countries, though less than in the USA. The importance of freight
transport is thus not merely the product of a different sectoral composition to the economy.

Since 1979 transport has been treated alongside energy as one of the
two most important constraints on China's economic development. This
chapter examines China's transport and communications from a regional
perspective. At the same time it considers telecommunications, since
under certain circumstances they can be a potential substitute for physical
transport, and may also have regional implications for development.

Two sets of problems have informed this investigation. The first is
the extent to which the Chinese authorities use transport or communications policy as a tool to achieve regional ends. The second is the extent

to which China's economic development is shaped by constraints of transport and communication. It is argued that policies on transport and communications have been aimed at objectives largely independent of any policy designed to encourage regional economic development. Moreover, the constraints represented by the nature and capacity of existing transport networks have shaped recent developments in a way that has acted to exacerbate regional disparities in favour of coastal and energy-rich areas, and are likely to do so increasingly in future as market forces gain ground in economic management.

Modes of transport

China's transport system is based predominantly on rail, though significant use is made of waterways and shipping, as well as road and pipeline. The railways carry nearly two-thirds of freight traffic. Yet in comparison with the size of the country, the rail network, at 52,000 km, is relatively small. This has resulted in very high traffic density on the system, in fact second only, by world standards, to the USSR. The rail network is not evenly distributed throughout the country. North-east China accounts for 23 per cent of the route length. That is largely an inheritance from the Russian-built Chinese Eastern Railway and the Japanese-built South Manchurian Railway. Another 52 per cent of the network covers the North, East, and Central-South regions. The remaining 25 per cent covers North-west and South-west China, but in 1985 these carried only 14 per cent of freight traffic. Rail capacity is even more concentrated than this might suggest: until 1979 nearly all double-track lines were north-south arteries within the eastern and north-eastern half of the country (Map 11). A characteristic of the rail network is therefore extremely intensive traffic flows.

The second most important mode of transport is inland and coastal shipping. It caters for slightly less than 20 per cent of freight movement. Geographical concentration here is, not surprisingly, even greater than for rail. Jiangsu, Zhejiang, and Shanghai possess an intricate network of canals linked to the north and south banks of the Yangtze (Changjiang). These provinces account for no less than a third of the length of navigable waterways. Guangdong accounts for another 10 per cent centreing on the Zhujiang (Pearl River). The heart of the navigable waterway system, however, is formed by the Yangtze and Heilongjiang rivers, accounting for 7,500 km out of the 109,000 km total. The Yangtze, which is navigable continuously for nearly 3,000 km as far as Yibin in Sichuan, is the main artery. Together, the main rivers account for roughly a third of waterway freight tonnage, and a considerably larger but unstated proportion of tonne-kilometres carried.

Next in importance as far as freight transport is concerned is the road network. At present it extends to nearly 960,000 km, but only carried, in 1985, 14 per cent of freight traffic. In relation to the size of the country, that is very small. At first sight the road network is somewhat better distributed than either rail or water. Nearly a third of road length is in the North-west and South-west Regions. Yet comparatively little is situated in the most populated or industrialized areas. For example, the Jiangsu-Shanghai-Zhejiang industrial belt in East China has about 5 per cent of road mileage. It is, however, responsible for 20 per cent of road tonnage, mainly moved over very short distances.

Pipelines account for about 4 per cent of freight movement, and have developed rapidly — particularly during the 1970s — to remove oil, oil products, and gas from the railways. The approximately 12,000 km of pipelines in use are mainly located in the Central, North and North-east Regions. The biggest network links the Daqing oilfield with the ports of Dalian (Luda) and Qinhuangdao, as well as the Yanshan (Beijing) and Qilu (Shandong) petrochemical centres, the Shengli oilfield with the port of Qingdao and the Yangtze refinery complex at Nanjing. Another trunk pipeline links the Yumen oilfields in Gansu with refineries in Lanzhou. There is a notable natural gas distribution network in Sichuan.

Air transport is as yet a minuscule proportion of total movement, especially of freight. On the other hand, it is particularly important to some of the more isolated regions. Xinjiang has the most developed airway network and the largest number of civil airports. Long road distances and climatic factors make it attractive to move some perishable goods this way. Indeed, air is the fastest-growing mode of transport, and with the construction of new airports, as well as the opening of military facilities for civil use, it now represents a realistic — if still limited — option for intercity passenger travel.

Transport problems

A general feature of all transport in China is that the ratio of freight to passenger traffic is very large by international standards — around four times that in Western Europe, for example. Networks have obviously been developed with freight rather than passengers in mind. Urban construction with mixed industrial and residential districts, for instance, has not encouraged radial commuting patterns around cities and the construction of commuter rail networks as in Japan.

The small size and relatively intensive use of transport networks in China is largely attributable to the relatively low priority given to transport in investment before 1979, and the concentration of resources on 'productive' sectors, particularly heavy industry. The development of transport facilities has not kept pace with economic growth. For instance, over the three decades to 1980, rail freight turnover increased more than thirtyfold, while the length of the network only grew by 130 per cent. Remarkably, the number of locomotives in operation increased by 150 per cent, and the number of wagons by 460 per cent. The result has been a chronic deficiency of capacity, exacerbated by low running speeds. Moreover, speeds are kept down by poor track quality and out-dated signalling — manually operated semaphore signals are common, even on newly-built lines. Marshalling yard capacity has not been expanded in line with traffic requirements. These inadequacies have had regional repercussions. In East China, where network expansion has been slowest, certain main lines (notably the Tianjin-Pukou artery) were reckoned as far back as 1980 to be meeting only 50 to 70 per cent of demand. Three of China's four worst rail bottlenecks are stated to be in the East China region.[1]

A similar problem exists with the road network. Between 1949 and 1986 road space is estimated to have risen in urban areas by 2.9 times, whereas urban passenger vehicles increased (to 1984) by seventeen times.[2] The same is true, to a lesser extent, of the road network as a whole. The bald statistics do not give an adequate indication of its carrying capacity. Less than 20 per cent of the network has asphalt surfacing. Much of the rest has no sealed surfacing. A large proportion is narrow, or unusable at certain times of the year. A particular problem limiting road capacity is the need to share space with slow-moving agricultural traffic, such as walking-tractors and animal-drawn vehicles.

The waterway network is also restricted in its capacity. From less than 74,000 km in 1949, it was expanded (notably during the period of the Great Leap Forward) to reach over 162,000 km in 1962. Yet a great deal of this has since been lost through construction of dams without shiplocks and through silting. Legislation in force since 1987 has sought to outlaw such inefficient construction, but future development is clearly limited. Of the entire navigable waterway network, roughly half is less than one metre deep. Only 16,000 km is open to boats of over fifty tonnes, and 8,000 km to those over a hundred tonnes.

Because of China's physical geography, much of the waterway net-work is either suitable only for localized traffic flows, or favours east-west flows. There are very few north-south canals. Potentially the most useful of the north-south links, the Grand Canal, is still in the course of being enlarged and dredged to take boats of a reasonable size. Part of its significance lies in the fact that it connects the systems of the Haihe, Huanghe, Huaihe, Yangtze and Qiantang rivers, and therefore relieves the poorly-developed rail networks of Anhui, Jiangsu and Zhejiang pro-vinces. However, it is still not navigable throughout its whole length.

The principal east-west artery in the south of the country, the Yangtze, forms with its tributaries a transport network of around 18,000 km, and is therefore a vital link to South-west China, parallel rail lines being very difficult to construct. The Huanghe (Yellow River), the more northerly of the two great east-west rivers, is too silted to be navigable for more than short lengths by shallow-draught boats. Seasonal floods and droughts affect large parts of the water network, and form an added limitation on capacity.

Investment priorities

Physical and other restrictions on the capacity of the transport networks, as well as the rapid growth of the traffic using them, underlie the relative investment priority given to transport. In its 1985 report, the World Bank estimated that transport investment in China was just over 1 per cent of GDP, quite a low figure compared with other countries, and the Bank advised that this share should be doubled.[3] Fast traffic growth has been accompanied by relatively low investment, at least until very recently. Any acknowledgement by increased spending on transport infrastructure would be expected, of course, to have significant regional implications, if only because stress on the transport system is unevenly distributed. As a general rule, provinces with a high share of heavy industry face the highest traffic densities, and if alleviation of transport bottlenecks were to be taken as the main investment criterion, those provinces would be the main recipients of any additional resources.

The future development of transport clearly has important implications for different sectors of the economy. Energy in particular is heavily dependent on transport for its development. In 1985 over 40 per cent of rail-loaded tonnage consisted of coal: another 5 per cent consisted of oil. Whereas the quantity of oil freight has not risen since the early 1970s — indeed, there is evidence of a recent decline — coal has slowly grown as a proportion of rail freight traffic. Allocation of resources to the transport sector is therefore likely to be governed by energy policy and the location of exploitable coal reserves. Indeed, the greatest expansion of the rail network has occurred in recent years in those provinces (with few exceptions) where coal-mine development has taken place: Hebei, Shanxi, Inner Mongolia, and outstandingly Anhui (with a 19 per cent increase during 1981–5).

Not only is the energy sector dependent on transport for its development, but of course transport is in turn dependent on fuel. Coal is hardly a problem. The transport sector consumed less than 6 per cent of total output in 1980, and the proportion is likely, if anything, to have declined since then. A more serious question arises over the availability of oil. Given likely rates of growth of domestic oil output in China, the World Bank has estimated that the proportion of refined oil used for transport purposes could rise from 38 per cent in 1980 to almost 50 per cent by 2000.[4] Competing non-fuel uses for oil are likely to be even more important then that now, and choices will have to be made, possibly under duress, about whether to import oil or to allow its scarcity to determine transport policy. At issue most importantly is whether private cars will be allowed a significant role in China, and hence what priority is given to personal mobility. High personal mobility will shape the urbanization process and will place stress on factors other than fuel, notably land.

Transport and the enterprise

The development of regional transport systems is clearly of more than passing significance to individual enterprises. Any change which occurs in the cost environment of an enterprise, particularly in the transport costs which it faces, will influence decisions on its location, on the regional division of labour, and on patterns of labour mobility or land use.

A characteristic of the Chinese economy is the large number of relatively small enterprises, in contrast to Soviet-style economies, and the extremely small number of large-scale enterprises (about 250 employees), in contrast not only to other centrally-planned economies, but also to those of the west. This may have its roots to some extent in an ideological preference for devolved forms of socialism. It may also be founded in a desire to save capital expenditure.[5] But important considerations in practice have been an explicit commitment to local self-sufficiency in production, and deficiencies in the material supply network arising from bureaucratic compartmentalization. These considerations have manifested themselves in a proliferation of plants, of sub-optimal scale, making the same products in the same locations, and often producing goods of inferior quality. Frequently cited examples include the steel and cement industries. Plants controlled by various levels of local government and national ministries are often sited in the same city, each with a more or less secure source of supply within the control of its administrative network, but tending to compete for markets. Self-sufficiency has also led to vertical integration, with many stages of the manufacturing process being carried on in the same factory, and workers' facilities sharing the same site. These characteristics are, of course, not universal in Chinese industry. But they are significant features which have a bearing on patterns of transport.

Although these practices may have minimized the transport of some goods, most probably intermediate products, the centralized administrative control systems to which enterprises have been subject have undoubtedly led to substantial amounts of cross-haulage. Superior or cheaper sources of supply near at hand may not be available to factories, which might have to procure supplies of inferior quality at a distance. The same materials or products might meanwhile be transported in the opposite direction to supply a plant located in another area, thereby adding to pressure on the transport system. Current reform of the industrial system centres on increasing enterprise autonomy, allowing enterprises to choose their own inputs and the markets for their products, with contractual relationships between enterprises replacing administrative orders from above. Other elements of the present reforms are encouragement of investment flows across administrative boundaries and (latterly) the inception of market-based systems of land tenure.

All these developments, though so far only in their early stages, tend to make enterprises more mobile, as well as more able to choose their supplies and markets according to economic criteria. Elimination of vertical integration, and increased specialization in production, may increase demand for transport. But the breakdown of departmental and local authority control of industrial enterprises may have the effect of reducing economically perverse activities such as cross-haulage. The net effect on transport demand is therefore not easy to assess.

Reform and deregulation

Reform of the financial regime under which the railway system operates, and deregulation of waterway shipping management, may have implications for the prices, and therefore the types, of traffic which are carried, and hence for the economic viability of enterprises in various locations. Cross-subsidization of traffics has been an important feature of Chinese transport policy. The practice of supplying remote areas with agricultural supplies at a nationally-fixed price has been a key element in regional assistance. It is likely that in the future, direct and explicit subsidization of local budgets will displace that practice. Departure from the pricing system used since 1955 on the railways, for example, involved abandoning their largely artificial incentive role in affecting wholesale prices of goods (and perhaps their tendency to favour transport over very long distances), in favour of a rate structure reflecting marginal transport costs and relative congestion of the network.[6] It is therefore unlikely that financial reform of transport will act in favour of remote areas.

Since the most congested parts of the transport system, particularly of the railways, are in East China, and the worst bottlenecks are felt in north-south traffic, any policy which makes the railways more difficult or expensive to use is likely to favour coastal shipping. Location of enterprises, particularly those with large requirements for bulk raw material supplies, may increasingly tend towards the coast as a way of minimizing land transport. This factor has already influenced the siting of large-scale projects around Shanghai (the Baoshan steel complex and the Jinshan chemical plant) and on the lower reaches of the Yangtze.

In the rural and inland areas, where the responsibility system and price increases for agricultural produce have resulted in rapid economic growth, there is a requirement for an extensive road network suitable for short-distance traffic. Otherwise wider economic development may well be seriously impaired. Vehicle inaccessibility has been a long-standing obstacle to the development of rural areas, particularly in western China, where the marketing of local produce in exchange for staples is often vital to the survival of communities.

Changing policy perspectives

The change in priorities for transport since the Third Plenum of the Eleventh Central Committee of the CCP in December 1978 has addressed what have been seen as long-standing inadequacies. As indicated in chapter 1, since 1965 development of the transport network had been concentrated heavily in the interior provinces as an integral part of the establishment of the Third Line. In April of that year, a CCP Central Committee meeting had decided that, in view of the escalation of hostilities in Vietnam by the United States, it was necessary to develop an industrialized base area in South-west China. Considerable resources were devoted to this effort. In particular, an extensive railway network was established in great haste. The Sichuan-Guizhou railway was speedily finished and opened during 1965; the Yunnan-Guizhou line was completed in 1966; and the Chengdu-Kunming line in 1969. Industrial centres, such as Panzhihua in Sichuan, were established.

The developments of the late 1960s required a large amount of investment, derived in the main from industrial production in the coastal provinces. Because of this reorientation of investment, hardly any significant transport facilities were set up or expanded in the coastal areas during the period up to 1978. An exception was the port expansion plan initiated during the mid-1970s to cope with increasing foreign trade. Inland transport capacity became inadequate to cope with the demands of the continually expanding output of heavy industry. This inadequacy was heavily concentrated on the key transport arteries of East China — the Beijing-Guangzhou and Tianjin-Pukou railways were the worst affected — and by the late 1970s was recognised as a drag on the whole economy. While industrial output grew by 125 per cent between 1966 and 1976, total transport volume grew by less than 77 per cent, of which rail transport only registered a 28.2 per cent increase. From 1970, at the height of the industrial expansion boom, until 1977, rail traffic failed repeatedly to reach its planned targets. The main casualty was coal supply from the two main mining centres, Shanxi province and the Kailuan coalfield near Tangshan in north-east Hebei province, to the Shanghai area, Wuhan and points south. Coal backlogs and deterioration in stockpiles became regular problems during the late 1970s.

Since 1979 the key transport priority has been the easing of coal transport out of Shanxi. This effectively put an end to the more ambitious inland lines under construction at the time (for example, the Qinghai-Tibet railway) and would appear to have slowed progress on others (such as the southern Xinjiang railway). The switch in priorities should be seen against the background of changes in foreign relations and in the political atmosphere, with a decline in the importance of the military in government and a more realistic assessment of the likelihood of war on China's frontiers.

Though affected by the cutbacks in investment during 1981–2, several transport projects — notably high-capacity rail links from Shanxi to the surrounding provinces — were incorporated in the Sixth Five-Year Plan (1981–5). Railway lines in the Taiyuan-Datong-Beijing-Qinhuangdao corridor were targeted for double-tracking and electrification, as was the central access line from Taiyuan (the capital of Shanxi) to Shijiaz-huang and Dezhou, connecting with the north-south Tianjin-Pukou railway. A southern corridor was opened up by building a line from the Yanzhou coalfield in Shandong to the new coal shipment port of Shi-jiusuo. A further connection from Jiaozuo in western Henan to Jining and Yanzhou was initiated so that coal from southern Shanxi could also travel over this route.

The initial impulse for the construction of those particular routes seems to have been the need foreseen in 1978 to export coal to Japan, but an important consideration since that time has been the need to free the north-south rail corridors of as much coal traffic as possible by substituting coastal shipping. Transport constraints in the interior have therefore contributed to enhancing the importance of the coastal ports.

Changing financial perspectives

The development of Shanxi and the area around that province as the country's main energy base (chapter 8) — with an associated emphasis on meeting its transport requirements — can be seen as one response to the problems facing the economy. Another has been the attempt to divert traffic away from the railways so as to reduce congestion. Since 1984 the relative prices of transport have been adjusted with the intention of transferring short-distance passenger and freight traffic from rail to road or other appropriate transport. The ultimate objective of this exercise has been to encourage inland passengers to use road transport for journeys of under 200 km, and freight to use road for journeys of less than 100 km, or 1,000 km for perishable goods. Favourable treatment has also been given to the use of water transport in the coastal regions and along the Yangtze. Coastal or combined transport is to be encouraged in those areas, as well as in North and North-east China. Passengers travelling over 1,000 km have been encouraged to travel by air.[7]

There had in fact been long-standing incentives to use coastal and combined transport, but price differentials in a period when enterprises had little autonomy, and pricing policy was confused, certainly appeared not to have had the desired effects. The long-term consequence of this attempt to shift traffic between modes of transport is likely to be a greatly enhanced role for the road network.

Transport has been one of the economic sectors expected to produce a surplus for the state during the 1980s, particularly because of the railways. With the rapid growth of traffic, by 1982 they were producing well over 2 billion yuan RMB in profits handed to the authorities. Yet this was the very sector most in need of investment funds. Fresh sources of funds were opened up in 1983 with the inception of a 20 billion yuan RMB construction fund for energy and transport raised from local governments, enterprises and state departments, and from 1987 by a new energy and transport tax levied on collective and individual businesses, equal to 7 per cent of after-tax profits.

The inception of the contract system on the railways in 1986 radically altered the financial framework within which they have had to operate. Instead of the free allocation of funds by the state, the railways were to be allowed loans of 25 billion yuan RMB to cover improvements during the period of the Seventh FYP (1986–91). The Ministry of Railways was responsible only for paying a 5 per cent business tax, and was allowed to retain any operating surplus. Individual railway bureaux under the ministry (of which there are now twelve) were placed under contract to fulfil various operating objectives. Overall, there was an incentive to maximize the operating surplus. One consequence of this change is bound to be an emphasis on improving railway facilities in the over-stretched parts of the system, that is, in East and North China.

During 1986 the media began to identify the loss-making parts of the railway system. It was stated that in 1982, a year in which the railways produced an overall surplus for the state of over 2 billion yuan RMB, a total of 10,000 km of line, built since 1966, had lost 830 billion yuan. The implication was quite clear, that in future priority would be given to lines generating revenue, rather than to new lines opening up the interior but not likely to attract sufficient freight traffic to cover their allocated expenses.

It was also at this time that a comprehensive rail modernization programme for East China was announced. The most important parts of this were links between Henan, Anhui, and Zhejiang, designed to create a line from Shangqiu, on the east-west Longhai main line in Henan, to Hangzhou in Zhejiang, running parallel to the Tianjin-Shanghai line, but avoiding Shanghai. Similarly, it was announced that the Beijing-Tianjin-Shanghai line itself would be modernized and electrified to transform it into a model high-speed trunk route, using the most advanced technology in the country. The total cost of the East China rail projects scheduled for the period of the Seventh FYP was given as 7 billion yuan RMB, or roughly a fifth of the entire rail investment budget.

From the interior to the coast

On the whole, the result of these changed perspectives during the 1980s has been that attention has shifted from the interior to the coastal areas. This new focus for the development of transport is reflected, not only in the pattern of foreign investment, but also in discussions within China of new policies to be adopted for vehicle use and the location of industry.

The willingness of Japan and the World Bank to finance high-capacity rail lines in East and North China has certainly influenced the redirection of investment away from the interior. Japan's interest in assuring supplies of coal is obvious. The Beijing-Qinhuangdao and Yanzhou-Shijiusuo lines, together with facilities at the terminal harbours, have been financed by a series of Japanese loans since 1979. The World Bank has funded the inland sections of these lines, from Datong to Beijing, and Xinxiang to Heze (between the provinces of Henan and Shandong). Current foreign-currency loans are being made for improvements to the Longhai Railway between Zhengzhou and Baoji, and to the Beijing-Guangzhou line between Zhengzhou and Wuhan.

Projects financed by foreign-currency loans must at least contribute to the generation of foreign exchange to service the loans. It is not surprising, therefore, that the arrival of large lending programmes for transport infrastructure has served to increase the emphasis on investment in coal-carrying railways and roads in the already developed areas of China. Initial developments of roads built to expressway standards are situated in industrialized areas. The Zhujiang (Pearl River) delta, and links between Beijing and Tianjin as well as Shenyang and Luda, have seen the first of these projects. However, short sections of what are intended to be long-distance expressways between Beijing and Guangzhou, and between Shanghai and Xinjiang (connecting with the USSR), have been started.

However, the potential of roads to stimulate wider economic development cannot be realized unless the mix of vehicles on them is altered. Fewer walking tractors, and fewer of the standard trucks will be needed; more small vans and light pickups, plus heavier vehicles needed to carry containers, will have to be built. So far, the mix of vehicles has varied widely across the country, with the coastal areas having acquired imported cars and vans much more rapidly than elsewhere. Some authorities have contended that poor maintenance and inefficient use of roads is a greater obstacle to accessibility than a deficiency in the size of the network.[8] Moreover, it seems that before a coherent policy on road development is drawn up, consideration will also have to be given to the extent to which vehicles can be allowed to use fuel which (as chapter 6 indicates) is in extremely short supply, and for which there clearly are competing demands.

With the start of the Sixth FYP in 1981 it was proposed that heavy industrial projects should be built using large quantities of raw materials close to the sources from which they came. This trend has accelerated since the beginning of the Seventh FYP. Areas which are benefiting from this locational policy are those where resources can be found close together, or those which permit coal transport to be minimized. Southern Shanxi and western Henan are good examples. These areas are close to coalfields, but also have mineral resources particularly attractive in making products which are either in short supply or represent import replacements. A programme for developing aluminium production is under way, with those sites intended to use coal as an energy source located on coalfields — for example, at Jiaozuo (western Henan). Fertilizer plants, where they too are intended to use coal, have similarly been sited on coalfields — for example, at Lucheng near Changzhi in southern Shanxi. In this way, recognition of transport constraints is leading to something of a reconcentration of heavy industry in energy-rich areas of the country.

At the present time a large proportion of the money-consuming transport projects in China are concerned with the transport of coal. New railways under construction from Baoji on the Longhai Railway to Zhongwei in Ningxia, and from Houma in southern Shanxi to Yueshan in western Henan are aimed at opening up new coal transport links. Shanxi province has also seen a significant road-building programme recently, with the aim of improving coal transport. Projects aimed at easing coal movement, and at facilitating exports, have taken a large slice of transport and communications funding, which was stepped up in 1987 when capital construction on transport and communications was raised from an originally scheduled 12 per cent to 14.8 per cent of total state capital construction spending. New techniques are being introduced to increase freight throughput at the ports. Lighter operation is now being tried out, modelled on the system in use in Hong Kong. Bulk handling facilities using the most modern technology are in use at the main grain and mineral ports.

Spending on transport and communications infrastructure seems therefore to be going to coastal areas and to be serving to concentrate economic activity there rather than in the interior, unless the location happens to be an energy-producing area. The types of transport infrastructure associated with increasing low-technology vehicle access are receiving a relatively low priority in the allocation of resources.

Telecommunications

An alternative to physical transport, particularly of passengers, is thought to lie in the use of telecommunications. At the present time, a large part of passenger travel in China is concerned with business or administration, and relatively little, except at the Chinese New Year, involves leisure trips. One reason for the prevalence of business journeys, and perhaps the most important, must be the difficulty of using the telecommunications network.

At the end of 1986 there were only eight million telephones in China.[9] Of these, by far the greater part were concentrated in the coastal areas. Guangdong province alone was stated to have 5,224 long-distance lines, 270,000 urban lines, and 250,000 lines in the rural areas. Of the 467,000 new switchboard lines added in 1986, Guangdong received 77,200, Shanghai 20,000, and Beijing 10,000. A total of 253,000 lines was available at the end of 1986 on programme-controlled telex switchboards: these were all located in twelve cities. Priority has indeed gone to equipping the coastal open cities with automatic exchanges, telex links, and other equipment so as to increase their attractiveness to foreign business. Once again, many of the larger projects are funded with foreign exchange, increasing the pressure to relate development of the system to economic activities likely to aid repayment.

Some technological developments, however, might be expected to have a beneficial effect on inland telecommunications accessibility. Perhaps the most significant of these is the introduction of satellite links. At the present time, Beijing, Guangzhou, Lhasa, Urumqi and Hohhot are connected in this way. Another form of technology which serves to increase the capacity of telecommunications links is optical-fibre cable. Communications using optical fibre are said to be available in twenty-three cities in eighteen provinces,[10] although it is unlikely that these cities are linked by optical fibre throughout. A Chinese domestic optical-fibre production capability has only recently been acquired with the use of Japanese technology in Xian.

Microwave links, however, have been used in a more localized way. The mainland and Hainan Island are now linked in this fashion, and microwave links are an important part of the Yangtze delta telecommunications project, for example. Another extensive system is being established in the Zhujiang (Pearl River) delta in Guangdong, where, in the semi-rural industrialized hinterland of Hong Kong, a large volume of intercity or long-distance calls are made to, or from, relatively far-flung locations.

The development of telecommunications has been marked by two apparent tendencies. The first, as already indicated, is the concentration of telephones or terminals in urban areas, particularly in coastal regions.

By 1990 the number of telephones should reach 13.5 million. Of the proposed increase during the Seventh FYP, about half is scheduled for urban areas; additional long-distance lines will connect urban areas as well. The second tendency is to spread the technology thinly according to administrative precedence. The targets in Guangdong for the current FYP envisage the installation of automatic long-distance dialling in all cities above the prefectural level. However, major cities and counties in the Zhujiang (Pearl River) delta will also receive those facilities. It is intended that by 1990 most of the rest of Guangdong's counties should have semi-automatic dialling.

Despite the rapid rate of increase in the number of telephone lines, there are obvious signs of shortage which must disadvantage the rural and inland areas. The waiting list for telephones was officially put at 230,000 at the end of 1986, despite the high connection charges, which may reach 800 yuan RMB. In rural areas, priority in connection may be given to a potential subscriber willing to pay the cost of installing the trunk line to the village. Another symptom of demand is the size of post office waiting-rooms: in rural or inland areas it may take several hours to have a call put through. Thriving businesses are reported in urban centres where business people may pay to have messages collected from public telephones.

The supply and distribution of telephone facilities may not be greatly improved by 1990. One estimate puts the number of telephones by then at 20 per 1,000 peple in developed provinces and cities such as Guangdong, Zhejiang and Shanghai; at 10 per 1,000 in Central China; and only 5-6 per 1,000 in 'remote and backward' provinces and autonomous regions.[11] The benefits of extending telephone service to rural areas seem to be well recognized. Estimates of increased output value by rural businesses have been given, though how they have been calculated is not clear. The effect of improved telecommunications on the relative benefits to different locations is disputed even in the west, where the subject has been researched.[12] Their effect on transport use has also been studied in the west,[13] but may be expected to be much more pronounced in China, where markets and information systems are not as well developed.

Issues for the future

The tendency for China's transport and communications systems to be developed further and faster in the already developed parts of the country has been strengthened by two factors in recent years. One is the introduction of economic criteria in the evaluation of projects. This has taken the form of mandatory submission of important projects to consultancy bodies, who have the task of identifying costs and benefits.

Regional development criteria do not fit easily into such studies, even where the methodology and information are sufficiently well known to allow such kinds of issues to be addressed. Projects will be selected on the grounds of their net benefit to the economy as a whole, and investment will be drawn to those areas where transport acts as a significant and immediate constraint on economic growth. These are largely in East China and the industrialized areas of North and North-east China. Unless some preferential treatment is given to inland projects — which presupposes an alteration of central priorities — the tendency is unlikely to be reversed in the foreseeable future.

Deregulation is the second factor that has further emphasized the uneven development of transport and communications. Devolution of effective powers to lower levels or subordinate agencies will probably not work to counter the favouring of developed areas. The financial fragmentation of the railways under the recent contract responsibility system seems likely to exacerbate the trend. Any system which allows increased retention of investable funds would be expected to have that result. As for road, water and air transport, a combination of both the policy of dismantling the former all-embracing agencies and the practice of increasing operational autonomy has already resulted in the expansion of capacity in developed regions. In telecommunications, control has been highly devolved for some time, and development has been uneven.

Market-oriented (if not market-based) criteria for investment in transport and communications have been reinforced in their effect by foreign-trade-related factors such as loans. Shortage of foreign exchange or foreign technology is, of course, one more priority to be balanced against the needs of the less-favoured regions. The reconcentration of heavy industry in the energy-rich areas of northern China, largely a product of transport constraints, provides an opportunity to spread economic development inland. Yet locational factors relevant to light industry may cause this to remain concentrated elsewhere. For example, light industrial products will tend to have lower transport costs associated with their inputs, and prefer to remain close to their markets.

Two specific problems face the future role of roads. The road network has the ability to provide the greatest access for freight and passengers, but whether this is realized depends on future fuel policy. For instance, the World Bank in its 1985 report recommended a reduction or abolition of the agricultural diesel fuel subsidy, which was claimed to lead to wasteful use in rural transport and a reduction in road capacity.[14] The second problem is whether a rapid expansion of personal mobility, if a high car-use strategy is pursued, will lead to investment being drawn further into coastal and city areas.

The development of transport facilities, or their absence, is clearly of crucial significance in the location of new economic enterprises. In particular, the emphasis on economic criteria of management may well have consequences for the increased mobility of enterprises. As specializations develop, so too may concentrations in optimal locations. The emergence of the area around Zhongguancun (in north-west Beijing, the university and higher education sector of the capital) as an electronics and computing centre — a Chinese small-scale version of Silicon Valley — is but one recent example. The constraining aspects of transport are then likely to affect the location of those concentrations, but not their existence.

In general, the most successful regions are likely to be those which can adopt easily complementary combinations of transport and communications technologies. A combination of physical accessibility and telecommunications facilities must be more productive than either alone. However, the potential of telecommunications to spread productivity geographically is probably most significant in a 'post-industrial' phase of development, in which intellectual inputs form a greater proportion of the national product.

Despite the argument that it is the eastern, coastal, and urban areas of China which are likely to benefit disproportionately from the apparent trends in the development of transport and communications, regional development is not simply an issue to be regarded in terms of the coastal-interior, east-west, or urban-rural polarities. Political change for example, has facilitated trade across the northern and western borders of China, and those possibilities have spurred construction of transport links, which in turn will probably stimulate economic growth in the adjacent areas. However, the most powerful imperatives remain those which emphasize the development of the coastal areas. Indeed, transport expansion in the context of an increasing role for the market is likely to contribute to the reinforcement of those pressures. In the interior, the development of transport facilities will be a pre-requisite of economic development. None the less, it is unlikely to contribute to narrowing the gap in economic development between the interior and the more developed, coastal regions of China.

Notes

1 *Beijing Review*, 5 January 1987, p. 6.
2 Ye Zuoliao (1986) *Banyue Tan* (Half-Monthly Talks) no. 1, abstracted in *(Ta Kung Pao* (Weekly Supplement), 26 June 1986.
3 *China: The Transport Sector*, (1985) Washington, DC: World Bank, p. xvi.
4 Ibid., p. 60.
5 For example, see section XI of Mao Zedong's speech of 1957 'On the

correct handling of contradictions among the people', translated in
Selected Works of Mao Tsetung, Volume V (1977), Peking: Foreign
Languages Press.

6 *Tielu Yunshu Gongzu/o Zuzhi (Organizing Railway Transport)*, Beijing:
Renmin Tielu Chubanshe, 1964); JPRS translation 28854, 1965, section
xvii, 'Railroad Freight Rates in a Socialist Economy'.

7 *Economic Daily*, 15 October 1984, cited in Seiichi Nakajima (1984)
'Reform of China's Transport System', *JETRO China Newsletter*, no.
55, p. 11.

8 Chen Zuyun (1987) 'On Highway Construction and Reform in
Yunnan', *Yunnan Ribao*, 13 March, p. 3 translation in JPRS
CEA-87-042, 12 May 1987.

9 'China now has 8 million telephone sets', *Xinhua*, 7 January 1987,
SWB-E, 28 January 1987.

10 Ibid.

11 *China Daily*, 16 December 1987.

12 See for example, Goddard, J.R. and Pye, R. (1977) 'Telecommunications and Office Location', *Regional Studies*, vol. 11, no. 1, pp.
19–30.

13 Nilles, J., Carlson, F., Gray, P., and Hannemann, G. (1976) *The
Telecommunications Transportation Trade-off*, New York: Wiley
Interscience.

14 *China: The Transport Sector*, op. cit., p. 46.

Chapter six

The energy sector

Michèle Ledić

China's production of primary energy increased nearly forty times between 1949 and 1987. China now ranks fourth in the world as a fuel producer, and third as a fuel consumer. There is low per capita fuel consumption, and China is a very inefficient energy consumer, although there has been an improvement in recent years. There have been prolonged energy shortages since the 1960s, and it is estimated that at present roughly 20 per cent of industrial capacity suffers from fuel shortages. Household energy consumption has also had to be kept at a low level. Coal is the main commercial fuel, followed in importance by oil. Biomass and other non-commercial fuels account for over 80 per cent of rural energy supply, while 80 per cent of total rural energy is consumed in peasant households.[1]

China's aim is to quadruple her GVIAO (Gross Value of Industrial and Agricultural Output) between 1980 and the year 2000, but even the most optimistic estimates foresee only a doubling of primary energy production during this period. Coal reserves are ample, but accessible oil reserves are a cause of anxiety. More oil and gas will be needed from inland, offshore and unconventional sources, such as oil-shale, which is abundant. Hydroelectricity output is expected to quadruple by the year 2000. China now relies almost entirely on its own energy resources. It exports large quantities of oil, but oil exports are likely to fall, whereas coal exports are planned to grow. From the regional perspective there are definite problems. Some 40 per cent of total national output is produced by, and nearly 40 per cent of population are located in, eight provinces of South and East China. These provinces have measured coal reserves of only 2 per cent of the national total. Oil also is unevenly distributed, and hydroelectric power is often inaccessible. Consequently, as detailed in chapter 5, the transport of energy is a major concern for the economy. For example, the transport of coal accounts for 33 per cent of the annual throughput of railways, 20 per cent of waterways and 25 per cent of highways.

China's main energy problems are, therefore, lack of accessible oil reserves, uneven distribution of coal and oil (with consequent heavy transport needs), inefficient energy consumption, and the need to increase fuel supplies in rural areas — particularly with the great increases during recent years in rural industries — while ensuring self-sufficiency. In the recent past there have been plans for substantial investment in nuclear power to help solve energy shortages in East and South China, and to reduce pollution from coal, but for the present these have been deferred. Efforts are now being made to find alternative means of coal usage, such as coal gasification. Shell, for example, have designed a highly efficient process.[2] Rural regions will need to diversify their energy sources and also economize in fuel use. As part of the Seventh Five-Year Plan, emphasis has been placed on improving energy efficiency, as well as measures to reduce pollution.

Energy production

As already noted, China is both one of the world's largest fuel producers, and one of its largest energy consumers. However, per capita consumption is very low, at only about one-tenth of the average for more advanced economies, though well above the level of the low-income developing economies (for example, more than double that of India). At the same time China is a very inefficient user of energy. When measured in terms of energy intensity, China uses 40 barrels a day of oil equivalent (bdoe) per US $1000 GNP, as compared with 10 used in the United States, 6 in Japan and West Germany, 14 in India and 10 in Pakistan. If greater energy efficiency could be achieved, China's present consumption of energy per capita would be compatible with much higher national output per head.

China's energy production is dominated by the coal industry. It employs some five million people, and provides about three-quarters of the country's energy needs. In 1987 coal accounted for 73 per cent of total commercial energy production in China. Crude oil accounted for 21 per cent, and natural gas and hydroelectricity for 2 per cent and 4 per cent respectively.

Just over 46 per cent of the total of coal production (430 million tons) was produced in pits owned by the Ministry of Coal in 1987, but only approximately 20 per cent of China's total output comes from fully mechanized faces. Over a quarter of total output comes from small mines, owned collectively or by one man. These small mines are very inefficiently operated, but their number went up threefold between 1980 and 1984, while their output rose by over 80 per cent, to 217 million tons. Most of this coal is used locally, with only some 30–40 million tons per annum entering the state distribution system. Some 54 per cent of the country's mines are now mechanized.[3] Over 65 per cent of China's coal production is in the North, North-east and East Regions, including 25 per cent in Shanxi. As a result there is a major need for coal transportation, notably from the north to the coal deficit areas of the south, and the southern coastal provinces.

Description of China's commercial energy production, as shown in Table 6.1, excludes energy for rural households and residential use, such as biomass and other non-commercial fuels (crop by-products, fuelwood, dung for production of bio-gas). However, biomass fuels are the second most important energy source (after coal) and they account for an estimated 30 per cent of final energy consumption.

Table 6.1 Commercial energy production, 1980–7

Energy sources	1980	1983	1986	1987	Average annual growth rate (in %, 1980–7)
Coal/lignite					
(million tons)	620	715	894	920	5.8
(million bdoe)	6.0	6.9	8.7	9.1	
Crude oil					
(million tons)	106	106	131	134	3.4
(million bdoe)	2.12	2.12	2.62	2.68	
Natural gas					
(billion m^3)	14.3	12.2	13.4	13.7	−0.6
(million bdoe)	0.26	0.22	0.24	0.25	
Hydroelectricity					
(billion kWh)	58.2	86.4	94.5	99.5	8.0
(million bdoe)	0.33	0.47	0.51	0.54	
Total commercial					
(million bdoe)	8.7	9.7	12.1	12.6	5.4

Sources: Statistical Yearbook of China for 1984 and 1986; State Statistical Bureau Communiqué, 20 February 1987 and 26 February 1988.

China's oil industry has developed virtually entirely since the foundation of the People's Republic in 1949. In 1987 China produced 2.68 million barrels a day compared with 400,000 barrels a day in 1970. During the period 1967 to 1978 oil output grew at 20 per cent per annum and natural gas production at 23 per cent per annum, as compared with a growth rate for coal output of 10 per cent per annum. In recent years, however, the growth of coal output has exceeded that for oil and natural gas. Between 1980 and 1987 coal production rose by 49 per cent as compared with 26 per cent for oil, but natural gas production fell by over 4 per cent.

Some 90 per cent of crude oil comes from the North, North-east and East regions, estimated to contain 50 per cent of China's recoverable on-shore oil reserves. Some 40 per cent of the oil (388 million barrels) comes from one field — Daqing in Heilongjiang province. By 1979 the oil industry of China was suffering severe strains because of the rapid growth of the previous twenty years. There was a slump as the industry underwent a period of readjustment, and as the production methods employed in the oilfields, at Daqing in particular, were reaching their limits. By 1982, with the help of imported technology and assistance, total oil output began to rise again, and by 1987 had increased by more than 30 million tons over 1982. Foreign bids were welcomed for major off-shore, as well as — recently — on-shore, oilfields.

China has emerged in recent years as Asia's second largest refiner after Japan. Its downstream petroleum industry has total crude-oil processing capacity of over 2 million barrels a day and is now the sixth largest in the world, with 1987 annual throughput of 1.94 million barrels a day. The high wax content of Chinese domestic crudes, and the fact that they yield an average of 70 per cent of heavy products, has led to the need for widespread use of secondary processes to upgrade the heavy ends into gasoline and diesel fuel. The total yield of light products has now reached about 55 per cent.

The China Petrochemical Corporation (SINOPEC) runs the country's major refineries, petrochemical plants, and chemical fertilizer plants. It produced 46.4 million tons of oil products — gasoline, kerosene, diesel fuel, and lubricants — in 1987. This compares with refinery output of 40 million tons in 1984, and a planned output of 63 million tons in 1990.[4] In 1987 gasoline accounted for 36.4 per cent of total refinery output, kerosene for 9.4 per cent, diesel fuel for 50.4 per cent and lubricants for 3.8 per cent.

The main challenge facing China's downstream sector of the oil industry is to meet the rising demand for gasoline and other light products. SINOPEC is concentrating on the modernization of existing capacity, rather than the construction of new refineries. Foreign technology has been imported in order to reduce fuel oil yields. Further imports will certainly be required, particularly as the programme to substitute coal for oil in power plants goes ahead. As a result, more crude will be available for secondary refineries. A large proportion of oil products is at present processed in Singapore's refineries, and that will probably continue in the future.[5]

Since the off-shore natural gas discovery south of Hainan Island, in 1983, by Atlantic Richfield and Santa Fe, with total reserves exceeding 100 billion cu.m., China has had to reassess the role of natural gas in its economy. Previously gas development had been almost totally ignored in favour of crude oil. Natural gas production had already decreased between 1980 and 1982, when it reached a low level of 12.2 billion cu.m. Since then production has increased by some 1.5 billion cu.m., or approximately 12 per cent, but has not yet reached the 1980 level of production. It still represents only 2 per cent of China's primary commercial energy production.

In addition to natural gas, LPG (liquified petroleum gas) production was between two and three million tons in 1986, but only a third of this was commercially available. Beijing has been active in promoting gas for household use — pipeline as well as bottled gas. Gasworks or 'town' gas is also widely used: obtained from metallurgical coke production and also as a primary product of bituminous coal.[6]

At present electricity generated by hydroelectric power accounts for only 4 per cent of total primary energy production in China, but provides about one-quarter of China's total electricity generation, the remainder coming from coal-fired thermal plants. Twelve large and medium-sized hydropower stations are under construction, and emphasis has also been placed on the rapid expansion of small-scale hydroelectric plants as a means of expanding rural electrification. The potential for both large- and small-scale hydroelectric power is great, but a number of factors hinder development, including cost and the problem of displacing people and cropland. As already indicated in chapter 2, the Three Gorges (Sanxia) scheme for the Yangtze river, is one such project.

Energy consumption

Energy consumption in China has been closely allied to available supply. The main exception during the last decade has been oil (Table 6.2). A quarter of oil output is exported, in crude or refined form. While coal exports have been growing, they are still far below oil exports and represent only a minute fraction of coal production.

In recent years China has revealed energy shortages, estimated (for 1987) at 20 million tons of coal, 10 million tons of petroleum, and 60–70 billion kwh of electricity. Energy shortages contribute to China's claimed 20 per cent underutilization of manufacturing capacity. In addition, the Ministry of Agriculture has estimated that energy shortages in China's rural areas could reach 50 per cent by 1990.[7] Despite these shortages, economic growth in recent years has been very rapid, and restricted supply has enforced improved efficiency in several sectors.

Between the mid-1950s and 1978 there had been a rise in the consumption of electricity per unit of GDP, and the progressive replacement of coal by oil. Both trends were sharply reversed after 1978. Energy efficiency improved by over 20 per cent between 1978 and 1982. Almost the whole growth of the economy has been met by coal. Between 1982 and 1987 energy consumption of standard coal for every 10,000 yuan RMB in GDP declined from 12.72 tons to 10.38 tons — efficiency in the use of coal improved by an additional 18.4 per cent.[8] This improvement

Table 6.2 Primary commercial energy production and consumption, 1965–87

Energy sources	1965	1975	1985	1986	1987
Oil (mn tons)					
Production	11.3	77.1	124.9	131.0	134.0
Crude export	0.2	9.9	30.0	28.5	27.2
Product exports	0.1	2.1	6.5	5.4	4.9
Consumption	11.0	65.1	88.4	96.8	101.9
Coal (mn tons)					
Production	231.8	482.2	872.2	894.0	920.0
Exports	3.5	3.4	8.1	10.3	13.5
Consumption	228.3	478.8	864.1	883.7	906.5
Natural gas (bn m³)					
Prodn & cons	1.1	8.9	12.9	13.4	13.7
Primary electricity (bn kWh)					
Prodn & cons	10.4	47.6	92.4	94.5	99.5
Total electricity					
Production (bn kWh)	67.6	195.8	410.7	450.0	496.0

Sources: Statistical Yearbook of China for 1984 and 1986; State Statistical Bureau Communiqué, 23 and 27 February 1988.

in energy efficiency is to a great extent a result of government awareness of the interaction between the growth of the economy and the role of the energy sector. A policy of switching emphasis from energy-intensive heavy industry to light industry has therefore been adopted. Energy conservation has also been encouraged, as well as the moving of industry nearer to the sources of primary energy[9] (see chapters 5 and 8).

China has two major problems in the energy field which affect the balance between production and consumption. One is the serious regional imbalance. The other is the differing patterns and major structural division between rural and urban areas as regards energy consumption. The 80 per cent of the population located in rural areas consume less than 40 per cent of the energy. Well over 80 per cent of their consumption is from local sources, such as biomass and locally-produced commercial energy. Only 10 per cent of rural consumption is met by allocation from nationally controlled sources. The policy that rural areas should be self-sufficient in energy, and should rely on nationally distributed commercial energy as little as possible, is to continue.

Consumption in urban areas accounts for roughly 85 per cent of the total consumption of commercial energy in China. A striking feature is that a predominant share (60 per cent) of total commercial energy consumption is in the industrial sector (see Table 6.3). The share consumed by transport is exceptionally low (8 per cent as compared with 18 per cent in India, for example), as is commercial energy consumed to meet residential and commercial needs (20 per cent).

Table 6.3 Shares of final energy consumption, 1980 (%)

Sector	Oil	Coal	Natural gas	Elec-tricity	Total commercial energy	Biomass	Total energy
			A Energy composition (%)				
Agriculture	29	47	—	24	100	—	100
Transport	52	47	—	1	100	—	100
Industry	13	60	5	22	100	—	100
Other	39	50	—	11	100	—	100
Residential/commercial							
% comm energy	2	88	0	10	100	—	—
% total energy	1	28	0	3	32	68	100
Total							
% comm energy	16	63	3	18	100	—	—
% total energy	11	44	2	13	70	30	100
			B Sectoral shares (%)				
Agriculture	15	6	—	12	9	—	6
Transport	25	6	—	1	8	—	5
Industry	50	58	98	74	60	—	43
Other	8	3	—	2	3	—	2
Resid comm	2	27	2	11	20	100	44
Total	100	100	100	100	100	100	100

Source: The World Bank Report on China (1985), China: Long-Term Development Issues and Options, Annex C: Energy, Washington, DC: The World Bank, p. 4.

Biomass is the second most important source of fuel in China. Small quantities are consumed in some urban areas and in some rural industries, but most of it is used in rural households. Biomass fuels account for some 30 per cent of total final energy consumption in China. It has been estimated by the World Bank that crop by-products (for example, corn cobs and stalks, wheat and millet straw) account for 46 per cent, fuelwood (for example, small branches, grass and leaves) for 38 per cent, and dried dung — which is an important input for the production of bio-gas — for some 3 per cent of biomass fuel consumption.[10]

Table 6.3 shows energy consumption by sector for 1980, the latest year for which comprehensive figures are available. In 1980 over 80 per cent of industrial energy was consumed by heavy industry, including chemicals (23 per cent), metallurgy (20 per cent) and the energy industry itself (15 per cent). Coal is by far the most important fuel in most sectors of the economy (accounting for some 75 per cent of total energy consumption in 1985), including transport and household use. The situation recently has changed to some extent with the introduction of diesel locomotives on the railways, but in the 1980s coal has accounted for over half the energy used in transport. Oil accounted for about 17 per cent of total energy consumption in 1985, having fallen from a peak of 23 per cent in 1976. Petroleum products have been in very short supply during recent years. Transport is the biggest consumer of oil products, using about 38 per cent of the total. Other significant consumers are heavy industry, agriculture and the power-generation industry.

Natural gas is still relatively unimportant, accounting in 1985 for about 2.5 per cent of energy consumption. The great majority of the supply is consumed by industry, but some has been diverted to urban areas to reduce pollution from household coal usage. Hydroelectricity is growing rapidly in importance, but still accounted, in 1985, for only about 5 per cent of total energy consumption. Over three-quarters was consumed by industry in 1980. There are many small hydroelectric stations serving local areas. About one-third of the electricity used in agriculture comes from such small-scale plants. At the end of 1985 it was estimated that there were some 74,000 small hydroelectric plants providing electricity for some 60 per cent of China's rural households.

Regional energy production

Regional imbalances in energy production have often been remarked upon. The high energy demand of recent years resulting from rapid economic growth, especially in industry, has highlighted the acute need to tackle regional energy imbalances. Regional shares of commercial energy production in 1985 are set out in Table 6.4.

Coal is produced on a large scale in several regions, with the North being predominant, producing nearly 36 per cent of the total. Mines which produce over 10 million tons per annum in the North include Datong and Yangquan in Shanxi, and Kailuan and Fengfeng in Hebei. Shanxi is the most important province for both coal production and coal reserves. It produced only one-fifth of China's coal in 1981, as compared with one-quarter in 1985. New mines are planned, and it is expected that Shanxi will produce one-third of national output by the year 2000.[11]

Over half of total oil production comes from the North-east, with most of this in turn from the Daqing field in Heilongjiang, discovered in 1959. In 1985 six oilfields accounted for 90 per cent of China's total oil production: Daqing (41 per cent) and Liaohe (7 per cent) in the North-east, Huabei (8 per cent) in the North, Shengli (22 per cent) in the East, Zhongyuan (4 per cent) in the Central-South, and Karamay (4 per cent) in the North-west. The newest of these is Zhongyuan, and the most remote Karamay.

Table 6.4 Regional shares of commercial energy supply, 1985 (%)

Region	Coal	Oil	Gas	Electricity Total	of which Hydro
North	36.3	11.3	6.0	17.3	1.2
North-east	15.1	53.4	31.5	16.4	8.8
East	14.5	22.2	9.1	28.7	14.3
Central-South	15.0	7.2	4.9	20.4	40.4
South-west	11.0	0.0	43.8	9.2	21.3
North-west	8.1	5.9	4.7	8.0	14.0
Total (%)	100.0	100.0	100.0	100.0	100.0
Total (amount)	872.2 (mn tons)	124.9 (mn tons)	12.9 (bn m³)	410.7 (bn kWh)	92.4 (bn kWh)

Source: Statistical Yearbook of China, 1986.

Natural gas is produced in two main regions, the South-west and the North-east, the two together accounting for over 75 per cent of output in 1987. Sichuan in the South-west is the most important province for production, with some sixty gasfields accounting for 45 per cent of total production. Associated gas is produced at all the main oilfields, with Daqing and Liaohe in the North-east generating nearly a third of gas output, and Shengli (in the East) about 9 per cent. A gas distribution network is centred on Sichuan covering itself and neighbouring provinces. A smaller network has been developed in Zhongyuan, in Henan province, since 1980. Gas from other areas is used locally. With the help of a World Bank loan, China intends to use western equipment to modernize the Sichuan gasfield and greatly increase its output.

Arco and Santa Fe had reached agreement with the China National Off-shore Oil Corporation (CNOOC) to develop their Yacheng field (Yinggehai) in the South China Sea, but this has been delayed. It was recently decided that the plan for the Yinggehai natural gas well, whose reserves are such that an estimated 3.2 billion cu.m, of gas can be extracted every year for more than twenty years, is to change. It is no longer to be developed to supply the Zhujiang (Pearl River) delta but, instead, priority supply is to go to Hainan Island, recently upgraded administratively in line with its new status as China's new major special economic development zone.[12]

The most important region for the generation of hydroelectricity is the Central-South, with Hubei the leading province. The importance of Hubei will be greatly emphasized if the Three Gorges project is given permission to go ahead. As has been already indicated, thermal power plants account for over 75 per cent of electricity production. Coal-fired plants account for over 80 per cent of thermal capacity, with the remainder being fuelled by oil and (to a small extent) natural gas. The region with the largest output is the East, but there is substantial output elsewhere. It has to be remembered that thermal power generation consumes primary energy. Its location depends on the location of demand for electricity, unless a grid is constructed to bring electricity from power stations in primary energy areas to the consuming areas. In fact, the policy of building mine-mouth plants has been fostered by the Ministries of both Coal and Power since the late 1970s, partly to reduce the need to transport coal. As indicated in Table 6.5, in general terms the North and North-east regions together supply more than half of total commercial energy. Coal dominates the energy picture in every region but the North-east, where oil production in 1985 was actually greater (in oil equivalent terms) than coal production.

Table 6.5 Composition of regional commercial energy supply, 1985 (% of bdoe)

Region	Coal	Oil	Gas	Hydro-electricity	Total output (%)	Total output (mn bdoe)	Share (%)
North	90.9	8.5	0.4	0.2	100	3.32	28.8
North-east	46.4	49.4	2.6	1.6	100	2.70	23.5
East	65.2	29.9	1.1	3.8	100	1.85	16.0
Central-South	76.2	11.0	0.7	12.1	100	1.64	14.2
South-west	81.9	0.2	8.6	9.3	100	1.11	9.7
North-west	74.8	16.3	1.2	7.7	100	0.90	7.8
Total						11.52	100.0

Source: Statistical Yearbook of China, 1986.

The output of the main sources of energy by region during the 1980s is given in Appendix Tables 6A.1 to 6A.4. As regards coal (Appendix Table 6A.1), the largest percentage increase of output has been in the most productive region, the North. As for oil (Appendix Table 6A.2), the leading producer region, the Northeast, showed a low rate of growth, while the Central-South grew very rapidly, from less than 1% of total output in 1980 to over 7% in 1985. Natural gas output (Appendix Table 6A.3) fell over the period, with the three most productive regions (the Northeast, the East and the Southwest) falling by more than the average. The Central-South region saw a very big rise in gas output from a low base in 1980. The change in electricity production (Appendix Table 6A.4) was much more uniform between regions, as is to be expected of a non-primary source of energy, with above average increases in the Central-South, the South-west and the East.

Regional energy consumption

Data for energy consumption by sector are not generally available.

The most recently published estimates are for 1980, produced by the World Bank (see Table 6.3). There are no published data or estimates on energy consumption by region, and it is therefore necessary to estimate this by indirect means. Industry accounts for about 60 per cent of commercial energy consumption, and the residential-commercial sector accounts for 20 per cent (Table 6.3). There are figures available for the Gross Value of Industrial Output (GVIO) by region, as well as for its distribution between heavy and light industry (see Appendix Table 6A.5). Residential-commercial use of energy is likely to be related to a certain extent to population. An approximate idea of likely energy demand by region can be estimated if industrial production and population are weighted by the percentages just mentioned, thus taking account of the relative strength of demand for industrial purposes and for residential-commercial purposes. The resulting weighted average of commercial energy consumption by region is shown in Appendix Table 6A.6.

There is one further refinement that can be made. Figures are available for energy consumption (in metric tons of standard coal), by province, for every 10,000 yuan RMB's worth of total industrial output value in 1985 — that is, they show energy efficiency. These figures of energy efficiency are given by province, but regional figures can be inferred.[13] Regional energy consumption estimates have been adjusted by those figures, and the results are given in Table 6.6. The table therefore indicates, broadly speaking (and in the absence of other information), the composition of commercial energy demand by region. The estimates can of course be subject to detailed criticism, but it does not seem likely that the broad picture they provide of the distribution of energy consumption by region is too far from the true position.

Table 6.6 Regional commercial energy supply and demand, 1985

Region	Energy[1] production (%)	Energy[2] consumption (%)	Energy intensity (tc/10,000Rmb)	Weighted consumption (%)	Balance (%)
North	28.8	13.9	8.03	17.7	+11.1
North-east	23.5	13.4	7.57	16.1	+7.4
East	16.0	36.2	4.44	25.5	−9.5
Central-South	14.2	21.1	5.93	19.8	−5.6
South-west	9.7	10.0	8.09	12.8	−3.1
North-west	7.8	5.4	9.43	8.1	−0.3

Notes:
1. See Table 6.5.
2. See Appendix Table 6A.6.
Sources: Statistical Yearbook of China, 1986; State Council Communiqué, 9 August 1986.

If the figures for regional energy supply (Table 6.5) are compared with the estimates for regional energy demand, then a clear (if somewhat crude) indication of the regional energy balance emerges, as Table 6.6 details. It cannot be a precise measure of the energy balance, partly because of the nature of the estimates that have been made, and partly because all primary fuels have been considered together. A comparison of the first and fourth columns in Table 6.6 (energy production and weighted consumption) reveals two surplus regions — the North and the North-east. All the other regions are in deficit, particularly the East and the Central-South regions. These last two regions would be in even more serious deficit were it not for their energy efficiency, which is relatively high by Chinese standards.

Internal and external trade

Oil is the most important fuel in China's foreign trade, with 26 per cent of output being exported in crude or refined form, earning about US $3.8 billion or 18 per cent of total foreign exchange in 1986. The picture was rather different in 1985, when China exported about 29 per cent of its oil output. It brought China some US $7.8 billion and accounted for 22.3 per cent of total foreign-exchange earnings, at that time the single most important provider of foreign exchange.[14]

Exports of coal are at present only a very small proportion of output, and imports of coal represent about one-third of exports. In 1985 exports were 0.9 per cent of total coal output generating some US $320 million or 0.9 per cent of foreign-exchange earnings. During 1987 China exported 13.13 million tons of coal or some 1.5 per cent of output, earning US $464 million, or 1.1 per cent of total export earnings. With the exception of oil, therefore, nearly all of the energy produced in China is consumed domestically. Because of the large regional imbalances in energy supply and demand, there is a need for very large movements of all fuels, both within and among regions. As indicated in chapter 5, one alternative that has been considered is the relocation of a proportion of industrial activity in the energy-rich provinces. However, doubts remain about the practicalities of such a policy.

Railways are the chief means of transport for coal, carrying about 60 per cent of output. Shanxi's coal exports are the largest in the country, with (in 1985) some 60 per cent of the province's output being transported elsewhere by rail. However, there is a need for the construction of additional railway lines particularly from Shanxi, because of the intended large increases in its coal output. Several of the planned lines are major state construction projects in the Seventh FYP. There are also large rail projects in Inner Mongolia where the lack of rail capacity has led to the closure of some mines.[15] Although they are major coal producers, the eastern and central provinces have faced some of China's most serious shortages of fuel and power in recent years. Several of China's worst transport bottlenecks are in eastern China. There are plans to increase railway investment in the region very substantially in 1987 and subsequent years, but serious shortages will remain for many years, as chapter 5 has shown.

An alternative solution to the problem of coal transport has been sought in the expansion of port facilities, in order to move coal along the coast by sea. Large investments are in progress and planned, including the construction of railway lines leading to ports. There has also been greater use of inland waterways for moving coal. There is much investment in canals and rivers, including the construction of additional and improved wharves.[16]

The bulk of oil is transported within China by pipeline, although significant quantities are also shipped by rail. By 1984 China had built over 11,000 km of pipeline, transporting some 65 per cent of its oil and gas output. There are two major pipeline systems taking oil and gas from the Daqing and Shengli oilfields to refineries, other consumption outlets, and to the ports, for coastal or ocean shipping. Some refineries are close to oilfields, but others are far away and require oil to be moved over long distances.

There is a shortage of both oil production and refineries in the southern provinces. New refineries are needed in the south to meet the growing demand for petroleum products in Guangdong and Fujian. The discovery of the Shengli (Eastern region) and Dagang (Northern region) oilfields during the 1960s was important because they are within reasonable reach of the main industrial areas. Because of the rapid expansion of production at Shengli in recent years, transport has become a problem, and new pipelines are having to be built. However, the best prospects for future oil finds are in the West and North-west regions, more than 2,000 km from the main consumption areas. Natural gas is transported largely by pipeline. A new pipeline is being built from Zhongyuan in Henan to Shandong and Hebei provinces, and will link up with pipelines from the Shengli and Dagang oilfields, forming China's first gas grid.

Problems of both production and transport are combined in the severe shortages of electric power in China. Coastal areas began experiencing frequent shortages of power during the late 1970s. Now power shortages are common in every part of the country, and the development of electricity generation has been given top priority for the next five years. Over 50 per cent of state investment in energy will go on power plants, transmission lines, and other facilities. Thermal power plants account for 70 per cent of installed capacity and 78 per cent of output. Large movements of coal are needed to ensure power stations are supplied, although the emphasis is now being placed on mine-mouth power plants. This reduces the need for the transport of coal, and is part of a broader strategy of encouraging energy-rich zones to industrialize further. There are plans for an expansion of hydroelectric output, but many of the most promising areas are remote, and would entail problems in transporting power to the regions where it is most needed.

Outlook for the energy sector

Serious regional imbalances characterize China's pattern of energy production and consumption. That regional pattern raises severe problems of energy transportation, and very heavy investment is now going ahead to remedy some of those transport problems. A partial solution being pursued is to base more industry in energy-rich areas of the country.

In addition to the problems of transporting energy, and the regional problems of scarcity on this account, there are severe difficulties arising from an overall shortage of the energy required to satisfy China's needs and its plans for growth. Between 1980 and 2000, output is planned to rise by a multiple of four while energy output is expected to double, thus necessitating a doubling of energy efficiency. There are serious doubts about whether this target can be achieved. Measures to reduce the size of the problem include reducing the ratio of heavy to light industry; switching from oil to coal in heavy industry; and replacing old boilers, furnaces and inefficient equipment. A system of rationing has also been introduced, with penalties for overconsumption and bonuses for underconsumption.

The very high growth rate of industrial output in recent years has outpaced the growth of agricultural output, as well as that of electricity and total energy output. In the period 1981–7 total industrial output grew in real terms by 13 per cent per annum — light industry by 14.6 per cent and heavy industry by 12.2 per cent. Pressure has consequently been brought to bear on other economic sectors, which have not kept pace with industrial production. For example, agricultural output increased at a rate of only 6.5 per cent per annum at most (taking inflation into account), creating a shortage of some farm products. During the same period, crude oil production had an average annual growth rate of 3.4 per cent, coal of some 5.9 per cent, electricity of about 10.5 per cent, and total commercial energy production of about 5.5 per cent. This inability of the energy sector to meet greatly increased demand has created severe shortages, and these will certainly continue into the foreseeable future hampering industrial output, as well as contributing to the transport shortage through lack of fuel for road transport.

Locational imbalances between energy supply and demand (which do not of course necessarily coincide with regional or provincial boundaries, but occur because of imbalances between the important areas of energy supply and the main areas of energy consumption) make the problem worse. The deficit areas, where industry is most highly concentrated, will suffer additional shortages because of the problem of transporting energy to them from the North and North-east. If, therefore, there is a general energy shortage, the pressure to deal with locational imbalances will become even stronger.

If sectoral consumption needs do not match the mix of energy sources, international movements of energy will be needed.[17] China's international energy trade balance may well deteriorate from its present sizeable surplus to a much smaller one, or even become a deficit. Even bigger changes could be in prospect: if in the future controls on foreign trade should be eased, there might be considerable alterations in present energy flows. The surplus areas might well find it more profitable to export much of their oil and coal, while the deficit areas might find it more desirable to import a substantial part of their energy needs. Whether such policies or practices are adopted will depend, among many other considerations, on estimates of what the likely effects might be on China's foreign-exchange position.

Appendix Tables

Table 6A.1 Coal production by region 1980–85 (%)

Region	1980	1981	1982	1983	1984	1985	*Percentage change 1980–85*	*Average annual rate of growth (%) (1980–85)*
North	33.1	34.5	34.6	34.7	35.4	36.3	+54.4	9.1
North-east	15.9	15.0	15.1	15.1	15.4	15.1	+33.1	5.9
East	17.0	16.7	16.0	15.7	15.2	14.6	+20.7	3.8
Central-South	15.5	15.3	15.7	15.9	15.3	15.0	+36.6	6.4
South-west	10.4	10.5	10.7	10.8	10.8	10.9	+47.2	8.0
North-west	8.0	7.9	7.8	7.9	7.9	8.1	+41.1	7.1
China	100.0	100.0	100.0	100.0	100.0	100.0	+40.6	7.0
Total output (mn tons)	620.1	621.6	666.3	714.5	772.2	872.2		

Source: Statistical Yearbook of China for 1983, 1984, 1985, 1986; World Bank Report on China, 1985.

Table 6A.2 Crude oil production by region 1980–85 (%)

Region	1980	1981	1982	1983	1984	1985	Percentage change 1980–85	Average annual rate of growth (%) (1980–85)
North	18.6	15.2	14.1	12.9	11.7	11.3	−26.5	−6.0
North-east	57.8	57.9	58.1	57.2	55.3	53.6	+13.7	2.6
East	17.7	16.3	16.4	17.7	20.6	22.2	+53.6	9.0
Central-South	0.8	4.7	5.5	6.1	6.5	7.2	+1,137.5	62.6
South-west	0.0	0.0	0.0	0.0	0.0	0.1	+20.0	3.7
North-west	5.1	5.9	5.9	6.1	5.9	5.6	+30.8	5.5
China	100.0	100.0	100.0	100.0	100.0	100.0	+17.3	3.3
Total output (mn tons)	106.4	101.2	102.1	106.4	114.6	124.8		

Note:
0.0% = negligible.
Source: Table 6A.1.

Table 6A.3 Natural gas production by region 1980–85 (%)

Region	1980	1981	1982	1983	1984	1985	Percentage change 1980–85	Average annual rate of growth (%) (1980–85)
North	5.6	5.7	6.5	5.9	5.5	6.0	−2.9	−0.61
North-east	36.9	35.6	34.6	34.1	32.5	31.5	−22.7	−5.1
East	10.2	8.4	8.4	8.6	9.3	9.1	−19.0	−4.1
Central-South	0.4	1.5	2.5	3.1	3.5	5.0	+1,288.0	66.7
South-west	44.2	45.6	44.1	44.3	45.3	43.8	−10.1	−2.1
North-west	2.7	3.2	3.9	4.0	3.9	4.6	+51.3	8.6
China	100.0	100.0	100.0	100.0	100.0	100.0	−9.4	−2.0
Total output (bn m^3)	14.27	12.74	11.93	12.21	12.42	12.93		

Source: Table 6A.1.

Table 6A.4 Electricity production by region 1980–85 (%)

Region	1980	1981	1982	1983	1984	1985	Percentage change 1980–85	Average annual rate of growth (%) (1980–85)
North	17.8	17.8	17.6	17.3	17.4	17.3	+32.5	5.8
North-east	18.0	17.5	17.2	17.0	16.8	16.4	+24.8	4.5
East	27.9	28.3	28.1	27.9	28.3	28.7	+40.7	7.1
Central-South	19.1	19.7	20.1	20.7	20.2	20.4	+45.5	7.8
South-west	8.9	8.7	9.0	9.2	9.3	9.2	+41.6	7.2
North-west	8.3	8.0	8.0	7.9	8.0	8.0	+31.2	5.6
China	100.0	100.0	100.0	100.0	100.0	100.0	+36.6	6.4
Total output (bn kWh)	300.7	309.3	327.7	351.4	377.0	410.7		

Source: Table 6A.1.

Table 6A.5 Indicators of commercial energy consumption — 1985 (%)

Region	Percentage of population	Total	Percentage of industry (GVIO) Heavy	Light
North	11.5	14.7	16.1	13.3
North-east	9.2	14.8	19.1	10.5
East	29.1	38.5	33.1	44.0
Central-South	26.9	19.2	17.4	21.0
South-west	16.1	8.0	8.4	7.5
North-west	7.2	4.8	5.9	3.7
Total	100.0	100.0	100.0	100.0
	1,045 (million)	829.46	418.1 (billion RMB)	411.36

Source: Statistical Yearbook of China, 1986.

Table 6A.6 Regional shares of commercial energy consumption — 1985 (%)

Region	Percentage of total population (A)	Percentage of GVIO (B)	Percentage of estimated energy consumption (C) [(C) = (A) x 0.2 + (B) x 0.6]
North	11.5	14.7	13.9
North-east	9.2	14.8	13.4
East	29.1	38.5	36.2
Central-South	26.9	19.2	21.1
South-west	16.6	8.0	10.0
North-west	7.2	4.8	5.4
Total	100.0	100.0	100.0

Source: Statistical Yearbook of China, 1986.

Notes

1 Lu Yingzhong (1986) 'Economic Development and Energy Use in PR China', International Round Table on Energy, Technology and Economy, Laxenburg: IIASA, p. 6.
2 Burgt, M. van der and Klinken, J. van (1986) 'The Shell Coal Gasification Process', Suzhou: Fourth Advanced Coal Gasification Symposium, November, p. 3.
3 *Xinhua*, 1 January 1988, in SWB-E 0008 A/6, 13 January 1988.
4 Johnson, T.M. and Fridley, D. (1985) 'China: The Future of Crude Oil and Petroleum Product Exports', Honolulu, Hawaii: East-West Center, p. 15.
5 Ibid., p. 6.
6 Johnson, T.M. (1987) *China: Energy Sector Outlook*, London: Economist Intelligence Unit, pp. 42–5.
7 Statement by Deng Kouyou, Ministry of Agriculture, Animal Husbandry and Fisheries, *Xinhua*, 8 November 1987, in SWB-E 0022 A/4, 18 November 1987.
8 *Xinhua*, 7 April 1988, in SWB-E 0022 A/4, 20 April 1988.
9 On China's recent efforts at energy conservation see *The Present State and Future of China's Energy Problem*, Tokyo: National Institute for Research Advancement, 1986, pp. 86–95.
10 The World Bank Report on China (1985) *China: Long-Term Development Issues and Options*, Annex C: Energy, Washington, DC: The World Bank, 1985, p. 137.
11 See chapter 8.
12 Gorst, I. (1986) 'China: Onshore Key to Increased Output', *Petroleum Economist*, vol. 53, no. 12, December, p. 456.
13 'Energy and Power Consumption Indices for 1985', State Council Departmental Communiqué, 9 August 1986, in SWB-E 1403 A/6, 20 August 1986.
14 Ledić, M. (1987) 'China: Energy Key to Economic Growth', *Petroleum Economist*, vol. 54, no. 11, November, pp. 405–8.
15 See chapter 8.
16 See Mao Yushi and Hu Guangrong (1985) 'China's Transport and its Energy Use', China Academy of Railway Sciences, Beijing: ERG Review Paper no. 073, p. 28; and chapter 5.
17 Ledić, M. (1987) 'PR China's Energy Prospects: Net Exporter or Net Importer?', in *Proceedings of RIIA-NIRA Conference on China, International Conference Report Series 7*, National Institute for Research Advancement, Tokyo, p. 135–51.

Chapter seven

Special Economic Zones
David R. Phillips and Anthony G.O. Yeh

China's Special Economic Zones, in common with many other export-processing zones in South-East Asia, are identifiable entities, isolated to a considerable extent legally and physically from the rest of the country. Their objectives may appear to be 'aspatial', but they nevertheless do contribute *de facto* to the regional balance or imbalance: they have specific locations and are becoming quite significant economic forces in their own right. Most important, perhaps, from a regional perspective, is their concentration in the coastal provinces of Guangdong, Hainan and Fujian (see map on page xv).

This chapter examines the evolution of the SEZs as part of the PRC's 'open door' policy in its drive to modernization. They are spatial expressions of that policy and, in many ways, the designation and changing fortunes of the SEZs have been strongly influenced by, and have mirrored, its evolution during the past decade. In spite of recent criticisms and some re-evaluation, their strategic locations and sociopolitical significance cannot be underrated. These factors will almost inevitably maintain the SEZs' prominence for both local and foreign investors, and sustain interest in them for researchers.

Special Economic and Export-Processing Zones

Many developing countries, particularly in South-East Asia, have developed Export-Processing Zones (EPZs).[1] Their creation has been associated with major shifts in policy towards export-orientated industrialization rather than import-substitution industrialization. A policy of export-orientated industrialization, with its concomitant requirements of efficient, cheap and modern production, has often led NICs to attempt to concentrate and attract industry (particularly foreign investment) in EPZs or free trade zones. These are administratively distinct areas in which legislation confers preferential treatment on investors. By mid-1984 the number of EPZs world-wide had grown to include at least seventy-nine significant special economic zones, export-processing zones, and science parks, in thirty-five different countries and territories. Some 57 per cent of known employment in such zones in 1984 was concentrated in Asia.[2] Significantly, during the 1980s some Third World countries, particularly the NICs, have become more concerned to promote high-technology enterprises rather than export industries in general.

Most EPZs, and especially those in Asia, have been developed in free enterprise economies, although India with its mixed economic system is an exception. China, by contrast, has its own form of socialism and, when zones were first designated there, central state control of the economy was even more evident than it is a decade later. As a result, the fundamental setting of the Chinese SEZs is somewhat different from those of other Asian EPZs. The objectives of the Chinese zones have differed too, and while initially rather unclear, they seem to have evolved along with the Chinese economy as a whole since 1978. Generally, the most important aims have been to attract foreign investment, to earn foreign exchange via exports, and to encourage technology transfer. In addition, the acquisition of knowledge of modern business practices and commercial-managerial skills has been desired.

Although unstated at the time, it seems likely that an important consideration in establishing SEZs must have been the creation of an economy free of the allegedly stultifying effects of state regulation. As was later stated quite explicitly, SEZs could on that basis be regarded as experimental, with greater direction reintroduced if necessary. It is also evident that the concept of the 'special economic zone' in China has changed. Initially the zones were envisaged almost as replicas of the EPZs of other countries in East and South-East Asia, and were regarded as 'special export zones'. The term was later changed to 'special economic zones' to emphasize their socialist nature and comprehensive development.[3]

The Chinese SEZs also differ from other EPZs in several other ways. Three of the five zones (Shenzhen, Xiamen and Hainan) are now considerably larger territorially than is the norm elsewhere. Foreign participation in services and infrastructural development, as well as in industry has been encouraged. More unusually still, the SEZs incorporate significant tourist, recreational, housing and retail sectors which inevitably present physical and economic features not totally congruent with their export orientation. The development of often luxurious housing for foreign employees, visitors, and higher grade staff, as well as the tolerance of types of retail provision which have enabled the import of goods into China for locals (rather than creating exports), have also influenced the nature of the SEZs, especially in their earlier years. Table 7.1 compares some of the characteristics of the Chinese zones with those of EPZs elsewhere, although the considerable variety of such zones (and, indeed, differences among the Chinese SEZs

Table 7.1 The PRC's SEZs and EPZs elsewhere — comparisons on selected aspects

	Export-Processing Zones	Chinese Special Economic Zones
Strategic aims		
Sociopolitical objectives	Not usually	Yes
Emphasis on attracting overseas investment	Yes	Yes
Emphasis on managerial and skill training	Not usually	Yes
Technology transfer	Sometimes	Yes
Employment generation	Often important	Not a key issue
Financial/legal		
Relaxation of customs duties	Yes	Yes
Fewer restrictions on profits transfer	Yes	Yes
Lower company taxation	Yes	Yes
'Tax holidays'	Often initially	Initially
Export-orientated	Usually	Yes but not totally
Access to local market	Sometimes	Officially restricted
Reduced environmental controls	Often	Uncertain
Planning/geographical		
Physical size	Usually small: many under 100–500 hectares	Variable: some larger than most EPZs
Specific designation of boundaries	Yes	Yes
Restrictions of free movement of goods/people	Usually	Usually
Central zone control/administration	Usually	Yes
Physical site planning/delimitation	Yes	Yes
Regional development/regional policy objectives	Sometimes	Not clear
Social and infrastructural		
Constraints on labour/union organizations	Often	Probably
Greater use of female labour	Usually	Probably
Social infrastructure for workers	Sometimes	Under construction
Cheap industrial sites in zone	Yes	Yes
Standard factory units available	Often	Yes
Residential facilities for overseas staff	Sometimes	Yes
Recreation facilities for tourism	Rarely	Yes
Hotels included	Rarely	Yes
Retail facilities	Unusual	Yes

Source: After Phillips (1986) 'Special Economic Zones in China's modernization: changing policies and changing fortunes', *National Westminster Bank Quarterly Review*, February, pp. 37–49. Reproduced with permission.

Table 7.2 SEZs — comparative data for 1985

	Shenzhen	*Zhuhai*	*Shantou*	*Xiamen*
CITY				
Land area (in sq. km)				
Whole city	2,021	1,630	10,346	1,516
City proper	328	654	245	555
Permanent population				
Whole city	478,600	411,700	9,202,400	1,026,700
City proper	231,900	155,000	760,800	546,400
SEZ				
Land area (in sq. km)	327.50	15.16	52.60	131.00
Permanent population	231,200	15,900	23,700	n.a.
Industrial output				
(in million US $)	604	33	11	n.a.
Exports (in million US $)	527	23	43	170
Retail sales				
(in million US $)	584	85	19	n.a.
Utilized foreign investment				
(in million US $)	324	73	8	n.a.
Total workers	193,000	15,600	6,800	n.a.
Workers in joint				
enterprises	31,700	5,200	3,000	n.a.
% Total workers in joint				
enterprises	16.42	33.33	44.12	n.a.
Per capita industrial output				
(in thousand US $)	2.61	2.06	0.48	n.a.
Per capita exports				
(in thousand US $)	2.28	1.45	1.81	n.a.
Per capita retail sales				
(in thousand US $)	2.53	5.35	0.80	n.a.

Note Hainan Island is not included above, since it was designated an SEZ only in 1988.
Sources: Guangdong Yearbook 1987, pp. 512–3 (for Shenzhen, Zhuhai and Shantou SEZs).
Almanac of China's Foreign Economic Relations and Trade 1986, pp. 737–8 (for Xiamen SEZ).
China Urban Statistics 1986, pp. 219–20, p. 223 (for city data).
(US $1 = 3.9 RMB)

themselves) can render generalizations misleading. Table 7.2 provides background data on the four original Chinese zones.

The designation of SEZs and other 'open areas'

The official designation of four SEZs in 1979 was perhaps the initial major recognition that increased foreign investment in China's economy was inevitable and desirable. The four zones were among the first of the huge and bewildering proliferation of new regional organizations that have followed. (Hainan Island, off the coast of Guangdong and originally part of that province, was designated a fifth SEZ in April 1988 following its establishment as a separate provincial-level unit.) However, in spite of their concentration in the south-east — three were in Guangdong and one in Fujian — it seems that there was not, at least initially, any significant regional planning behind their creation. At that stage, they were not intended to act as direct stimulants to the economies of their environs. Rather, they appeared to be regarded as variants of the concept of the 'growth pole' (*pôle de croissance*),[4] in which 'aspatial' growth poles within the economy might establish and develop.

Of course, the SEZs do have very distinct regional identities. Their boundaries, though subsequently modified in some cases, were strictly defined. However, direct linkages with the local economies in which they were set were not initially actively sought or anticipated. Indeed, only certain parts of the cities to which the SEZs belonged were demarcated as special zones. It seems that their sitings were probably decided by broader strategic considerations and their ability to attract overseas investment.

The image of business-predatory Cantonese might have been reinforced by the apparent gift of special zones exclusively in the south of China. The southerly bias of the initial geographical location of 'open sites' was undoubtedly a cause of some resentment and presented an opportunity for political criticism from the north, and Shanghai in particular. However, since designation of the SEZs, at least two other important steps have been taken. First, fourteen coastal cities and Hainan Island were identified in 1984 as 'open areas' and, in the case of the cities, economic and technological development zones have been set aside for foreign participation. Second, a number of other wider areas have been designated for foreign involvement and priority investment, including the Changjiang (Yangtze River) delta, the Zhujiang (Pearl River) delta zone and the Minnan Delta Economic Region in southern Fujian Province.

The geographical distribution of such areas goes some way to redressing the southerly bias of the SEZs, as ten of the fourteen cities are north of Fujian and emphasis has focused on Shanghai, Tianjin, Dalian (Luda) (as well as Guangzhou) since 1986, rather than treating all of the cities equally. Nevertheless, two of the three main 'open' delta regions are in the south — the Zhujiang (Pearl River) and the southern Fujian deltas — and there is currently considerable emphasis on Hainan Island, which, as already noted, became a fifth SEZ and new province in 1988. As Lockett describes in chapter 4, the emphasis is on the south and the coastal orientation of development. The identification of the Shandong and Liaodong peninsulas as integrated units and development zones, and the encouragement for domestic reasons of the North China Energy Zone, the Shanghai Economic Zone and the Huaihuai Economic Region seems intended to redress the regional imbalance emerging in the Chinese economy.

Pragmatism and sensitivity to political and economic realities have determined the sites of the SEZs. During the late 1970s, the selection of Shenzhen and Zhuhai, on the borders of Hong Kong and Macau respectively, seemed sensible, since those foreign colonies were 'hot spots' of international economic activity (albeit of very different scales). Xiamen faces Taiwan directly and is in Fujian, the home of many millions of Overseas Chinese. Similarly, Shantou is the home of four million or more Overseas Chinese, who are widely scattered throughout South-East Asia. If the patriotic feelings of successful Overseas Chinese businessmen could be tapped, it was thought that they might be persuaded to invest in their homelands, given suitable investment and production environments. The choice of Shenzhen and Zhuhai is an early demonstration of the thinking that permitted the 'one country, two systems' agreements on the future of Hong Kong and of Macao. The 'demonstration effects' to Taiwan of the success of such a policy are likewise of great significance. Hainan Island has many more natural resources than the original SEZs, and also lies conveniently on a major sea route from East Asia (Japan, Taiwan and Korea) to South-East Asia, especially Singapore.

Objectives and attractions

The early evolution of the administrative structures of the SEZs is extremely confused, and in part reflects their ambiguous or overambitious objectives. The zones lacked a blueprint and had multiple and ill-defined objectives. In no particular order of priority, they were to be sites for foreign investment in enterprises which would produce exports to earn foreign exchange to underwrite modernization; they were to be 'classrooms' in which locals could observe and learn management practices and business skills; they would be places in which high-technology equipment and knowledge could be acquired and transferred; they were to be laboratories in which western 'business culture' and techniques could be observed and those aspects most suitable to Chinese socialism selectively adopted. The SEZs were therefore vaguely being asked to be 'windows' and 'pioneers' in China's modernization. They were expected to attract foreign investment and advanced technology for their development, as well as to establish an export-oriented economy — all of which were very ambitious goals at the time of designation.

There is some variation among the SEZs on the details of inducements or concessions offered to investors, but broadly they cover a range of variables.[5] These inducements are often in addition to, or modifications of, the provisions promulgated in October 1986 for encouraging foreign investment, from which various rules and regulations have subsequently emerged.[6] Managerial and technical staff from overseas may work in the zones, especially when providing training for locals. Local workers may be hired directly by enterprises or through the SEZ labour-service companies. Employment is not guaranteed in the zones, and staff may be subject to discipline, warnings and dismissal, representing the breaking of the 'iron rice bowl'. Labour rates in the SEZs are generally competitive with those in Hong Kong and Macau, but are not as low as in most other parts of China. The zones differ somewhat on specific features; for example, Shantou is levying rent, land fees and labour-service charges about one-third lower than those in Shenzhen. Wong identifies the introduction of contract labour and a new wage system, and the adoption of a tender system for construction works, as two significant SEZ reforms which have spread to other parts of China.[7]

Certain tax exemptions have been designed to encourage foreign investment, including import tax exemptions for equipment and raw materials. Enterprise income tax exists but 'tax holidays' may be negotiated for new firms, with further periods at reduced rates of taxation. Other financial inducements include the ability to remit earnings and profits in hard currencies, which had previously been a problem in China. In the SEZs, the relaxation of rules relating to foreign exchange is a considerable bonus to foreign investors who can maintain foreign bank accounts and settle foreign-exchange matters through Chinese, or some overseas banks, registered in the zones. Foreign enterprises may remit abroad after-tax profits, foreign employees' salaries, and agreed capital and revenue funds after operations cease. The availability of and access to foreign exchange (officially and unofficially) has been a major attraction for domestic businesses to invest in the zones but, concomitantly, the illicit use of foreign currencies has been a cause of problems to the authorities and a cause of criticism of the SEZs.

For foreign investors, the access to a potential market of over one thousand million people has been a major psychological attraction. It has been agreed generally that firms will be able to negotiate the sale of a certain proportion of some types of products from the SEZs on the domestic market, but, in essence, this is contrary to the desired export orientation of the SEZs. The problems of corruption and abuse in the 'open areas' with regard to the resale of imports have been discussed for a number of years, and the adverse balance of China's trade after 1985 led to serious review of import sales arrangements in the SEZs and elsewhere. The precise effect of these remains unclear, although China's trade imbalance had been largely corrected by 1988.

In addition to inducements and concessions, the SEZs as a whole offer foreign investors (in particular) a range of other advantages. The zones are supposed to offer 'open attitudes' to foreign involvement and, although other parts of China are now also developing such attitudes, this was an initial advantage. The zones are located close to the peripheral parts of China best known to foreign businessmen, and the SEZs themselves are more convenient and comfortable to live and work in than many other parts of the country. An assortment of serviced sites, factory buildings, housing for domestic and foreign employees, hotels, retail services and good communications (particularly with Hong Kong and Macau but also more widely) all add to the zones' attractiveness.[8] Labour costs are cheaper than in Hong Kong, and labour more readily available, if at lower skill levels than in the territory. Finally, the easing of entry and exit formalities was a significant initial advantage, but this has faded somewhat as other parts of China have become more readily accessible to foreigners. Indeed, as Chu notes, many other parts of China are now offering comparable concessions and are, in effect, quasi-special economic zones.[9] The impact of such competition on the SEZs is discussed later.

Nevertheless, the SEZs have offered attractive inducements to overseas investors, and domestic firms have also taken advantage of them, often in ways not originally intended. Typically, for example, a Chinese enterprise may set up an agency in Shenzhen, where it will sell its products, often at greatly reduced prices, to bargain-hunting foreign traders. With the foreign exchange thereby earned, it may buy consumer goods for the local market and might also diversify its activities into more profitable avenues. The loss of goods at cheap rates and the abuse of foreign-exchange arrangements has been one of the more important criticisms of the SEZs during the mid-1980s. It has contributed to the high retail volume of the zones' activities (especially Shenzhen), and their relatively low industrial production.

Developments within the SEZs

The establishment of the SEZs occurred in a somewhat uncoordinated manner. Their territorial and *de facto* existence actually pre-dated the official declarations giving them authority to develop and accept investments on preferential terms. It appears that the process through which the SEZs came into being, involving the creation of new administrative entities with uncertain initial levels of authority, was accompanied by considerable flexing of muscle by various administrative agencies unwilling to lose control over parts of their territories.

The promulgation of four important SEZ laws (on the registration of enterprises, land usage, visas, and labour and wages) only in fact came about in Guangdong at the Thirteenth Session of the Standing Committee of the Fifth Provincial People's Congress in November 1981. In short, the framework for the operation of the SEZs was set up only after the zones in the province had been growing for some two years. During the establishment of Shenzhen SEZ its administrative structure was upgraded several times. In February 1979 Shenzhen's status was changed from that of (county) town (*xiancheng*) to 'city' under the direct authority of the province. In October 1981 it was further upgraded to a provincial municipality, with status equal to that of Guangzhou (much larger in terms of population). As Kwok notes, this upgrading of the SEZ appeared to be in response to the experimentation and practical experience gained while it and the other zones were growing.[10] Increasingly, it appeared that the SEZ required greater administrative autonomy to achieve at least some of its objectives. This, one suspects, would also enable it to negotiate with foreign enterprises without recourse to conservative or perhaps inexperienced officials elsewhere in the bureaucracy.

The Office of the SEZs was established in 1982, under the Premier, and this controls the SEZs in Guangdong and Fujian. However, the provincial administration of the Guangdong zones was established earlier, in 1980. The Shenzhen SEZ was established in December 1979, but this had been preceded by the establishment in January 1979 of the Shekou Industrial Zone in its western sector, which was itself part of the SEZ but organized by a company (the China Merchants' Steam Navigation Company) under the Beijing Ministry of Communications. It is small wonder that there was confusion and a lack of clear signals to foreign participants and local officials as to the levels of responsibility allocated, and co-operation expected.

In spite of simplifying various aspects of foreign collaboration, the bureaucracy of the SEZs remains cumbersome and their government is no less complicated than elsewhere in China. If anything, the presence of representatives and interests of powerful central ministries and provinces, as well as relatives and friends of important leaders, renders the bureaucratic and political web even more complex. The situation is worsened by the unclear lines of responsibility between the SEZ governments, the Guangdong and Fujian provincial authorities and the policy-making SEZ office under the State Council. Indeed, the high profile of the SEZs, and their controversial nature, renders then a constant target for bureaucratic interference and criticism.[11]

Since designation there have been certain obvious changes in the SEZs, most notable of which is their physical growth in terms of infrastructure, buildings and service provision.[12] The infrastructure of the SEZs was substantially in place in 1984-5. Two of the zones, Shantou and Xiamen, have had their original sites considerably extended. Xiamen SEZ now includes the whole of Xiamen and the Gulangyu Islands; Shantou's area has been extended to some 52.6 square km, far larger than the 3 square km originally designated for industry and port.

Shenzhen and Zhuhai have prospered relative to the other zones. The decolonization negotiations over Hong Kong and subsequently Macau proceeded satisfactorily from the Chinese viewpoint after 1982. In spite of some international nervousness and loss of local confidence in Hong

Kong at certain stages of the negotiations, by and large, it and Macau remain economic 'going concerns', and the adjacent zones continue to benefit from their investment. In the future, the land borders between the zones and ex-colonies could conceivably be removed or, alternatively, the SEZs might remain as buffer zones between a nominally socialist China and capitalist enclaves which will continue largely unchanged for the next fifty years (under the 'one-country, two-systems' arrangement). This might be realistic since, although official rhetoric suggests that China's standard of living will be considerably higher by the end of the century and productivity nearing that of Hong Kong, the shock of over-exposure to Hong Kong or Macau might be softened by the physically intervening, strictly defined, SEZs.

Xiamen has also succeeded relatively well, especially in terms of attracting high-technology investment. It has been suggested that it might gain free-port status (or something similar) which would presumably further reduce customs duties. The success of this zone might provide reassurance for Taiwan about a future reintegration with the PRC. The development of Shantou remains more backward and relies, it seems, on the initiatives of specific Overseas Chinese entrepreneurs. Fewer statistics to indicate its economic success are readily available; recent data suggest it is developing something of a modern agricultural orientation over a considerable amount of its area.

Recent achievements: areas of debate

During the early 1980s, the SEZs — and Shenzhen in particular — were being cited as models of modernization and enterprise for the rest of China. In early 1984, Deng Xiaoping praised the zones highly after an official visit, and subsequently fourteen coastal cities were identified as being 'open' to foreign investment. However, by the second half of 1985, doubts were being expressed by some about the SEZ experiment, and Shenzhen in particular was this time cited as an example of what should not be done. The other SEZs were also suffering to some extent. Critics pointed to the expense of establishing the zones in relation to their returns, the types of enterprise attracted to the Shenzhen zone in particular, and the destination of the SEZs' products. The SEZs were said to have failed to attract sufficient foreign investment, advanced technology and export-oriented industry.

The precise contribution of the SEZs to the national economy is hard to judge, and this necessarily influences assessment of their success and potential future development. In June 1985, Deng Xiaoping voiced publicly the misgivings expressed by many others that the SEZs were somehow straying from their purposes. At the same time it was announced that the development of only four of the fourteen open cities would now be regarded as a priority. This was perhaps a pragmatic reassessment of foreign investment, as well as an indication that China could easily overstretch the financial and human resources available for modernization. A narrower focus on the four open cities and SEZs was a practical attempt to head off the critics of the policy of the 'open door', and to reaffirm it in a specific manner.

Nevertheless, three major criticisms of the SEZs have emerged. First, the costs of establishing the SEZs have been criticized as excessive. These have been variously estimated and are very difficult to assess, especially because of the calculation of land and labour prices. By 1985 some observers were suggesting that the Shenzhen zone had involved China in expenditure of over US $1,000 million, and some conservative estimates even suggested that US $1,600 million had been spent in its development during the five years up to 1985, of which only about half or less came from outside China. For example, one estimate suggests direct foreign investment of some US $840 million by early 1985. The Shenzhen zone itself claimed investments of some US $2.4 billion from overseas, although this appeared to include planned development of infrastructure, as well as a power-station which would only provide longer-term returns. [13]

Chinese estimates suggest that 6.3 billion yuan RMB were invested in capital construction in Shenzhen between 1979 and 1985, of which more than 40 per cent went towards urban construction, communications, and post and telecommunications installations. Large-scale projects such as the Shekou and Chiwan wharves, a helidrome, and double-line electrification of the Guangzhou-Kowloon railway have inevitably been very costly, as have road construction and factory-building. However, the balance of returns to investments has not been impressive, and the China Academy of Planning and Design indicates a utilization of fixed assets in Shenzhen at about 49 per cent, compared with a national average figure of about 75 per cent. [14] In part this may be explained by the lack of completed projects, but bottlenecks in power, communications and housing have also caused problems. Chan and others have noted that the largest proportion of investment in the zones has come not from foreign sources but from central and local city governments. [15] Foreign investment seems to have peaked during the early 1980s and to have tailed off relatively ever since (Table 7.3). It seems that today there is heavy reliance on local accumulation and domestic loans, in Shenzhen at any rate. The relative decline in foreign investment might be related to the world economic situation or it might also reflect the competition from increased opportunities to invest elsewhere in China. Table 7.4 indicates the main sectors of foreign investment in Shenzhen.

A second criticism involves the nature of activities attracted to the zones. It was envisaged that the SEZs would develop thriving,

122

Table 7.3 Sources of capital construction investments in Shenzhen City 1979–85

Source	1979	1980	1981	1982	1983	1984	1985	Total (1979–85)
Central government	23,850	33,000	22,740	47,380	43,700	21,060	42,850	234,580
%	47.81	26.43	8.41	7.49	4.93	1.29	1.55	3.69
Govt ministries & provinces	12,240	13,160	24,440	57,930	70,240	141,850	378,420	698,280
%	24.54	10.54	9.04	9.16	7.93	8.67	13.70	10.98
Foreign investment	5,470	53,920	135,330	191,380	222,120	264,980	360,650	1,233,850
%	10.97	43.18	50.05	30.25	25.07	16.19	13.06	19.40
Domestic loans	0	7,030	31,630	202,910	334,050	721,750	563,510	1,860,160
%	0.00	5.63	11.70	32.07	37.71	44.10	20.41	29.25
City govt & enterprises	8,320	17,760	53,350	113,960	175,080	430,420	1,182,840	1,981,730
%	16.68	14.22	19.73	18.01	19.76	26.30	42.84	31.15
Others inc. domestic enterprises	0	0	2,900	19,090	40,740	56,640	232,980	352,350
%	0.00	0.00	1.07	3.02	4.60	3.46	8.44	5.54
TOTAL	49,880	124,870	270,390	632,650	885,930	1,636,700	2,761,250	6,361,670
%	100.00	100.00	100.00	100.00	100.00	100.00	100.00	100.00

Source: Shenzhen SEZ Yearbook 1986 (for 1979–83 data), pp. 592–3; Shenzhen SEZ Yearbook 1986 (for 1984–5 data), pp. 436–7.

Table 7.4 Sectoral distribution of actual foreign investment in Shenzhen SEZ 1979-85 (in HK $1,000)[1]

Sector	1979	1980	1981	1982	1983	1984	1985	Total (1979–85)
Industry	17,270	79,910	320,860	222,060	409,410	629,070	496,310	2,174,890
%	23.59	38.90	42.20	43.26	44.27	43.27	37.57	41.41
Real estate	41,140	87,380	302,020	197,540	386,480	214,270	279,240	1,508,070
%	56.20	42.54	39.72	38.48	41.79	14.74	21.14	28.71
Tourism	2,420	5,140	17,770	11,610	17,000	129,870	331,420	515,230
%	3.31	2.50	2.34	2.26	1.84	8.93	25.09	9.81
Commerce	9,590	27,060	99,320	68,730	90,460	408,950	94,850	798,960
%	13.10	13.17	13.06	13.39	9.78	28.13	7.18	15.21
Transport & communications	2,420	5,150	17,760	11,620	21,470	68,720	113,650	240,790
%	3.31	2.51	2.34	2.26	2.32	4.73	8.60	4.58
Agric. & animal husbandry	360	770	2,670	1,740	0	2,960	5,690	14,190
%	0.49	0.37	0.35	0.34	0.00	0.20	0.43	0.27
Others	750	3,760	7,770	13,440	7,530	310,830	1,208,140	1,552,220
TOTAL	73,950	209,170	768,170	526,740	932,350	1,764,670	2,529,300	6,804,350
TOTAL (exc 'others')	73,200	205,410	760,400	513,300	924,820	1,453,840	1,321,160	5,252,130
%	100.00	100.00	100.00	100.00	100.00	100.00	100.00	100.00

Note:
1. In 1988, US $1 = HK $7.80
Sources: Shenzhen SEZ Yearbook 1985 (for 1979–83 data); Shenzhen SEZ Yearbook 1986 (for 1984–5 data).

remunerative enterprises and attract high-tech, modern projects from which China could learn and develop skills. However, industry, although increasing, contributed less than 30 per cent of the income of the Shenzhen SEZ in 1984, whereas building and service industries accounted for 33.7 per cent and 27.3 per cent of income respectively. Most of the economic activities in Shenzhen are not industry-oriented but tend more toward construction and trade, which in general do not employ advanced production technology, although advanced high-rise construction techniques (of dubious necessity) have been introduced.

Many of the initial projects in Shenzhen and Zhuhai, in particular, involved tourism, recreation, retail and luxury housing developments. By 1987, there were over 300 large tourist resorts, restaurants, hotels, and guest houses in Shenzhen, with some 50,000 beds available. In 1985 this SEZ received some 2.2 million tourists and visitors. Many were domestic, on shopping excursions, but many were also short-term visitors from Hong Kong. While the income from these visitors has been considerable, commerce and trade have in a sense become the mainstay of the Shenzhen zone (and to some extent the Zhuhai zone also), which conflicts with the original objectives.

Chinese sources suggest there is insufficient macro-control over commerce in the SEZs; for example, certain industrial, cultural and educational enterprises have diversified (or deviated) into profit-making and highly profitable commercial undertakings, even reversing the relative contributions of their main functions and new sidelines. The retail structure of the SEZs is also generally unbalanced, since many shops have entered the highly profitable electrical and clothing consumer sectors, while everyday goods, especially foodstuffs, are sometimes difficult to buy.[16] Occupancy rates of some hotels are low, and there are too few cheap or moderate hotels and guest houses, and too many high grade ones; there are also numerous expensive and underused taxis. Overall, accurate figures of the balance of income contributed to the zones by industry and commerce-retail are difficult to find, since even the identification of enterprises (by name) may not indicate accurately the major thrust of their profit-making activities. As noted some figures suggest that, in Shenzhen, for example, industry and commerce contributed roughly equal amounts to income (each about 30 per cent) while the building industry contributed a further one-third.

There are, however, strong indications that productive industrial enterprises in the SEZs are now contributing more to income than previously, and the proportion of larger rather than smaller enterprises is growing. Nevertheless, in 1985 only four large- and twenty-two medium-sized enterprises were noted out of some 907 in Shenzhen (size definitions are not given), but those twenty-six enterprises contributed 39 per cent of industrial output value.

A third, more fundamental, criticism of the SEZs has been their alleged lack of export orientation. In part this has been highlighted by the nature of enterprises attracted to the zones early on: the direct export orientation of hotels, tourist activities and retail outlets is naturally limited, although certain of those activities might attract hard currency or foreign investments. Initially it was intended that the SEZs should be both industrially modern and export-oriented. However, it seems that an 'outward-looking' economy has been slow to develop in the SEZs. Retail sales and the development of property and infrastructure have hindered what was arguably the chief objective of the SEZs in 1978, to promote with foreign collaboration those domestic industries which had potential.

This criticism certainly applies to both Shenzhen and Zhuhai until at least 1987. Estimates made in mid-1985 suggested that as much as 70 per cent of Shenzhen's 1984 production actually was for the domestic market; some estimates indicated an even lower export ratio from this zone of perhaps only 20 per cent of its total industrial output. At that date it was reported that Beijing had stated that by 1988 60 per cent of Shenzhen's industrial production should be for export.[17] Obviously such an achievement is important if fundamental criticisms of the SEZs' effectiveness are to be averted and a deficit balance of payments in the zones avoided.

Recently there has been some evidence that the SEZs have become more export-oriented. Shenzhen, for example, has attracted and developed more modern plant and industry, with more varied functions and higher export potential than previously. However, relative to other EPZs in the region, Chinese assessments state that 'the industrial basis of Shenzhen is still rather weak, the export-oriented industrial structure has not yet taken firm shape, and the economic results are not so satisfactory'.[18] More critical observers (foreign and domestic) highlight a major hindrance to export orientation in the greater profitability to be gained from the sale of imports on the domestic market than from the development of exports.[19]

The reorientation of the SEZs to achieve greater efficiency in exporting began after criticisms during mid-1985. The long-term development plans for Shenzhen, for example, recognize the difficulties of excessive reliance on trade and real estate, with their mainly domestic involvement, and stress the need for outward orientation and stronger macroeconomic guidance. However, the source and means of such guidance remains unclear. The plans for the new Hainan Island SEZ stress that the island must not sell imported goods on the mainland for high profits, and that other places must not take advantage of Hainan's preferential policies to indulge in tax evasion and illicit foreign-exchange acquisitions.

Nevertheless, as Tables 7.5 and 7.6 indicate, the SEZs are contributing significantly to the exports of Guangdong and Fujian, even if their national contribution is relatively small. The export orientation of the smaller SEZs has recently also been re-emphasized. In particular, Shantou has claimed considerable success in the types of activity it has pursued. For example, it is stated to have exported 78 per cent of its industrial output value in 1986, and 85 per cent of its farm and aquatic production. The various foreign-funded enterprises exported 84 per cent of their total output. Perhaps Shantou's later development and its concentration on food, pottery, clothing and electronics have helped to achieve this more impressive balance. Shantou claims to be relatively more successful economically than the other zones, but it is very strongly dependent on the continued patronage of Overseas Chinese. Indeed, it is estimated that 90 per cent of the investment in the zone is from Overseas Chinese, foreigners of Chinese origin, and Hong Kong and Macau 'compatriots'.[20]

Table 7.5 Exports (in million US $)

	1985	% of province	% of nation	Per capita export (in 0,000 US $)
Guangdong's SEZs:				
Shenzhen city[1]	563.00	18.40	2.17	1.18
Zhuhai city[1]	57.44	1.88	0.22	0.14
Shantou city[1]	275.00	8.99	1.06	0.03
TOTAL GUANGDONG	3,059.33	100.00	11.80	0.05
Fujian's SEZ:				
Xiamen city[1]	170.00	35.19	0.66	0.17
TOTAL FUJIAN	483.12	100.00	1.86	0.02
NATIONAL TOTAL	25,915.61	—	100.00	0.02

Note:
1. See note to Table 7.6.
Source: Almanac of China's Foreign Economic Relations and Trade 1986, pp. 732–8.

Table 7.6 Composition of exports in 1985 (%)

Exports	Shenzhen city[1]	Shantou city[1]
Agricultural and native products	46.10	37.26
Light industries, electronics and textiles	51.70	60.60
Metals, chemicals, machines and minerals	2.20	2.14
TOTAL	100.00	100.00

Note:
Agricultural and native products include chicken, pigs, pond fish, vegetables. Light industries include yarn, cotton, household appliances, watches and furniture
[1]These figures include the county, city proper and SEZs concerned.

127

Regional relations

It is often difficult to discern precisely the local and even regional effects of developments such as the SEZs. However, in addition to their international links and the attraction of foreign investors to the zones, they have developed an important, although less explicit, network of domestic economic relations. Indeed, local demonstration and trickle-down effects may, in practice, have a greater long-term significance than the zones' export production *per se*, for it may well be overtaken by developments in other parts of the country. The establishment of domestic economic relations between Shenzhen and its environs seems significant, and it and other zones are developing commodity exchange and economic and technological co-operation with their hinterlands. In July 1984, for example, Fujian approved a series of regulations concerning economic association between the Xiamen SEZ and inland areas of China. It is difficult to measure precisely what might be called the multiplier effects of these zones, though they clearly have a number of sets of impacts or relations which affect their local regions and, indirectly, promote the national modernization programme.

Two main forms of domestic economic relations have developed, namely, commodity exchange and economic-technological co-operation. Commodity exchange entails the SEZ becoming associated with the domestic economy as both a supplier and consumer of certain goods. Economic-technological co-operation involves the exchange and diffusion of ideas, techniques and technical knowledge generally into the wider economy. It is possible to identify at least four types or levels of economic and technological co-operation between the SEZs and the rest of China.[21] There exist, first, co-operation (and competition) among the four SEZs themselves; second, co-operation between a zone such as Shenzhen SEZ, Shenzhen city, and Bao'an county; third, co-operation between the SEZ and its direct neighbouring areas (in the case of Shenzhen, the area includes Guangzhou); and, fourth, co-operation between SEZs and ministries (or commissions) of the State Council, and provinces, municipalities and autonomous regions. This involves wider, national domestic co-operation, some aspects of which are sectorally oriented, others geographically directed. Indeed, domestic co-operative enterprises in Shenzhen now form the largest category of enterprises in the SEZ. Co-operative enterprises run jointly by Shenzhen and the hinterland now number over 600, with almost 300 other forms of joint domestic ventures (some of which also involve foreign investment).

The basic function of developing domestic economic relations between an SEZ and its hinterland might be said to be to enhance the local economy and generally improve the district's ability to absorb and utilize modern technology and foreign investment. This is now more of a priority than it was when the SEZs were first established. The SEZs were all located in areas with relatively weak existing infrastructures and economies, with the possible exception of Xiamen. Since designation, the SEZs have developed links with their neighbouring areas in a number of ways. First, there are links involving the provision of construction capital. For example, the hinterland of Shenzhen is said to have provided about one-sixth of the total construction capital for the SEZ, particularly by investment in the buildings materials industry.

Second, the hinterlands have provided numerous workers for the SEZs and, to an extent, scientific and technical personnel (although these have perforce been recruited over a much wider area). Some 90 per cent of workers in enterprises in Shenzhen are estimated to have come from its hinterland. Naturally, an SEZ such as Shenzhen with very limited prior development was unable to supply sufficient numbers of high-grade personnel and virtually all have moved into the zone, from many parts of China.

Third, neighbouring districts have supplied directly construction materials required for developing the SEZs. It is estimated, for example, that some two-thirds of the investment in the Shekou industrial district of Shenzhen has gone to buy domestic, mainly local, construction materials. Finally, the hinterlands have provided the SEZs with industrial raw materials as well as agricultural supplies and foodstuffs. The purchase of consumer goods by hinterlands (directly or indirectly, and openly or covertly) has helped the SEZs to enlarge their markets, although the extent to which this has diverted their export orientation is a matter of concern. The SEZs are also outlets for locally and nationally supplied goods via their retail shops, restaurants and hotels.

There is now strong support for various levels of co-operation and liaison between the SEZs and their hinterlands, and the zones are felt to have assisted the development of their hinterlands in a number of ways. However, there is likely to be an element of competition and jealousy and it is questionable whether harmonious co-operation on a commodity or economic-technological basis will be maintained when wider areas become more open economically. For example, the Zhujiang (Pearl River) delta region and the southern Fujian triangle have been more recently designated as priority investment and development areas. Their opening may compete more directly with the SEZs and cause internal local competition for investment, personnel and resources. Indeed, when compared with their neighbouring cities, do Rosario suggests that the SEZs are over-built, over-borrowed, inefficient and uncompetitive.[22] The dangers of spreading resources too thinly have been noted in the decision to focus selectively on fewer of the fourteen open cities. Whether such a reorientation of policy with regard to the hinterlands of the SEZs will be necessary, or whether, as is more likely, the benefits of subregional agglomeration of economic and technical development will outweigh such potential problems, remains to be seen.

Conclusion

China's 'open door' policy has progressed to the extent that the SEZs are now but one of a wide range of types of geographical area designated for foreign and domestic priority investment. Their importance has therefore altered in a few short years: many feel that they should pay their way in terms of export-earning revenue rather than acting as entry points for foreign imports into the country. The change in political, administrative and economic objectives for the SEZs is understandable in the context of the PRC's overall development since they were first established. From being regarded as unusual and highly privileged, they have become one among several types of location for foreign involvement, if still the chief one. While remaining, to a large extent, isolated from the majority of the population, their psychological and economic originality is now muted.

In many ways, therefore, the SEZs are beginning to become less 'special'. Many of their innovative economic reforms have by 1988 been tried in or extended to other parts of China. These include the introduction of wage and contract labour, the adoption of a tender system in construction, the home-purchase scheme for workers, and a re-evaluation of the practice of heavy state subsidies for housing. The SEZs no longer have a distinct edge over the rest of the country in terms of the inducements they can offer to investors. Indeed, higher costs of living and localized competition for labour and resources in the SEZs have raised costs and may persuade some investors to look elsewhere in the future. The designation of other parts of the PRC for economic development may well further undercut the attractions of the SEZs.

Competition will probably be less strongly felt in Shenzhen and Zhuhai than in Shantou and Xiamen. Shenzhen and Zhuhai are rapidly becoming industrial extensions of Hong Kong and Macau, and the relatively abundant and cheap labour supply of those SEZs make them attractive locations for industries which are having problems in finding workers. With the return of Hong Kong and Macau to the PRC in the late 1990s, the present borders may effectively become less significant and the two SEZs become assembly plants and processing areas for industrialists in Hong Kong and Macau.

The creation of SEZs, open coastal cities, and open economic (delta) regions represent the present regional bias of national development which emphasizes the coastal regions first, in the hope that economic development will later spread to inland provinces. As indicated throughout this volume (particularly in chapter 5), whether that will occur depends very much on the future efficiency of the transport network and internal linkages within China. It is doubtful that such results will be likely without a determined central initiative to distribute some of the economic gains of the coastal regions to the inland provinces.

It may be that the initial and continuing costs of developing the SEZs will have been too high, especially as neighbouring countries' zones have outperformed them without the benefit of such special policies or subsidies. This is certainly one trend of current thinking about the SEZs. Alternatively, it is possible to accept another current official view, that it is too early to judge the achievements of the SEZs. There is little question, however, that the SEZs are in reality among the least economically efficient places in the PRC, despite their designated roles as the vanguard of reform and modernization. In particular, a number of problems are clearly identifiable.

The SEZs are suffering from excessive capital construction costs and physical over-building, especially in Shenzhen, and there is a plethora of unnecessary high-rise buildings (though that criticism may also be applied to other parts of the PRC). In the SEZs many projects are financed by loans. It is doubtful that in economic terms their favoured status can remain justified, and that may well provide a brake on development. Land prices are on the increase and, in a first land auction held in Shenzhen during December 1987, a parcel of residential land fetched more than double the price of a comparable parcel leased only four months earlier. Considerable concern has resulted that land prices will no longer be cheap in the SEZs.[23]

More fundamentally, the objectives of the SEZs during the early 1980s were too vague, with no clear guidelines for investment or priority sectors. The SEZs were left to their own devices to make money quickly. The result was a number of ill-conceived and misguided schemes, as well as a range of more or less practicable projects. The SEZs have suffered from weak leadership, both locally and in terms of central representation, where a more powerful body is needed in Beijing. Their bureaucracy is neither as streamlined nor as efficient as it could be, and there remain unclear lines of responsibility from the SEZs to provincial and central levels.

Since they were established, the attractiveness of the SEZs has been eroded by the designation of open cities and other areas (in and after 1984) which offer broadly similar incentives. Their competitive edge has therefore been somewhat blunted. However, the SEZs are undoubtedly firmly established in the minds of foreign investors as 'special' places and they will therefore continue to receive political support. Indeed, as if to confound critics, and in spite of the increased competition for investment from other areas, the combined industrial output of the SEZs rose by over 50 per cent in 1987 compared with 1986, and exports more than doubled in value. The performance of the SEZs showed much better than the national average increases for both industrial output value and exports.

The development of the Shenzhen SEZ in particular quite closely related to the continued success of its Hong Kong connections. It has become the most successful SEZ mainly through its proximity to Hong Kong and its receipt of investments from the territory in real estate, industry, and tourism. However, while relatively cheap land and labour initially attracted Hong Kong investors to the SEZs, there is evidence that many industries from the territory have decentralized beyond Shenzhen's boundaries, to establish production in rural townships in the Zhujiang (Pearl River) delta, where labour costs and rents are even lower than in Shenzhen. This trend further erodes the competitive position of Shenzhen and Zhuhai. The dependence on Hong Kong for investment and support is likely to continue for a number of years until both Shenzhen and Zhuhai have established a sounder, independent industrial and economic base — a situation which is still some years distant.

Perhaps more worrying for the continued prominence of the SEZs themselves is the current emphasis on the development of all the coastal regions as export-oriented places. In early 1988 Zhao Ziyang spoke of the SEZs only in passing as one of a range of open areas.[24] The SEZs are possibly in danger of 'receding' to the status of the other open coastal cities and priority areas in China. Indeed, unless the central leadership remains committed to making the SEZs a success, their future is uncertain. On the other hand, despite criticism, there is at present no sign that Beijing's fundamental support for these important symbols of an 'open door' policy is weakening to any significant degree.

Notes

1 Wong, K.Y. and Chu, D.K.Y. (1984) 'Export processing zones and special economic zones as generators of economic development: the Asian experience', *Geografiska Annaler*, vol. 66B, no. 1, pp. 1–16; Rondinelli, D.A. (1987) 'Export processing zones and economic development in Asia', *American Journal of Economics and Sociology*, vol. 46, no. 1, pp. 89–105.

2 Currie, J. (1985) *Export Processing Zones in the 1980s*, Special Report no. 190, London: Economist Intelligence Unit.

3 Chu, D.K.Y. (1986) 'The Special Economic Zones and the problem of territorial containment' in Jao, Y.C. and Leung, C.K. (eds) *China's Special Economic Zones: Policies, Problems and Prospects*, Hong Kong: Oxford University Press, pp. 21–38.

4 Perroux, F. (1955) 'Note sur la notion de "pôle de croissance"',

Economie Appliquée, vol. 8, p. 307-20.

5 Phillips, D.R. and Yeh, A.G.O. (1983) 'China experiments with modernization: the Shenzhen Special Economic Zone', *Geography*, October, vol. 68, no. 4, pp. 289-300; Phillips, D.R. (1986) 'Special economic zones in China's modernization: changing policies and changing fortunes', *National Westminster Bank Quarterly Review*, February, pp. 37-49.

6 See, for example, *Beijing Review*, 11 May 1987.

7 Wong, K.Y. (1987) 'China's special economic zone experiment: an appraisal', *Geografiska Annaler*, vol. 69B, no. 1, pp. 27-40.

8 Phillips, D.R. and Yeh, A.G.O. (1987) 'The provision of housing and social services in China's Special Economic Zones', *Environment and Planning C*, vol. 5, pp. 447-68.

9 Chu, op. cit.

10 Kwok, R.Y.W. (1986) 'Structure and policies in industrial planning in the Shenzhen Special Economic Zone', in Jao, Y.C. and Leung, C.K. (eds) *China's Special Economic Zones: Policies, Problems and Prospects*, Hong Kong: Oxford University Press, pp. 39-64.

11 do Rosario, L. (1987) 'Models in a muddle', *Far Eastern Economic Review*, 1 October, vol. 138, no. 40, pp. 102-3.

12 See, for example, Wong, K.Y. and Chu, D.K.Y. (eds) (1985) *Modernization in China: the case of Shenzhen Special Economic Zone*, Hong Kong: Oxford University Press; Yeh, A.G.O. (1985) 'Physical planning', in Wong, K.Y. and Chu, D.K.Y. op. cit. pp. 108-30; Kwok, (1986) op. cit.; Phillips (1986) op. cit.; in China Academy of Urban Planning and Design and Shenzhen Municipal Planning Bureau (1987) 'Shenzhen experiment: economic development of the Shenzhen Special Economic Zone', *China City Planning Review*, March, vol. 3, no. 1/2, pp.79-115; Phillips and Yeh (1987) op. cit.

13 do Rosario, L. (1985) 'China: into the red zone', *Far Eastern Economic Review*, 19 September, vol. 129, no. 37, pp. 61-3.

14 China Academy of Urban Planning and Design (1987) op. cit.

15 Chan, T.M.H. (1985) 'Financing Shenzhen's economic development: a preliminary analysis of sources of capital construction investments 1979-1984', *Asian Journal of Public Administration*, vol. 7, no. 2, pp. 170-97.

16 Phillips and Yeh (1987) op. cit.

17 do Rosario (1985) op. cit.

18 China Academy of Urban Planning and Design (1987) op. cit., p. 91.

19 Fewsmith, J. (1986) 'Special economic zones in the PRC', *Problems of Communism*, November-December, pp. 78-85.

20 *Beijing Review*, 24 August 1987, p. 17-20.

21 China Academy of Urban Planning and Design (1987) op. cit.

22 do Rosario (1987) op. cit.

23 Cheng, E. (1988) 'Special economic zones face fight for capital', *Far Eastern Economic Review*, 24 March, vol. 139, no. 12, pp. 82-4.

24 'Zhao on coastal areas' development strategy', *Beijing Review*, 8–14 February 1988, vol. 31, no. 6, pp. 14–19; Geng, Y. (1988) 'The coast to intensify its export orientation', *Beijing Review*, 15–28 February, vol. 31, nos 7 and 8, pp. 4–5; *Beijing Review* 1988, 25 April–1 May, vol. 31, no. 17, p. 46; Yang, X. 1988 'Hainan Province — China's largest SEZ', *Beijing Review*, 2–8 May, vol. 31, no. 18, pp. 14–18.

Chapter eight

Shanxi: China's powerhouse

Shaun Breslin

Shanxi Province is situated in the north of China, with its capital, Taiyuan, lying some 500 km south-west of Beijing. The province covers an area of 58,000 square miles, which is roughly equivalent to the combined size of England and Wales, and has a population of around 26 million people. In modern times Shanxi's fame has centred on the warlord Yan Xishan (Yen Hsi-shan) who ruled the province by virture of his command of one of the most powerful armies in China after the fall of the Qing dynasty in 1911, Willian Hinton's *Fanshen* novels depicting life in a Shanxi village,[1] and the importance of Shanxi's coal deposits.

Shanxi's contemporary national significance has been highlighted by the establishment in 1982 of the Shanxi Energy Base Office of the State Council. The intention, as made manifest in the Seventh Five-Year Plan, is the development of Shanxi as the single most important energy base for national modernization. In the new national division of labour, it is targeted as the powerhouse to provide energy and raw materials for pro-duction units in the Eastern Coastal Region. It is calculated that if the Eastern Coastal Region could receive 1,000 tons of coal a year, its gross value of industrial output would increase by more than 17 billion yuan RMB.[2] Thus, the primary concern for the province in the 1980s has been to update and modernize its existing coal-mines, and to promote the development of new mines in order to achieve the planned 80 per cent increase in the amount of coal to be shipped out of Shanxi between 1986 and 1990.[3]

However, the province has to overcome major obstacles if it is to fulfil these aims and maintain its development into the twenty-first century. One crucial problem is that of funding. The establishment of new mines and the modernization of the coal and energy industries is a huge enterprise that will require high rates of investment. If the best results are to be achieved, then up-to-date foreign technology must be put to use in the province's mines. That is dependent on Shanxi obtaining access to foreign currency. Even if the province can boost its coal production, there is the added difficulty that the existing national communications network will not be able to cope with transporting increasing amounts of coal to the manufacturing industries of the Eastern Coastal Region.

This chapter examines the ways that these various problems are being tackled, as well as some of the emerging side-effects of the modernization process in Shanxi. Economic side-effects such as declining agricultural output are relatively easy to identify, but the same cannot be said of the political consequences of modernization in the province. The central government is playing a key role in directing the modernization process in Shanxi, particularly through the Shanxi Energy Base Office, but the nature of the relationship between centre and province is unclear. Beijing and the provinces of the Eastern Coastal Region may simply be exploiting Shanxi's wealth for their own benefit. Alternatively, there may be an attempt to create wealth in Shanxi through the development of the province's extraction industries, which can then be used as the springboard for all-round provincial economic growth. These two explanations are not necessarily mutually exclusive — centre and province are not necessarily in conflict. There may well be an emerging community of interest between the provincial and national leaders regarding the best strategy for Shanxi's modernization.

Shanxi's economic base

The geography and topography of the province have had profound effects on Shanxi's history, and promise to play a crucial role in its future development. Virtually isolated from its neighbours by mountain ranges and rivers, and with much of the interior mountainous and impassable, poor communications and low agricultural production have long caused problems for Shanxi's leaders. With half of the farmland situated in the mountainous areas, and the climate of northern China leading to droughts in the spring which are typically followed by floods in the summer, the province has always had severe difficulties in providing enough grain to feed the population.

On the other hand, nature has not been totally unkind to the province. Shanxi abounds in raw materials, with estimated reserves of 500 million tonnes of bauxite and 3 billion tonnes of iron ore. However, by far its biggest asset is coal. It is estimated that coalfields cover some 45 per cent of the province and contain 220 billion tonnes of coal, or, put more simply, the province possesses the biggest coalfield in China, and a third of the nation's verified and as yet unexploited coal reserves are beneath Shanxi soil.

The decision to exploit the province's coal reserves has historical precedents. In the 1920s and 1930s, despite paying lip service to the authority of the Guomindang government in Nanjing, Yan Xishan, one of the outstanding political figures of the period, developed his own independent economic policy for Shanxi. Recognizing the key role that its coal reserves could play in the modernization of both the province and the country, in 1932 he introduced a 'Provincial Ten-Year Plan of Economic Reconstruction' aimed at creating a new commercial empire.[4] Today Shanxi's coal is similarly seen as being a crucial element in the country's modernization plans. Hence the establishment of the Shanxi Energy Base Office.

During the 1950s and early 1960s, Shanxi benefited from substantial investment by central government. A total of 2.1 billion yuan RMB was invested in the province during the First FYP, with 75 per cent of the money coming from central sources. At the same time, existing industrial plants in the coastal region were closed down, and re-sited inland. For example, a Shanghai textile mill was dismantled and rebuilt near Taiyuan.[5] This high level of investment was facilitated by the existing industrial infrastructure in Shanxi dating back to the ambitious economic policies of Yan Xishan.

Before the era of the Cultural Revolution, natives of Shanxi were also well represented in the higher echelons of the party and state system: Peng Zhen was a member of the Political Bureau and — probably of equal importance to the province — both Bo Yibo and An Zhiwen were two of the state's key economic planners. While it is impossible to quantify just how far the level of investment was influenced by these three, the attitude of key central leaders to their home provinces has been (and remains) an important consideration affecting regional development in China.

Coal production: prospects and problems

Possessing reserves of raw materials is one thing, but turning potential into concrete results is an entirely different story, hence the current concerns of both central and provincial government. As Table 8.1 shows, at first glance the record of Shanxi's recent coal production appears to be quite good, with provincial output accounting for something like a quarter of the national total.[6] This level of production places Shanxi sixth in the ranking of world coalfields.[7]

On the other hand, although production has increased rapidly during the 1980s, many of the province's mines are still using old-fashioned equipment and work practices. The present rates of production are better than before, but they are still deficient. Moreover, the national communications system cannot adequately transport coal from Shanxi to manufacturing units in other provinces. Thus, Hunan province finds it more convenient, and ultimately cheaper, to use precious foreign currency reserves to import coal from Australia rather than obtain coal from Shanxi.[8]

Table 8.1 Shanxi's coal production, 1952–86

Year	Total production (mn tons)	Index of coal production (1980 = 100)
1952	9.94	12.03
1978	92.85	76.72
1980	121.03	100.00
1982	145.37	120.11
1983	159.18	131.52
1984	187.16	154.64
1985	214.22	177.00
1986	221.80	183.26

Sources: Shanxi People's Publishing House (1986) *Shanxi Jingji Nianjian (Almanac of Shanxi Economy)*, Hong Kong: China Book Company, p. 92.
'Communiqué on Economic and Social Development in 1986', *Shanxi Ribao*, 28 February 1987.
'Communiqué on Shanxi's Economic and Social Development in 1985', *Shanxi Ribao*, 20 April 1986.
'Communiqué on Shanxi's Economic Development in 1984', *Shanxi Ribao*, 27 March 1985.
'Implementation of Economic and Social Plan', *Shanxi Ribao*, 21 June 1984.

The problem of increasing the efficiency and cost-effectiveness of China's manufacturing industries lies at the heart of the present development of Shanxi province, and attempts to rectify these problems are affecting its pattern of economic activity. Rural communities in Shanxi are now being urged to deviate from traditional means of employment, namely agricultural production, and concentrate more on coal-mining and coal-intensive industrial production. In order to persuade peasants to change the habits of a lifetime, and to make the establishment of new mines economically viable, a number of financial incentives are offered, which in turn places a strain on the province's finances.

The emphasis on primary production means that the province produces few manufactured products and, furthermore, has restricted access to potential foreign markets. Shanxi has no history of economic ties with foreign countries, as is the case, for example, for Shandong with Germany, or Guangdong with Britain. Nor is it close to any potential international markets, as is the case with the Special Economic Zones. Thus it has problems in generating sufficient funds, or more particularly, foreign currency reserves, from within the province to provide incentives to rural mines, to purchase up-to-date foreign technology for existing mines, and to invest in the province's communications network.

As a result, Shanxi must rely on direct central investment, as well as centrally-directed investment — in the form of foreign loans and joint ventures with foreign firms — if it is to achieve its full economic potential. This will, of necessity, lead to a greater dependence on Beijing than is the case in provinces like Guangdong or Jiangsu, where individual production units are manufacturing finished products that are immediately attractive to both domestic and foreign purchasers.

Because of the extent of Shanxi's raw material deposits, the province has always been seen as a strategic area for development, but there has been a definite shift in emphasis during the 1980s. Whereas Yan Xishan's policies and those of the 1950s and early 1960s were based on investing in Shanxi to build up Shanxi's own industrial base, the policy today, as exemplified by the establishment of the Shanxi Energy Base Office, is to invest in Shanxi to build up the industrial base of the Eastern Coastal Region. However, the emphasis on the development of heavy industry has not been an exclusive concern.

The light industrial sector

One possible scenario for Shanxi's economic growth is that investment in the excavation and energy-producing industries will produce wealth for the province by attracting manufacturing industries to the source of their raw materials. In the light industrial sector, there is some evidence that the output of certain products has increased rapidly in recent years. For example, in 1986 the production of electric fans increased by 110 per cent over the figure for 1985.[9] However, such figures are often misleading. Large percentage increases may simply reflect a low base figure. The 1986 increase in output produced only 10,808 fans as against Liaoning's production of 442,000 fans in the same year.[10] Moreover, surges in production in an individual year may result from earlier falls. In Shanxi in 1985, a 110 per cent increase in the production of washing machines merely redressed a 97 per cent decrease in output during 1984.[11]

In 1986, light industrial production constituted only a quarter of Shanxi's total industrial output by value.[12] In contrast, although the value of Guangdong's total industrial output in 1986 was nearly 4 million yuan RMB lower than in Shanxi, its light industrial output value was almost 41 per cent higher than in Shanxi. The value of light industrial output in Heilongjiang, one of China's major bases for heavy industry, was a third of that province's total industrial output value.[13]

The value of Shanxi's light industrial output has risen steadily in recent years: from 4.4 billion yuan RMB in 1983 to 6.52 billion yuan in 1986. However, its importance relative to heavy industry has declined, with light industry's share of total industrial output falling from 42.5 per cent in 1950 to 31.3 per cent in 1980 (by value), and further decreasing to 26.2 per cent in 1986. Moreover, the speed at which the light industrial sector is growing has begun to slow down, with the value of provincial light industrial output increasing by only 9.3 per cent during 1986, as opposed to 16.5 per cent the previous year.[14] The development of Shanxi's light industrial base is still in its infancy.

The heavy industrial sector

The story in the heavy industry sector is one of growth based on the province's coal reserves. Outlining the prospects for Shanxi under the Seventh FYP, governor Wang Senhao announced that planned investment would be 17 billion yuan RMB, an increase of 75 per cent over the Sixth FYP. Of this, over four-fifths was for the coal and power industries, and railway projects.[15] The emphasis on the extraction industries is directly related to the development of the heavy industry sector as a whole. For example, thermal-powered electricity generating plants in Shanxi made use of the province's coal resources to boost output by 83 per cent between 1980 and 1986, and other coal-intensive industries such as pig iron and steel production have also benefited from being located locally.[16] Not all coal-intensive industries have been successful: the production of chemical fertilizers fell by roughly a fifth between 1984 and 1986.[17] None the less, those industries that supply the mining and energy sectors have seen their production levels soar. For example, the output of the mining equipment industry increased by 83.8 per cent during 1985, and then by a further 21.9 per cent the following year. The production of electricity transformers similarly increased by 31.9 per cent and 13.6 per cent during the same years.[18]

Although there has been some progress in the production of manufactured goods, all other industries in Shanxi exist in the shadow of the coal industry. State coal-mines alone employ 14.3 per cent of the provincial work force, and the industry's share of the output value of all industry is a massive 20.8 per cent. With the electricity-generating industry accounting for 6.4 per cent of the total, the two industries alone produce more output value than the whole of the light industrial sector.

Coal output is increasing, but, as might be expected, most of the coal does not stay in the province. In 1985, 65.9 per cent of Shanxi's coal was transferred to other provinces, and in 1986 the proportion increased to 68.7 per cent. Furthermore, the rate of increase in coal being transferred to other provinces during 1986 was greater than the rate of increase in coal production.[19] If that trend continues, it is unlikely that manufacturing units will move to Shanxi to be near their source of raw materials. Similarly, the creation of a manufacturing base in the province able to generate the funds required for long-term development and growth seems a less likely consequence of current economic strategy.

Agricultural production and rural Shanxi

In Shanxi, the fears of some in the national leadership that the production of grain and other essential products will decline as peasants chase higher profits in cash crops seem well founded. Shanxi's output of hemp, jute and flax more than doubled during 1985, but grain output fell by 5.7 per cent. Although the *Shanxi Ribao* stated that one of the main aims during 1986 had been to promote grain production, this fell by a further 11 per cent.[20] Some of the decrease is officially put down to 'natural calamities', but while total agricultural output fell during 1986, the proportion of forestry, animal husbandry, fishery and sideline production in the value of total agricultural output increased.[21]

A situation where peasants are increasingly engaging in sideline activities at the expense of growing grain is a problem by no means unique to Shanxi. However, it may well face bigger problems than other provinces. Historically it has always had problems trying to produce enough grain to feed its population, and so can afford further decreases in grain production even less than other areas. Although investment in industry is obviously necessary, 80 per cent of Shanxi's population lives in the countryside, and investment in increasing agricultural efficiency and output is also needed. Less than a third of the cultivated land in the province is irrigated, and this has had profound effects on agricultural output. According to the *Shanxi Ribao*, for example, one of the main reasons for the reduction in the province's agricultural output during 1986 was an unusually severe water shortage.[22]

Moreover, the emphasis on coal production in Shanxi has extended into the countryside, and is radically altering traditional patterns of economic activity. In part, this is a result of the rural population moving to the mining centres for employment. In the 1950s there were approximately 30,000 miners employed in Shanxi's state-owned mines, but by 1985 the figure had leapt to 400,000.[23] Under the guidance of the provincial Coal Resource Commission, township collectives and individuals living in rural and suburban areas have been actively encouraged to diversify from agricultural activity to coal extraction, and in the process agricultural production has been relegated to a secondary source of income in some areas.

The incentives to set up small mines are quite considerable, and include low-interest loans, no tax in the initial stages of production followed by low taxes later, personnel training by state-run mines, and access to equipment and technology at preferential rates. Between 1981 and 1985 the Shanxi Provincial Government granted 65 million yuan RMB per annum in low-interest loans for the technical transformation of key peasant-run mines.[24] Under these circumstances, coal production from non-state-owned mines has increased rapidly during the 1980s, with the 3,410 rural mines in Shanxi producing roughly half of the province's total coal output by 1984.

The high wages that can be earned in the small rural mines are also a considerable incentive. Unlike the state sector, there are no fixed wages in the peasant mines, with income dependent on the individual mine's output. Rural miners can earn half as much again as the average wage for underground workers in state-owned mines, and extra bonuses can be earned by fulfilling contracts to supply coal to the state. The idea behind the promotion of rural mining is that the miners should be primarily farmers, only engaging in coal extraction during slack periods. However in practice, agricultural output is falling, and earnings from mining now account for 51 per cent of peasant income in coal-producing counties.[25]

Despite the emphasis on developing Shanxi's heavy industrial base, the decreases in grain production have not been ignored. In June 1986 the Shanxi Provincial Government ordered the provincial Department of Agriculture and Animal Husbandry, and the provincial Grain Bureau, to make arrangements for creating eighteen special 'Grain Production Bases' in the province. The aim is to boost grain production by allocating funds to designated counties and cities in order to subsidize investment in water conservancy work, to popularize advanced agricultural technology, to experiment with new varieties of wheat, and to prevent the spread of plant diseases and pests.

Given its commitment to provide economic support for rural industry, the provincial government faces a problem in having to find sufficient funding also for agricultural projects. The solution lies partly in help from central government. The centre will provide 24 million yuan RMB annually to finance 40 per cent of the cost of each project, with the remainder coming from local funds. In return for these subsidies, the designated grain production bases have to accept specific targets for increases in grain production, and specific amounts of wheat that the counties and cities have to sell to the state each year.[26] The targeting of Shanxi as China's coal production base has thus led indirectly to a high level of dependence on central government if the province's agricultural base is to be modernized.

Limits to growth

Some 73 per cent of China's energy supplies comes from coal. Since energy is in such short supply that power cuts are commonplace, and factories often run well below capacity, a drive to increase coal production rapidly by concentrating resources on Shanxi seems to be a sensible move. There is, however, a certain paradoxical element about both Beijing's and Taiyuan's policy of boosting coal production in Shanxi.

In the 1920s, when Yan Xishan was trying to build his economic empire on Shanxi's mineral reserves, his plans were thwarted because he could not move coal and iron ore out of the province on a worthwhile scale. The problem has not simply disappeared, and indeed has been exacerbated as coal output has surged in the 1980s. Severe problems remain, with every year since 1980 seeing Shanxi's mines producing more coal than the transport system can handle.[27] A coal train leaves Taiyuan every six minutes, 85 per cent and 70 per cent of Shanxi's rail and road freight respectively are involved in coal transport, yet coal stockpiles are growing.

Growth rates in the coal industry are outstripping growth rates in the transport sector. Between 1979 and 1984 the average annual growth rate for Shanxi was 8.9 per cent, but transport capacity grew at only 4.3 per cent per annum. By March 1986 the result was that the 4.6 million tons of stockpiled coal in Shanxi represented a third of the national total from state-owned mines, and controls on production during the first quarter of 1988 led to output falling below the quarterly target.[28]

Moreover, since rural mines flourish and boost output of coal of often poor quality, large state-owned mines that have received new technological inputs to increase their capacity are being asked to restrict their output because the communications network cannot cope. For example, a large state-owned mine in Pinglu County is restricted to producing 1.5 million tons a year instead of the 2.5 million that it could produce at full capacity, and even then its own stockpile is still growing.[29] With wages in state-owned mines being fixed and not dependent on production, the restriction of output to a point below their full potential capacity is increasing the cost of producing coal in state-owned mines. The manager of the mine in Pinglu county has complained that in some sectors he now has three men employed to do one man's job.

Just as the province over-extended itself in construction projects during the early 1950s, more recently too much money has been pumped into industry too quickly, and without much consideration of the overall economic situation. Having recognized this problem, the provincial government has begun to take remedial action. For example, in February 1987 it announced the initial results of its attempts to control the scale of investment in fixed assets. During 1986 total investment in capital construction in state-owned enterprises was 5.3 billion yuan RMB. Although this amount represented a 4.5 per cent increase over the figure for 1985, the rise was considerably less than the 37.3 per cent increase during the previous year.[30]

None the less, if Shanxi is to reach the planned target of producing 400 million tons of coal per annum by the year 2000, investment and construction are still necessary. For example, in September 1985 the New China News Agency announced that over 80 per cent of Shanxi's 2,000 state-owned enterprises needed retooling or to undergo foreign technological renovation.[31] Thus, the provincial economic planners have to find a fine balance between overheating the economy, and providing sufficient investment to generate long-term growth.

One method of solving the problem of over-production was outlined by the then general secretary of the CCP, Hu Yaobang, on a visit to Shanxi in June 1985, when he called for as much coal to be consumed locally as possible.[32] As a result, 225 small pig-iron-producing furnaces went into operation in Shanxi in 1985, and construction was begun on another 303, with an estimated combined annual consumption of 4 million tons of coal.[33] The majority of those new furnaces have been constructed in rural or suburban areas, and are owned by individuals or collectives and not the state, thus providing another example of how traditional patterns of economic activity are being changed in Shanxi. 1985 also saw the start of construction on three small thermal power stations, with a planned capacity of one million kilowatts each.[34]

Although domestic consumption may solve the problem of stockpiled coal in the short run, it is not going to help Shanxi reach the planned 80 per cent increase in coal exports to other provinces by the end of the Seventh FYP. In any case, many of China's long-term industrial plans have been built around supplies of coal from Shanxi. For example, construction work began in April 1986 on a new power station in Hebei province, with the aim of remedying the energy shortfalls in Hebei, Beijing and Tianjin, three key centres of production in the Eastern Coastal Region. The coal for this new power station is to come from Yangquan in eastern Shanxi.[35]

Shanxi's role as a source of energy for China's future means that the centre is faced with having to play a direct role in almost every aspect of its modernization programme. An obvious example is the heavy emphasis placed by Beijing on the development of railway communications in Shanxi (see chapter 5). When improving the nation's railway network is officially mentioned, Shanxi is usually explicitly cited.[36] In October 1985 a national drive to build more railways was announced. The four priority areas were named as north-south trunk lines, port areas, inter-provincial lines, and Shanxi province, where three new lines were to be constructed so that eventually some 120 million tons of coal could be moved from Shanxi each year.[37]

The most important of those projects, and one which shows the centre's commitment to exploiting Shanxi's reserves more efficiently, is the line running from Datong in northern Shanxi to the port of Qinhuangdao in Hebei province. Named as a key project of the Seventh FYP, it is China's first electrified double-track railway, and will move 100 million tons of coal a year to Qinhuangdao, from where it will be transported by sea to other coastal ports.[38]

Investment and trade

It is essential for Shanxi to invest in mining technology if coal output and efficiency are to be improved in the future. Yet the province does not generate sufficient foreign currency reserves from exporting resources and manufactured goods. It has twenty-one corporations set up specifically to deal with import and export commodities, and has a total of 300 varieties of commodity available for export to the rest of the world, ranging from safes and fire extinguishers, to traditional medicines, and the potent *Fen Jiu* spirit. None the less, 58.8 per cent of Shanxi's income from the sale of commodities abroad comes from the export of coal, with Japan and North Korea being the two main importers.[39]

Because it is largely a single-commodity economy, Shanxi now faces a shortage of home-produced consumer goods and food staples. It has traditionally been a grain deficit province, and with the emphasis today on increasing rural mining and encouraging peasants to engage in small-scale, coal-intensive industrial activities, it is unlikely that self-sufficiency in grain production will be achieved in the foreseeable future. As well as having to try and earn much needed foreign currency by exporting coal abroad, it has to try to acquire daily necessities and consumer goods by exporting its coal to other provinces within China.

In keeping with the idea of regional specialization, Shanxi exchanges its coal for the commodities it needs in a style of barter that is usually referred to as compensatory trade. Coal has been exchanged for rice, edible oils, building materials and other such essential commodities, as well as Shanghai ready-made suits. The more developed provinces also trade with hard cash, services and expertise. For example, Tianjin trains personnel for a Shanxi calcium carbide factory, and Tianjin and Taiyuan have signed an agreement whereby Tianjin will train 200 college students from Shanxi at a total cost of 3 million yuan RMB each year in return for coal.[40]

Much hinges on Shanxi's production of coal, yet the province has been painfully short of investment. As already noted, one important solution has been central assistance. In 1986 the state invested 2.63 billion yuan RMB in fourteen key provincial projects, with 80 per cent of state investment centred on development of the energy industry and communications. Although coal may well provide a long-term solution to the problem, the 178 million yuan RMB in foreign income generated from sales during 1986 fell well short of the demand for foreign currency within the province.[41] Thus Shanxi has had to turn to Beijing not only for aid in the form of direct state investment, but also for help in attracting investment and low-interest loans from abroad.

Small-scale deals with foreign companies in the west are made by the individual enterprises concerned. For example, the First Conference on International Economic and Technological Co-operation held in Taiyuan during 1984 resulted in seventy joint projects being set up between firms in Shanxi and foreign enterprises.[42] Other projects are arranged and organized by the provincial government, which attempts to attract foreign firms to Shanxi by offering three- to five-year exemption from local taxes; tax reductions of 15–30 per cent after the initial period of exemption for low-profit forestry and agriculture projects, and projects in backward or remote areas; lower ground rents than in other provinces; foreign currency loans in the initial stages of operation; preferential terms on the purchase of Shanxi manufactured goods for sale overseas; deferred payment of foreign currency debts for firms introducing new technology into Shanxi; payment in Chinese currency at local prices for raw materials from Shanxi; and lowest-interest-rate loans from the Taiyuan branch of the Bank of China.[43]

Central government arranges and controls large-scale foreign loans, investment, and joint ventures through the State Council's Office for Planning the Energy Resource Base of Shanxi.[44] For example, mining experts from Sweden supervise the use of British-made equipment in the giant Gujiao coalfield, and by 1985 the first four mines funded by low-interest loans from Japan had already commenced production. While Czechoslovakia trades technology and skills for coal from the Shentou mine, individual companies such as the Harnischfeger Corporation from the United States, and the Demag Corporation from West Germany, have constructed excavator plants in conjunction with the local authorities in Shanxi.[45]

Undeniably, the agreements with foreign firms that have been arranged by individual units as well as the provincial government will greatly benefit the province, but the centre's role is crucial. Although the province's total earnings from exports in 1986 were US $302 million, by December 1986 the construction of China's largest mine, with a planned annual capacity of 15 million tons, in Pingshuo county in northern Shanxi, had already cost US $470 million. The mine is jointly owned by the Ministry of the Coal Industry and the Occidental Company of the United States.[46] A further US $240 million has been generated by a World Bank loan to the Changcun and Chengzhuang mines to buy advanced foreign mining technology.[47]

Shanxi's leadership

Although the centre's control over important projects in Shanxi appears stronger than in many other provinces, there is little apparent conflict between provincial leaders in Taiyuan and central leaders in Beijing. On the contrary, a community of interest seems to have emerged between central economic planners, who see Shanxi as the energy base for China's modernization, and provincial leaders who realize that the funds and technology that Shanxi desperately needs for its development cannot be generated from within the province alone.

The community of interest between central and provincial leadership is reflected in the centre's appointments to the provincial administration. The provincial party, state and military organs have undergone a virtual clean sweep of leading personnel during the 1980s. Of the seventy-five people who have held leading positions in the province during the past decade, only three — Ruan Bosheng, Yan Wuhong and Feng Sutao — held their positions from before 1980 to the start of the Seventh FYP. Even then, those three took up their positions only in December 1979. Those who now occupy the other nineteen leading positions in the province were all appointed after March 1983.[48]

This high turnover of personnel was not restricted to Shanxi, but resulted from a national policy designed to transfer power away from the older generations towards those committed to reform. Just as the State Council and its subordinate departments were streamlined in the spring of 1982, and over half of the Central Committee was replaced at the Twelfth Congress of the CCP in September 1982, so provincial leaderships were reorganized nationally in the spring of 1983 and again during the early summer of 1985.[49]

Provincial governor and deputy secretary of Shanxi's CCP Committee, Wang Senhao, is the epitome of the type of leader that the reorganizations were designed to promote. Born in 1933, Wang is one of the generation of young technocrats who are increasingly becoming the holders of power in the provinces. A one-time chief engineer in the Ministry of Coal, Wang has no connections with the Shanxi leadership of the Cultural Revolution era, nor with those assigned to restore order in the province after 1978.

However, not all of Shanxi's leaders share Wang Senhao's background. Although only three leaders retained their positions after the 1983 reorganization, others with experience of service in Shanxi continued to hold important positions. Shanxi's post-1983 provincial leadership shows a balance of young, centrally-trained technocrats, on the one hand, and leaders with experience of local affairs, on the other. Exactly half of those holding the top twenty-two positions in the party, state and military hierarchies, as of November 1987, were either natives of Shanxi or had served there before 1983, if not both.

Naturally, experience of working or living in a province does not necessarily presuppose loyalty to that province as opposed to the centre. Provincial Party Secretary, Li Ligong, for example, is a native of Jiaocheng County in Shanxi, and first served in the province in September 1981. However, Li's ties to the centre are perhaps stronger than Wang Senhao's, since he first came to prominence as a leader of the Communist Youth League, the same route taken by Hu Yaobang in his rise to central power. Similarly, deputy secretary of Shanxi CCP Committee, Wang Jiangong, has a history of service in Shanxi, but also has links with central leaders (and presumably Li Ligong) through having been secretary of the Communist Youth League until December 1982.

These leadership profiles indicate that intra-leadership conflict is less likely to be between central and provincial leaders than among different groups of allied provincial and central leaders. This dimension of the relationship between centre and province is nothing new. Commenting on the era before the Cultural Revolution, Jane Lieberthal makes precisely the same point with respect to the province's then leadership and its central allies, notably Peng Zhen and Bo Yibo, two of Shanxi's most influential native sons.[50]

During the 1950s and early 1960s, Peng and Bo held positions in state organs responsible for economic planning, and remain important figures today. Interestingly, Peng has retained links with political leaders in Shanxi even after the 1983 reorganization. For example, Ma Guishu, who served in the Taiyuan CCP Municipal Committee during the 1950s, and who was purged in 1968 while working in Tibet precisely because of his relationship with Peng, is now the vice-chairman of the Provincial People's Congress.

Future trends

Shanxi's coal production has soared as a result of increased mechanization, technology and knowledge. Whether the communications network can be improved so that it can cope with sustained high output in the future remains to be seen. At present the centre retains a high level of control through the State Council's Shanxi Energy Base Office, direct investment in state enterprises, control over the arrangement of foreign investment and loans, and subsidies for investment in agriculture. For the time being, Shanxi's leaders must accept this high level of control (compared with the more developed provinces of the Eastern Coastal Region) as the price they have to pay for the province to achieve its full potential in the drive to modernize.

One area where problems may emerge in the future is the competition among provinces for access to scarce foreign currency. If the individual units that earn foreign currency by exporting products abroad are allowed to retain their earnings, then the centre is going to face problems in helping units in provinces like Shanxi, where aid is needed to purchase modern equipment. The centre thus needs to retain economic control over the provinces of the Seventh FYP's Eastern Coastal Region in order to maintain its access to resources needed to help fund the development of the provinces of the Central (and indeed the Western) Region.

The question of foreign currency retention may also affect relations between provinces. For example, the centre is currently updating the national communications network so that Shanxi can supply energy to the manufacturing industries of East China. The manufacturing units are paid in foreign currency for the goods that they sell on the international market, yet acquire the energy used to manufacture the goods by paying in Chinese currency or with goods and services that are in demand in Shanxi. In a sense, Shanxi's extraction industries are losing out, since they do not receive any of the foreign currency that their exertions make possible.

Although it is obviously important for the most modern foreign technology to be employed in the province's industries, future problems may also arise over the repayment of debts. Despite a 22 per cent increase in the level of foreign trade in Shanxi during 1986, 96.6 per cent of the foreign currency actually used in the province was funded by loans.[51] It is therefore likely that while leaders in the Eastern Coastal Region urge the centre to allow more foreign currency to be retained by manufacturing units, Shanxi leaders are arguing that the centre should retain considerable control over foreign currency reserves, in order (among other reasons) to facilitate the continued development of Shanxi's economy.

Shanxi has made great strides forward, particularly in the heavy industrial sector. However, problems still remain, notably in agricultural production and transport. Given the emphasis on promoting rural industry at the expense of agricultural production, some comparisons with the experiments in rural industry attempted during the Great Leap Forward emerge. One obvious similarity is Hu Yaobang's call to consume coal within Shanxi by setting up small-scale furnaces, and the proliferation of 'backyard steel furnaces' that sprang up during the 1950s. Although grain production has fallen in Shanxi, and investment is being clearly targeted at the industrial rather than the agricultural sector, these comparisons should not be overstressed. Steps are being taken to control the runaway rates of investment that began to emerge during the early 1980s and that led to a 6.4 per cent increase in the cost-of-living index during 1986.[52] Moreover, despite the propensity for bad weather to hit Shanxi's agricultural base, increased trade with other regions within China has overcome some of the problems of feeding the population.

Notes

1 Hinton, W. (1972) *A Documentary of Revolution in a Chinese Village*, Harmondsworth: Pelican, and Hinton (1983) *Fanshen: The Continuing Revolution in a Chinese Village*, London: Secker & Warburg.
2 State Statistical Bureau cited in Lin Wancheng (1987) 'China's Three Railway Construction Projects', *Beijing Review*, 20 July.
3 'North-East Plans Coal Self-Sufficiency in China', NCNA, 21 July 1986, in SWB-E, 30 July 1986.
4 Gillin, D.G. (1967) *Warlord Yen Hsi-shan in Shansi Province 1911-1949*, Princeton: Princeton University Press, pp. 125-208.

5 Lieberthal, J. (unpublished) 'Shansi', p. 39 in Winckler, E.A. (ed.) *A Provincial Handbook of China*.

6 It is difficult to assess Shanxi's exact share of China's coal production due to discrepencies in official figures. See, for example, 'Rising Coal Exports From Shanxi Province', 1 September 1985, in SWB-E, 11 September 1985, and 'PRC Receives World Bank Loans to Develop Shanxi Province', NCNA 4 July 1985, in SWB-E, 17 July 1985.

7 Jing Wei (1984) 'China's Biggest Energy-Producing Centre', *Beijing Review*, 3 December.

8 Pauley, R. (1986) 'Adrift on a Sea of Coal', *The Financial Times*, 18 December.

9 'Communiqué on Economic and Social Development in 1986', *Shanxi Ribao*, 28 February 1987, in SWB-E, 25 March 1987.

10 Ibid. and 'Communiqué of Provincial Statistics Bureau', *Liaoning Ribao*, 12 February 1987, in SWB-E, 11 March 1987.

11 'Communiqué on Shanxi's Economic and Social Development in 1985', *Shanxi Ribao*, 20 April 1986, in SWB-E, 7 May 1986, and 'Communiqué on Shanxi's Economic and Social Development in 1984', *Shanxi Ribao*, 27 March 1985, in SWB-E, 1 May 1985.

12 'Communiqué on Economic and Social Development in 1986', *Shanxi Ribao*, 28 February 1987, and 'Communiqué on Shanxi's Economic and Social Development in 1985', *Shanxi Ribao*, 20 April 1986.

13 In Heilongjiang, light industrial output value accounted for a third of the province's total industrial output value. 'Communiqué on Economic and Social Development in 1986', *Shanxi Ribao*, 28 February 1987; 'Communiqué of Provincial Statistics Bureau', *Heilongjiang Ribao*, 7 March 1987, in SWB-E, 8 April 1987; and 'Communiqué of Guangdong Provincial Statistics Bureau', *Nanfang Ribao*, 22 March 1987, in SWB-E, 15 April 1987.

14 'Communiqué on Economic and Social Development in 1986', *Shanxi Ribao*, 28 February 1987 and 'Communiqué on Shanxi's Economic and Social Development in 1985', *Shanxi Ribao*, 20 April 1985.

15 'Leaders of Shanghai, Jiangsu, Shanxi and Xinjiang on 1986–90 Plan, NCNA, 10 May 1986, in SWB-E, 15 May 1986.

16 'Communiqué on Economic and Social Development in 1986', *Shanxi Ribao*, 28 February 1987, and Shanxi People's Publishing House (1986) *Shanxi Jingji Nianjian (Almanac of Shanxi Economy)*, Hong Kong: China Book Company, pp. 91–4.

17 'Communiqué on Economic and Social Development in 1986', *Shanxi Ribao*, 28 February 1987. 'Communiqué on Shanxi's Economic and Social Development in 1985', *Shanxi Ribao*, 20 April 1985; 'Communiqué on Shanxi's Economic and Social Development in 1984', *Shanxi Ribao*, 27 March 1985.

18 Ibid.

19 Provincial coal production increased by 3.6 per cent, whereas the amount of coal leaving the province increased by 10.1 per cent; 'Communiqué on Economic and Social Development in 1986', *Shanxi Ribao*, 28 February 1987; 'Communiqué on Shanxi's Economic and

Social Development in 1985', *Shanxi Ribao*, 20 April 1985.

20 Thus, grain output fell from 8.72 million kg in 1984 to 7.32 million kg in 1986. 'Communiqué on Economic and Social Development in 1986', *Shanxi Ribao*, 28 February 1987; 'Communiqué on Shanxi's Economic and Social Development in 1985', *Shanxi Ribao*, 20 April 1985; 'Communiqué on Shanxi's Economic and Social Development in 1984', *Shanxi Ribao*, 27 March 1985.

21 From 26.7 per cent to 28 per cent. 'Communiqué on Economic and Social Development in 1986', *Shanxi Ribao*, 28 February 1987.

22 Ibid.

23 Jing Wei (1985) 'Miners Past and Present', *Beijing Review*, 11 March.

24 'Shanxi's Coal Output — Growing Rate of Peasant Mines', NCNA, 24 August 1985, in SWB-E, 18 August 1985.

25 'Rural Coal Mines in Shanxi', NCNA, 9 May 1985 in SWB-E, 22 May 1985.

26 'Shanxi Contracts For Grain Production Bases', *Shanxi Ribao*, 30 July 1986, in SWB-E, 30 July 1986.

27 'Shanxi Develops Industries To Consume Surplus Demand', NCNA, 25 February 1986, in SWB-E, 5 March 1986.

28 Jing Wei (1984) 'China's Biggest Energy-Producing Centre', op. cit., and *Zhongguo Xinwen Shi*, 20 April 1986, 'Shortage of Rail Transport Causes Stockpiles', in SWB-E, 30 April 1986, and NCNA, 'Shanxi Controls Coal Output, in SWB-E, 4 May 1988.

29 Jing Wei (1984) 'Large-Scale Development Mapped Out', *Beijing Review*, 17 December.

30 'Communiqué on Economic and Social Development in 1986', *Shanxi Ribao*, 28 February 1987.

31 'Shanxi Province's Trade and Co-operation Upgrading Enterprises', NCNA, 10 September 1985, in SWB-E, 18 September 1985.

32 'PRC Official Hu Yaobang in Shanxi and Shaanxi Provinces Discusses Economic Development', NCNA, 22 June 1985, in SWB-E, 25 June 1985.

33 'Shanxi Develops Industries To Consume Surplus Demand', NCNA, 25 February 1986.

34 'Development of Shanxi Province's Coal and Power Industries', NCNA, 14 May 1985, in SWB-E, 22 May 1985.

35 'New Thermal Power Station For Hebei Province', NCNA, 18 November 1985, in SWB-E, 27 November 1985.

36 'Progress With Railway Electrification', NCNA, 1 December 1985, in SWB-E, 11 December 1985.

37 'More and Better Railways', NCNA, 6 October 1985, in SWB-E, 16 October 1985.

38 Lin Wancheng (1987) 'China's Three Railway Construction Projects', *Beijing Review*, 20 July.

39 'Communiqué on Economic and Social Development in 1986', *Shanxi Ribao*, 28 February 1987, and 'Communiqué on Economic and Social Development', NCNA, 14 January 1986, in SWB-E, 22 January 1986.

40 Jing Wei (1985) 'Joint Exploitation Absorbs Foreign Capital', *Beijing Review*, 18 February.

41 'Communiqué on Economic and Social Development in 1986', *Shanxi Ribao*, 28 February 1987.

42 Shanxi Foreign Economic Relations and Trade Bureau, Shanxi Provincial People's Government, *Shanxi Province Foreign Trade* (no publication details).

43 Jing Wei (1985) 'Joint Exploitation Absorbs Foreign Capital', op. cit.

44 Vice-Governor Bai Qingcai quoted in Jing Wei, ibid.

45 Jing Wei (1985) 'Joint Exploitation Aborbs Foreign Capital', op. cit., and Shanxi Provincial Radio Service, 20 March 1986, 'Heavy Construction Equipment Produced in Shanxi Province', in SWB-E, 2 April 1986.

46 'Rising Coal Exports From Shanxi', NCNA, 1 September 1985, in SWB-E, 11 September 1985; 'PRC-USA Jointly Owned Coal Mine in Shanxi', *Renmin Ribao*, 6 December 1986, SWB-E, 31 December 1986.

47 'Foreign Funding For Coal Mining Projects', NCNA, 21 December 1984, in SWB-E, 9 January 1985.

48 All biographies and data regarding provincial leaders are from ESRC Project E0023-2173 on *Provincial Leadership in the People's Republic of China*. A computer database is available at the University of Newcastle upon Tyne.

49 Mills, W. de B. (1981) 'Leadership Changes in China's Provinces', *Problems of Communism*, no. 3, May-June.

50 Lieberthal, 'Shansi', op. cit., p. 61.

51 'Communiqué on Economic and Social Development in 1986', *Shanxi Ribao*, 28 February 1987.

52 Ibid.

Chapter nine

Shandong: an atypical coastal province?

Peter Ferdinand

The Eastern Coastal Region has been correctly characterized as the most developed part of China. The Seventh Five-Year Plan envisages that, because it is the most industrialized region, it will take the lead in the modernization of traditional industries and the training of industrial personnel, as well as the introduction of new high-tech industries to China. However, the region is far from homogeneous. The north-eastern provinces of Liaoning, Jilin and Heilongjiang have had a long (pre-revolutionary) tradition of heavy industrial development. Jiangsu, Zhejiang and Guangdong, in the south-east, have had an even longer-established reputation for agricultural and light industrial products. In contrast, and apparently atypically for a province in the Eastern Coastal Region, Shandong is somewhat undeveloped and unindustrialized. This chapter considers the development of Shandong (which is roughly in the centre of the Eastern Coastal Region) in order to illuminate the problems associated with both the northern and the southern parts of the region.

As indicated earlier, one of the features of economic policy during the Mao era was the imposition of uniformity throughout the country. In particular, almost every province was instructed to industrialize. During the 1970s they were instructed to develop their heavy industrial base under the slogan 'Take steel as the key link'. In response, all provinces set up heavy industrial plants, especially steel mills, regardless of the local supplies of raw materials. In many provinces valuable resources were wasted in vain attempts to unearth coal and iron reserves, even though previous geological surveys suggested that it would be a waste of time. Among the provinces of the Eastern Coastal Region, Jiangsu and Guangdong, for example, squandered vast sums in searches for suitable coal for their own heavy industries.

Similarly, in agriculture (as indicated in chapter 1), the central line of the 1970s was to 'grow grain everywhere'. Pastureland in Inner Mongolia was ploughed to grain. In Jiangsu, Zhejiang and Guangdong mulberry fields and subtropical crops such as sugar were cut back to favour grain, and there was a prejudice against cultivating aquatic products — obviously suitable for the coastal provinces — even though they did not compete with grain for land at all. The effect of national policy was at least in part to hold back the more developed areas, particularly those on the south-eastern coastal strip.[1]

Economic reforms since 1978 have consciously attempted to revive traditional regional specializations. One immediate aim is to take advantage of local concentrations of raw materials that can be produced relatively cheaply. Another is to build on the centuries-old local skills which create products with a nation-wide reputation. Two such revived or re-encouraged skills are the production, for example, of calligraphy paper in Anhui and Shaoxing wine in Zhejiang. Thus one major thrust of policies during the 1980s has been the revival of traditional regional economic specializations and links. Provinces have been given greater freedom to develop pursuits which they have always been good at, including, as will be discussed later, business itself.

The economic base

In 1984 Shandong had a population of some 76.37 million people. It was China's most populous coastal province and the third most populous province overall, after Sichuan (101.12 million) and Henan (76.46 million). Some 48.5 per cent of Shandong's population live in cities or towns, and it is consequently a far more urbanized province than either Sichuan or Henan. Indeed, it is the fifth most urbanized province (after Shanxi, Jilin, Liaoning and Heilongjiang) apart from, obviously, the provincial-level municipalities of Beijing, Shanghai and Tianjin.

Climatically the province enjoys distinct changes with the seasons. It is in the monsoon belt, and summers are hot and wet. Winters, however, are cold and dry. There are roughly 180–220 frost-free days per year. The geography of the province is varied and complex, ranging from mountain areas — including one of China's traditionally most sacred mountains, Tai Shan — to the long and indented coastline culminating in the Shandong peninsula.

The province is quite well endowed with mineral resources. Over ninety minerals are mined, including coal, oil, natural gas, iron, gold, copper, aluminium, diamonds, graphite, gypsum, magnesium and barite. It also produces a great variety of agricultural and industrial products. Among the most important are grain, cotton, edible oil, tobacco, hemp, fruit, aquatic and livestock products, petrol and petroleum products, electric power, steel, pig-iron, machine tools, vehicles, synthetic ammonia, tractors, cotton yarn and cotton cloth, raw salt, watches and gauges.

It does not, however, occupy a particularly vital strategic place in China's defence plans, especially now that relations with Japan are quite cordial. With the exception of some naval and air force bases that are responsible for covering the approaches to the Gulf of Bohai, it is not a province whose development has benefited from defence considerations.

On the other hand, it has been an important transport centre for the whole of northern China since the turn of the century, when a German consortium was granted the concession to build a railway linking the provincial captial, Jinan, with the treaty port of Qingdao. More recently the importance of the province to communications has been emphasized by the decision to include the ports of Qingdao and Yantai among the fourteen ports designated as 'open coastal cities' — the special status granted by the central government in 1984 to stimulate foreign trade.

Since 1949 Shandong has seen major industrial development, which has overtaken the traditional pre-revolutionary strength of the textile industry. In particular, heavy industry has grown considerably in importance instead of the previously predominant cotton industry. By 1984 the province accounted for 6.5 per cent of China's gross industrial output and 9.4 per cent of gross agricultural output (in both cases measured by value), which together represented 7.4 per cent of total industrial and agricultural output. Of all the provincial-level units of government, Shandong ranked fourth for industrial output (after Shanghai, Jiangsu and Liaoning); second for agriculture (after Jiangsu); and third for the two combined (after Jiangsu and Shanghai).

Reluctance to reform

Despite Shandong's relatively high levels of both agricultural and industrial output, the per capita level of development remains relatively modest. Thus in 1984 per capita industrial output was only 88 per cent of the national average by value. If anything, Shandong's economic performance since 1978 has been stronger in agriculture than in industry, where, in 1984, per capita agricultural output was 129 per cent of the national average, again by value. Little had changed in that respect since the national economic reforms were launched during 1979–80. In 1985 Shandong's share of the nation's total imports and exports was only 7.3 per cent by value.

Shandong has thus performed creditably, but it is clear that the greatest transformation in its industrial and agricultural performance took place during the period before 1979. Since then it has merely held its own compared with the national average. In contrast, the party secretary of Guangdong commented that his province had seen as much development during the nine years since 1978 as in the preceding twenty-nine years.[2] That contrast suggests that Shandong's leaders might be more satisfied with the type of economic policies pursued in the past — Shandong was one of the provinces which took the lead in advancing the early phases of the Cultural Revolution — and that they would be less eager to change policy-styles in the early 1980s. Indeed one account of the economic development of the province has claimed that during the two years after Mao's death the policies of the Mao era — one-sided emphasis upon basic economic construction and investment, accompanied by neglect of non-state industries — were actually intensified.[3] This was at a time when market and other economic reforms were being advanced in other provinces. One consequence was that Shandong fell behind as market reforms gathered momentum elsewhere.

Shandong's economic performance during the 1980s reflects its decline relative to other provinces. In part that can no doubt be explained in terms of the greater priority and freedom of manoeuvre allocated to light industry. Jiangsu, Zhejiang and Guangdong, for example, had been held back by the resources which they had to allocate in the vain search for their own coal and other raw material supplies for heavy industry. Once that priority had eased, the southern coastal provinces were better able to return to their traditional strengths in light industry and forge ahead.

In Shandong, by contrast, light industry accounted for only 54.9 per cent of total industrial output in the province (1984 figures), which is rather less than in Zhejiang (64.2 per cent) and Guangdong (66.3 per cent). Indeed, light industry now accounts for a smaller proportion of industrial output in Shandong than in most other coastal provinces, with the exception of Manchuria.

On the other hand, these statistics do not on their own explain Shandong's relative economic performance. In neighbouring Jiangsu, for example, light industry similarly accounted for 57.8 per cent of output in 1984. Moreover, Shandong does have a substantial light industrial sector. There are a number of light industrial products that enjoy a national reputation and whose output has grown considerably in recent years, as, for example, paper, notably computer paper, and textiles.

An equally important factor explaining Shandong's relatively poor economic performance during the 1980s was its slowness to encourage the expansion of collectively owned enterprises, especially in the countryside. The point is highlighted by comparison with Zhejiang. Both provinces in 1984 had 3,400 state-owned enterprises. Yet in Zhejiang 35,500 were also collectively owned, whereas in Shandong there were only just over half that figure, 17,900, despite Shandong's rural population of 39.33 million, as opposed to 29.75 million in Zhejiang. Jiangsu too had 80 per cent more collectively owned enterprises (33,100) than Shandong, although it also has a larger rural population of 47.75 million, some 20 per cent more.

There is then more than a suspicion that Shandong's leaders were reluctant to turn their backs upon the economic policies and priorities of the 1970s. Apart from structural differences between the economies of Shandong and neighbouring provinces, however, there were also differences in business practices and in official attitudes towards them. The recently appointed mayor of the provincial capital Jinan has suggested that the rate of development after 1949 had not been ideal. He gave the backwardness of economic skills that were available in the province as a chief reason for that predicament. In his opinion, even those to be found in Jinan were not commensurate with what would be expected in a provincial capital. As a result, it took more time to develop new attitudes towards markets, as well as working practices that would make the most of market opportunities.

Moreover, though Shandong is on the coast, the capital is inland and the province is relatively inward-looking. Certainly it had far fewer traditional links with abroad — whether business or family — than, say, Guangdong. Consequently, the policy of opening up the country to the outside world initially ran into strong resistance in Jinan.[4]

Investment for the 1990s

Although Shandong's industrial development was only about average for the period 1979-84, during the early 1980s the provincial leadership (no doubt with the agreement of central government) appears to have taken the decision to step up industrial investment in the province. In 1982 Shandong had been the sixth largest provincial recipient of investment, but by 1984 it had become the largest. The proportion of that investment that went on industry (71 per cent) was the third highest of all provinces (after Jiangxi and Shanxi), while the proportion that went on housing (13.2 per cent) was the fourth lowest in the country (after Jiangxi, Henan and Shanxi). Moreover, Shandong also used more of its total investment on new construction (69.4 per cent), as opposed to expanding or re-equipping existing capacity, than any other provincial-level unit.

Despite other trends in economic management, and the practice in other provinces, in Shandong the provincial leadership has continued to play a very active role in allocating resources. In particular, it appears to have decided to give higher priority to building up the province's economy rather than expanding the provision of welfare services, including housing. Indeed, the Provincial Economic Commission appears to take a central role. One indication of this is the appointment of its former head, Jiang Qunyun, a native of Yantai, as the current governor of Shandong.

On the other hand, not all of this increased investment can be attributed solely to decisions by state or state-controlled bodies. As the 1980s developed, individual and collective investment began to increase. By 1984 Shandong was the province attracting the largest amount of such investment, some 4.778 billion yuan RMB — 760 million yuan more than Jiangsu and at least twice the amount in almost all other provinces. Although in the past Shandong may have seemed slow to develop individual and collective investment, it ought to benefit considerably once all this investment begins to show returns.

Shandong's agriculture during the 1980s has shown marked improvements in the output of key basic commodities such as wheat, maize and cotton. Indeed those improvements have been among the best in the country. For example, while the overall national grain harvest grew by 15 per cent between 1982 and 1984, in Shandong it grew by 28 per cent. The provincial maize output there grew by 17 per cent during the same period, while the wheat harvest was a staggering 55 per cent higher. No doubt it is for this reason that a Deputy Party Secretary from Shandong, Lu Maozeng, was elected a candidate member of the Central Committee between 1982 and 1987, and was then raised to full membership at the Thirteenth Congress of the CCP, for he is also a senior agronomist who has made contributions to cultivating superior varieties of wheat.

Cotton has traditionally been a major crop in Shandong. Between 1982 and 1984 national output grew by 74 per cent, but in Shandong, the nation's largest cotton-grower, with about a quarter of total production, output grew by 80 per cent. Perhaps to make room for the extra output in cotton and the other key commodities, the province reduced cultivation of some other products, such as tobacco. More southerly provinces, notably Guizhou and Yunnan, were thus able to increase both their output of tobacco and their share of the national tobacco crop.

Shandong's more recent development, then, would appear to have been following the priorities of central government. Given that the national leadership has expressed concern over provinces diversifying into products with higher financial returns while neglecting staple products such as grain, Shandong's economic growth would seem to conform more to what Beijing would favour. Even though the national emphasis is upon individual provinces doing more than in the past to adapt their production to local conditions, with much greater regional specialization, in Shandong this can work to the advantage of both the central and the local governments. Instead of pursuing a policy of planting a fairly varied set of crops, the provincial government is freer to devote more space to staple products for which its local environment happens to be particularly favourable.

On the other hand, this relatively close relationship with central government can have its drawbacks too. Cotton production provides a good example of the disadvantages. By 1984 output throughout the country far exceeded national needs. Consequently, in 1985 it was agreed that there should be a major reduction in the amount of cotton grown. Shandong, however, was disproportionately affected by this policy, since it is the nation's largest cotton producer. That year saw a 38 per cent fall in its cotton harvest, which compared with a 25 per cent cut in neighbouring Jiangsu. It is true that Shandong then diversified by expanding quite successfully into other cash crops such as hemp, but further attempts to increase cereal production were less successful.

Nevertheless, the province has also managed to expand the production of some secondary crops which are especially suited to local conditions as, for example, peanuts. Shandong accounted for 27 per cent of the national peanut crop in 1982, but in 1984 the figure had risen to 37 per cent, and output had risen 29 per cent. At present a large proportion of the province's peanut crop is sold for export. Fruit cultivation has been another success story. Although Shandong's share of the national fruit harvest fell slightly — from 20 per cent to 19 per cent during 1982–4 — it was still by far the province with the largest fruit production, growing 39 per cent more than the next largest, Hebei. It is therefore not surprising that Shandong is looking to export fruit in various preserved forms, including, possibly, irradiation.

Shandong and central government

The picture which emerges of relations between Shandong and central government is largely one of harmony and mutual co-operation. To a considerable extent the relationship between Shandong and Beijing is the result of geographical accident. Shandong is close enough — both physically and politically, for communications are excellent by Chinese standards — for the capital to cast a significant shadow in the province. However, there are several other clearly identifiable determinants of that relationship.

As already noted, agricultural co-operation is not a bone of contention. The climate favours the cultivation of crops which are high on the list of priorities of central government. In that sense therefore, by developing them, the province has been acting in conformity with the wishes and interests of the central government as well as its own.

Shandong also has minerals and raw materials readily available and relatively accessible for export. Of the central and southern coastal provinces, it is among the best endowed with mineral resources, especially fossil fuels. In 1984 it was the PRC's third largest provincial-level producer of crude oil, accounting for 13 per cent of total output; and the fourth largest provincial-level producer of coal, accounting for 7 per cent of total production. Shandong is clearly well placed to benefit from all the efforts being made to tackle China's enormous energy problems.

However, Shandong has more than fossil fuels in abundance. It also has significant gold deposits, which could acquire much greater importance if world supplies from other sources, such as South Africa, were disrupted for whatever reason. There are also large granite deposits in the province, ready to be supplied for export, either for building purposes or for gravestones, for example. There has long been a declining world supply of granite from the more traditional sources, notably Italy, which offers Shandong the opportunity to take over some of those markets and compete with other Asian suppliers such as Bangladesh.

The availability and accessibility of minerals and raw materials for export will be bound to enhance Shandong's importance in the future, particularly if, as at present, China is reliant upon the export of such materials to pay for the imports of foreign equipment and technology. Shandong will clearly benefit, but so too will central government, both in terms of foreign currency and in terms of the particularly large slice of SINOPEC's earnings (including presumably domestic earnings) which now go directly to central government. Thus central government has a particular and mercenary interest in seeing Shandong prosper.

Shandong is also well placed to benefit from the efforts to overcome national transport problems, especially now that export routes via the east coast figure so much more prominently than they did before. Shandong's location at the mouth of the Yellow River, with the deep water ports of Qingdao and Yantai — more southerly than those of Liaoning, and less subject to silting than Shanghai — means that the province will certainly acquire greater significance as an export centre, both for its own products and also for those provinces to the west, such as Shanxi. Indeed, there is the prospect of developing rail links with Xinjiang and even, possibly, with the Soviet Union, thus providing an alternative transport route to the Trans-Siberian Railway.

As was stressed in chapter 5, national transport policies have a crucial impact upon regional development. Clearly the availability of relatively developed transport links to the coast has played a major part in the rapid growth of particular provinces during the 1980s as China has opened up to the outside world. The east-west routes that link the hinterland with the coast cut across the more usual north-south divisions into East, Central and Western China and create their own economic links and regions.

Indeed, it is striking that several of the provinces which have enjoyed particularly rapid industrial development during the 1980s, as indicated in Table 3.3 could be said to have a 'Yangtze connection': that is, Hubei, Jiangsu and Zhejiang, as well as Shanghai itself. Since 1984 this 'Yangtze connection' has had a more concrete manifestation in the Nanjing Regional Economic Co-ordinating Conference in which the representatives of eighteen cities and local governments from Jiangsu and neighbouring provinces have participated.

Now there is the prospect that a parallel 'Yellow River connection' will emerge, with Shandong at its head, as the rail network and marshalling yards are built up around Qingdao. Between 1982 and 1984 Shandong was far and away the province which absorbed the greatest investment in railway construction. In 1984, for example, it received 600 million yuan RMB for railway development, more than twice the amount invested in railways in Shanxi and Guangdong, the next largest recipients of investment to that end. Most other provinces received less than a sixth of Shandong's figure.

A Yellow River Development Region, or some such nomenclature, stretching west from Shandong, is likely to acquire greater significance in the future. As yet there seems to be no institutional agency which looks after economic development in this region as a whole, but there is no doubt that some leaders in Shandong think in those terms and believe that Shandong should take a lead in its promotion and development. According to the mayor of Jinan, the city is a 'crevice' which is favourably located to benefit from growth in the areas on all sides of it.[5] It may also be relevant to note that the current leading party secretary in Shandong, Liang Buting, served as Second and then First Secretary in Qinghai in the north-west of the country between 1979 and 1983.

Apart from the opportunities for export through Shandong, there are possibilities for encouraging foreign tourism, especially from Japan. Shandong is famous for its seaside attractions, the historic sites in Jinan and elsewhere, the sacred Tai Shan, and most notably the birthplace of Confucius in Qufu. Provincial and municipal travel services have been set up to cater for and expand this tourist traffic.

Chapter 3 suggested that central government was feeling its position to be increasingly weak in its dealings with provincial governments, especially those of the Eastern Coastal Region, which ran their own budgetary surplus. Yet at the same time it is clear that relations between central government and the provinces are not so starkly opposed to each other. For example, in Guangdong the local leadership may well be suspect for tolerating far too much and too rapid change that undermines socialism — as the party secretary in the province recently admitted, it sometimes seems as though 'everyone there is engaging in business deals, reselling western goods, doing shady deals and smuggling'.[6] None the less, Zhao Ziyang, the current general secretary of the CCP, spent most of his career between 1949 and 1966 in Guangdong's politics, and he will doubtless be more sanguine about the local leadership's basic reliability. Moreover, Guangdong recognizes that it needs major improvements if it is to develop its own economy — as, for example, in electricity supplies and transport links — and that most of these will have to be financed by central government. Consequently, even its claims for autonomy, let alone its behaviour in practice, are likely to be moderated.

Shandong has even stronger reasons for co-operating with central government, for it clearly benefits immensely from central investment. As already indicated, national priorities demand the expansion of Shandong's agriculture and extraction industries. However, expansion both of these supplies, and also of the transport network to facilitate exports from Shandong and the provinces to its west, requires the kinds of massive investment that only central government can provide. One likely consequence is that central control will remain a major factor in the calculations underlying Shandong's development.

Access to foreign currency provides an excellent example of the extent of continued central control. Even that foreign currency which is to be used for local development — theoretically at the disposal of the provinces in general — requires prior approval from Beijing before it can be used. In 1984 Shandong had notionally US $200 million for developing overseas trade relations, including US $50 million from the province's own revenues, $50 million from Beijing, and $100 million in loans from the Bank of China. Nevertheless, all that amount required central approval before it could be spent.

Shandong, for its part, is likely to continue to accept fairly strong central control since, compared with other provinces, it is a major net beneficiary. Central government is prepared to invest such massive sums in Shandong's railways and energy base, but the province can determine the future use of these additional facilities. One consequence is that the province is unlikely to take the lead in pressing to retain a greater proportion of its own revenue, for under present arrangements central government still transfers significant investment funds into Shandong. In this respect Shandong has more in common with its neighbours to the north-east, Liaoning, Jilin and Heilongjiang, as well as to the west, as for example Shanxi, all of which have strengths in heavy industry, than it does with its southern neighbours, which are considerably more orientated towards light industry.

Conclusion

Possibly because of its dependence upon the centre, Shandong is not a pace-setter for reforms, as are Guangdong, Fujian and Jiangsu to the south, or Liaoning to the north. Nor does it have any great traditional reputation for financial skills or business acumen, the qualities which are once again at a premium and which are serving Guangdong and Shanghai so well. Before Liberation Shandong had a reputation for producing policemen rather than bankers or businessmen.

Nevertheless market reforms are gathering momentum. Foreign trade is developing. Since the province's own policies for development seem to fit in very well with national aims, there should be the basis for a harmonious working relationship with Beijing — at least for the time being. When the recent massive investments in infrastructure and the exploitation of raw materials begin to pay off, it may be that Shandong will become more self-assertive. For the moment, however, Shandong would seem to be among the least of the central government's worries. Perhaps that is one reason why the governor, Jiang Qunyun, has on several recent occasions been seen in group photographs of dignitaries from all over China standing quite close to Deng Xiaoping.

Notes

The author would like to acknowledge the comments made by Dr Bob Callow on an earlier draft. The views expressed here, however, are the author's own.

1 Chen Jiyuan (1981) 'Regional Economic Structure', in Ma Hong and Sun Shangqing (eds) *Zhongguo jingji jiegou wenti yanjiu (Research on China's Economic Structure)*, Beijing, ii, pp. 653–67.
2 Lin Ruo, 'Review of and prospects for the reform and opening up of Guangdong', *Hongqi*, 1988 (2), p. 2.
3 *Zhongguo shengqing (The Condition of China's Provinces)*, Beijing, 1986, p. 467.
4 Zhai Yongbo, 'Bound along the path of vertical and horizontal reform, develop vigorously and comprehensively Jinan's economy', *Zhongguo Jingji Tizhi Gaige*, 1988 (1), p. 35.
5 Ibid.
6 Lin Ruo, op. cit., p. 4.

Chapter ten

National minorities and the internal frontier

Terry Cannon

Impressions of ethnic tensions in China are so dominated by the case of Tibet that it is easy to forget that there are in all fifty-five recognized 'minority nationalities' incorporated into modern China's territory. Altogether there are some seventy million national minority peoples, of whom by far the largest group is the Zhuang, of Guangxi in south-west China, who number about thirteen million. More famous perhaps are the Mongols, Uighurs, and Miao.

Historically, relations between the Han (93 per cent of the population) and the minority nationalities have not been good, and the long record of conflict continues. During the past ten years, demonstrations and violent disturbances rooted in ethnic tensions are known to have occurred in Xinjiang, Yunnan and Inner Mongolia, in addition to the well-known case of Tibet. In 1981, several hundreds appear to have died in Kashgar (west Xinjiang) after local Kirghiz people seized arms from a military camp and revolted.[1] Reports of complaints from minority peoples of racist treatment are common, as are the CCP's pronouncements on the dangers of Han chauvinism.

The economic development of a minority nationality area provides no panacea. It often means economic change which is irrelevant to, or disruptive of, the nationality's existing livelihood, and can include the immigration of more Han. The political solutions of the past forty years have fared little better. In constitutional terms, where the non-Han peoples are concentrated in significant numbers, they are theoretically granted self-administration: hence minority nationality areas are designated as *autonomous* regions (at the provincial level), *autonomous* districts or *autonomous* counties. However, there is not even the pretence of self-determination. The boundaries of administrative units designated as autonomous on ethnic grounds are themselves defined by the Han rather than the minority nationalities. An extreme example was the transfer of huge areas of the Inner Mongolian Autonomous Region to neighbouring provinces in 1969, a Cultural Revolution 'wrong' which was righted in 1979.[2] Another problem is the precise definition of the territory of

Tibet, which for many Tibetans includes large areas of Sichuan, Gansu and Qinghai provinces.[3]

In the past, Han political domination manifested itself in the appointment of leaders to minority nationality areas.[4] As part of a general package devised in the early 1980s to improve Han-minority relations, the 1982 state constitution specified that heads of autonomous areas down to county level must be members of the relevant national minority.[5] However, the same constitution in a new clause prohibited acts that instigate the secession of any national minority. The inclusion of such a clause where none existed before suggests that there is some concern about such demands.[6]

This chapter examines the potential impact on China's minority nationalities of the current drive to modernize. In particular, it suggests that the benefits of modernization may be very different for the Han and the non-Han peoples of China. It concentrates on the Seventh FYP's Western Region because one notable feature of that region is its relatively high proportion of non-Han Chinese population. However, the various national minorities are not found exclusively in the West, and some of the provinces of the Western Region, such as Shaanxi and Sichuan, are traditionally Han territory.

The crucial questions in relations between the Han and the minority nationalities concern the uses to which the territory of the latter is put, the manner in which the Han determine policy for the entire country, and the consequent impact on the economies of the minority nationalities. Although they comprise only a small proportion of the country's population, their traditional territories extend over a huge proportion of the country, and include many resources and natural attributes (including grazing and arable land) of interest to the Han agrarian and industrializing economy. By itself the Xinjiang Uighur Autonomous Region covers one-sixth of China's land area, and is as large as Western Europe. Yet it contains only 1.3 per cent of the total population.

Antagonism between the Han and other nationalities is not new. However, China's pursuit of modernization places new demands on its 'frontier' zone by the rapidity of growth in the dominant economic system. Conflict is virtually inevitable, since Han goals involve means and objectives which differ from those that the other nationalities have normally used to organize their own economic and cultural systems.[7] Tolerance tends to be low: the Han have effectively imposed new ways of life and brooked no resistance.

The legacy of history

The revolution that brought the CCP to power in 1949 was predominantly a Han affair, based on the dual motors of agrarian reform and anti-Japanese nationalism. The minority nationalities were scarcely involved in either of those struggles, partly because their areas were not invaded by the Japanese, and partly because their economic systems were not agrarian, but pastoral, or — if based on agriculture — only in areas of little interest to the Han and their leaders, as, for example, Tibet until 1959. The revolution essentially involved a transformation of the Han economic and political system. The new government therefore had to devise new means to relate to the other nationalities in so far as it was felt valuable or necessary.

In Imperial times such value was seen in strategic terms, or as tribute-payment, or in the colonization of new agricultural land. Since 1949 the strategic concern has been not only to secure control over the other nationalities, but also to provide buffers against external threats. A more contemporary concern is the utilization of resources which lie in minority nationality areas. These range from raw materials to remote sites for nuclear testing and waste dumping.[8] The Han economy under communist leadership is no longer simply agrarian; it is rapidly industrializing. Since the CCP lays claim to the territory of the old empire, it feels that it has the right to extract resources from any part of the country.

The territory over which the CCP gained power in 1949 was little different in extent from the Imperial China of the Qing.[9] The CCP inherited an empire, but failed to devise sufficiently sensitive or adequate means by which to reflect upon the colonial relationships of that empire and bring them to an end. During the CCP's discussions in the 1930s there had been indications that rights of secession would be incorporated in a new constitution.[10] However, by 1954 and the first constitution of the PRC, that possibility had disappeared.[11] Instead, the system of local autonomy at various levels of the administrative hierarchy was introduced, along with a rubric on the need to combat Han chauvinism. Since that time minority nationalities must consider themselves part of China or be branded 'counter-revolutionary secessionists'.

As noted in chapter 1, the Seventh FYP in effect contains a model of regional comparative advantage. In its operation, the Western Region will experience a slower rate of growth than the other two regions, largely because throughout the twentieth century (and despite the development of *san xian* projects during the 1960s and 1970s) it has remained relatively undeveloped. For the future, the Western Region's main national function is as a source of energy and mineral resources. The Seventh FYP is also designed to lessen the burden the Western Region currently imposes on the rest of the economy. Thus, for example in agriculture, grain yields are targeted to rise in order to reduce grain imports from elsewhere in the PRC.[12]

Unsurprisingly, within minority nationality areas of local government there is a dual response to current policies as enshrined in the Seventh FYP. The Han inhabitants see benefits in joining the modernization programme of the national economy, and have requested further resources to ensure local development. Some of the minority peoples, in sharp contrast, regard the current developmental strategy as the imposition of Han needs upon their own economic systems. Many would prefer the withdrawal of both existing Han immigrants and any new resource exploiters.[13]

These issues were addressed in April 1988 — not long after major disturbances in Tibet — by Zhao Ziyang, general secretary of the CCP. He combined firm statements about the inviolability of national territory with reassurances to local leaders that any harmful effects of national development policies on the Western Region would be offset. In part Zhao was addressing the concern of many leaders of Western Region provinces and autonomous regions that current policies are leaving it behind in terms of national development. Other economists and party leaders have been expressing concern that the impact of reform and the open-door policy has been to create even more regional inequality.

The problem of regional inequality poses a set of interconnected and irresolvable dilemmas for the government. It cannot allow the gap to become too great without incurring criticism that its policies are unfair to the Western Region, not least from the large numbers of Han settlers required to live there. Indeed, there is already evidence of a 'brain drain' to the East of trained personnel — mostly Han — who have skills which are prized and will be better rewarded elsewhere. At the same time, to promote rapid development in the West runs the danger of provoking minority nationalist opposition because local resources are being exploited for Han needs, and at the expense of the local means of livelihood. In any case, there is little chance that the government will alter its priorities. Rather, it will continue to emphasize the development of the Eastern Coastal Region as the strategy for the benefit of the whole country. The leadership argues that if efforts are concentrated on the Eastern Coastal Region, then the greater wealth created there can be shared with the West.[14]

The East-West divide

Although there is a clear East-West divide in contemporary China, there is no reason to believe that the Western Region cannot experience rapid growth, nor that it is necessarily consigned to an existence on low levels of income. The 1984 provincial-level production statistics indicate some curious contrasts which seem to belie the overall impression of the Western Region as 'poor and backward'. For example, as Table 10.1 demonstrates, three important coastal provinces have lower levels of per capita consumption than the Xinjiang Autonomous Region. Tibet and Qinghai have higher per capita consumption than Hunan, Jiangxi and

Anhui (all of which are in the Central Region). The recently published *Population Atlas of China* — particularly useful because it presents data on a county-by-county (*xian*) basis — also provides some interesting examples of curious East-West anomalies. For instance, the counties with the highest agricultural output per capita are most of Jiangsu province (which is well known), and a number of counties in Tibet and Inner Mongolia, where animal husbandry (pastoralism) predominates and sales of livestock at high prices seem to be buoyant.

Table 10.1 Consumption for selected provinces and autonomous regions in 1984

Provincial-level unit	Consumption (yuan RMB per capita)	Region
Xinjiang	410	western
Zhejiang	365	coastal
Jiangsu	397	coastal
Guangdong	408	coastal
Qinghai	371	western
Tibet	359	western
Hunan	311	central
Jiangxi	311	central
Anhui	286	central

Source: *Statistical Yearbook of China 1986*, p. 558.

The rate of economic growth in the Western Region is likely to be high given the relatively low levels of past economic development. A comparison of the Gross Value of Industrial and Agricultural Output (GVIAO) in 1981 and 1985 for each of the provinces and autonomous regions in the Western Region is presented in Table 10.2 (comparative data for a number of other provinces in the Eastern Coastal and Central Regions are also provided). Table 10.2 suggests that the rate of economic growth in the Western Region can be as rapid as, or even greater than, elsewhere in China. However, there is a wide variation in rates of growth, both above and below the national average. Four of the provincial-level units which are well below the national average (Tibet, Yunnan, Gansu and Qinghai) have substantial populations of minority nationalities. Two with significant non-Han populations have slightly above-average growth rates (Xinjiang and Ningxia); and the two mainly Han provinces are about the average (Sichuan and Shaanxi). Although Guizhou has the highest rate of growth in the Western Region, it started from an abysmally low base.

Aggregate growth rates are not always the best way to assess development. They say little, for example, about the development of the economic infrastructure, and nothing about the quality of life. Moreover, in

Table 10.2 GVIAO by province and autonomous region in the Western Region, 1981 & 1985 (millions of yuan RMB, 1980 prices)

Province	1981	1985	% increase
Western zone			
Sichuan	46,700	75,949	62.6
Guizhou	8,500	14,476	70.3
Yunnan	13,000	20,457	57.4
Tibet AR	740	866	17.0
Shaanxi	15,500	25,587	65.1
Gansu	10,200	16,059	57.4
Qinghai	2,000	3,058	52.9
Ningxia Hui AR	2,000	3,295	64.7
Xinjiang AR	7,500	12,395	65.3
Other selected provinces			
Fujian	14,000	23,622	68.7
Guangxi Zhuang AR	15,400	21,377	38.8
Anhui	24,600	40,524	64.7
Liaoning	53,500	80,597	50.6
Shandong	54,300	89,547	64.9
Shanxi	17,200	28,507	65.7
China Total	749,000	1,216,753	62.4

Note: The figures for 1981 have obviously been rounded, and this will affect the accuracy of the percentage change figures.
Sources: 1981: *Beijing Review*, 1982, no. 33, p. 24.
1985: *Statistical Yearbook of China 1986*, p. 37.

interpreting the variable benefits of modernization, political perceptions — whether of national leaders, provincial-level officials, or local inhabitants — may be more important. Much of the Western Region is territory traditionally held by non-Han peoples and it is this ethnic dimension, and the political perception of an East-West divide, that shapes the attitude of central government. That attitude was reflected by Zhao Ziyang in April 1988:

In a country with such a vast territory as ours, uneven economic development in the eastern, central and western regions will exist for a long time. In the past few years, the difference in the level of economic development between some Chinese nationality areas and the coastal zone has been widened. It should be noted that this gap has emerged under circumstances in which national economic construction in nationality areas has experienced huge advances, but the coastal areas have developed at a still faster pace. Our goal is to seek common prosperity for all nationalities, but this cannot be achieved simultaneously.[15]

Economics and nationality

One of the most crucial differences among China's various nationalities (including the Han) is the distinct nature of the economic systems which each operates. One such distinction is well known, and in a sense caused the Han to build the Great Wall. For millennia the Han used agricultural land in the loess area and the lower Yellow River basin; to their north were herdspeople, pastoralists whose resources were animals and grazing land. Competition for the land, which could be used for either purpose, produced conflict. The military superiority of the mounted herders to the north determined the nature of the relationship for centuries, and inspired the Han to build the Great Wall.

Today that same distinction between farmer and herder marks out one of the major clashes of economic interest within the country's modern borders. Even among the agriculturalists, not all farm the land in the manner of the Han. The Uighur engage in oasis cultivation, based on ancient irrigation channels that bring meltwater from the snows of the mountains surrounding the inland basins of Xinjiang. In Yunnan some nationalities engage in slash-and-burn cultivation, using land temporarily and then moving on to allow it to regenerate. In this area of topographic extremes, mountain ranges stretch up in high folds parallel to deep valleys. The farmed hill lands separate narrow valleys containing more permanent agriculture. The patchwork of ethnic groups is as variegated in altitude as in space, with certain groups occupying the higher slopes and others the valley bottoms. The peopling of that area resulted at least in part from the marginalization to those lands of ethnic groups pushed there in previous centuries by the outward and southward expansion of the Han.

The various minority nationalities have distinct economic systems and patterns of social interaction. As a result, the pressure of an external nationality with a different conception of resources, land and social organization may lead not simply to a disruption of the indigenous economy, but also to resistance of a political nature.[16] The centuries-old interaction between Han and northern pastoralists, for example the Mongols, produced both conflict and compromise. Pressures by the Han on other border peoples have likewise produced a *modus vivendi*, though not without antagonism and sometimes leading to the defeat of the border peoples in the process of empire-building. However, the Han economy is no longer just an agrarian system seeking security, allegiance, tribute or (historically perhaps the most significant of all) farmland to colonize. In the present century, and most especially during the period since 1949, the Han have created an industrializing economy.

Where once the pressure was on land, in order to feed more mouths and to settle more colonists, now there is also a perceived need to find resources, provide power supplies and — because they are deemed to be part of China — to use the territories of the minority nationalities for the benefit of the Han-defined 'Chinese economy'. Although they do not seem to have gone about it in the most productive way possible, the Han have also required the allegiance of the border peoples (especially those in the Western Region) to secure the international borders of their own territory.

Since 1949 the CCP has had to devise means for dealing with the minority nationalities because, for the most part, it had had little involvement with them before. The results have been variable, depending largely on the degree to which policy at any specific time either regarded other nationalities as possessing inherently counter-revolutionary customs at one extreme, or saw their territory as essential to economic growth (thereby requiring more liberal treatment of ethnic attributes in order to promote easier access) at the other. That distinction is perhaps somewhat oversimplified, but the formulation is a fair representation of current policy, which has had to contend with considerable ill-will, created by the application of the opposite policy, especially during much of the Cultural Revolution decade.

A crucial plank of the approach typified during the Cultural Revolution was the enforcement of collective forms of economic and social organization on other nationalities. One source of ethnic tension was the lack of models for the incorporation of pastoralists into communes. Another was the minority nationalities' lack of a revolutionary history — they had not struggled in revolution to overthrow an oppressive system. Indeed, from their perspective the new collectivism was to be imposed by people who were ethnically no different from their previous imperial masters. In some respects the new government was even worse, for the degree of interference was in some cases greater than before.

Despite differences in policy between the era of Cultural Revolution and the 1980s, there is none the less a degree of continuity in the economic uses made of minority areas. Moreover, the underlying policy assumption of both periods is that, in their dealings with the minority nationalities, the Han government and people are basically dealing with inferiors. That attitude was expressed in the Cultural Revolution as the superiority of socialist collectivism over the various 'primitive' forms of social structure found amongst the feudal, tribal or primitive communist peoples of the Western Region. Today it is shown in criticism of minority nationalities as having backward forms of economic organization. These are said to lack the commodity form of production deemed necessary to encourage the full development of the productive forces so crucial to the improvement of their livelihoods (but perhaps of greatest value to the Han industrializing economy).

Han utilization of national minority areas has entailed four types of activity which are now being reinforced by the desire to further integrate the Western Region into the mainstream economy. The first has been the extraction of raw materials and energy resources. The second has been the use of land for farming by Han colonists. That land would have been farmed in different ways by the local inhabitants or been available for other purposes. The third has been the takeover of land for other purposes, including nuclear weapons testing, the establishment of labour camps, or the setting-up of industrial enterprises. In the early 1950s large numbers of troops were demobilized in the Western Region (especially Xinjiang), and some whose loyalty was doubted by the new government were forced to remain there. A more recent version of this strategy has been the expansion of tourism. The fourth activity has been to increase the impact of commercialization through the changing pattern of demand stimulated by market forces, for example, in livestock production or oasis produce.

The last of these four has had the greatest impact during the current reform period, and is seen as a crucial part of the desire to increase the Western Region's integration into the national economy. Local nationalities may even be party to this commercialization, and may well benefit financially, as with livestock profits in Tibet and Inner Mongolia. However, under different circumstances, when not obliged by the market to adopt such a strategy, their policies might be different and less harmful to the fragile environments of the Western Region. In any case, different minority nationalities appear to have very varied responses to the prospect of commercialization: the lack of interest shown by some is a matter of regret for some economists and party leaders.

Each of the first three broad strategies has historically resulted in Han immigration into minority nationality territories, and the scale is of immense significance. In Inner Mongolia the Han have for quite some time outnumbered the Mongols, accounting for 84 per cent of the total in 1982.[17] In Xinjiang, Han settlers (including state farm workers) number 40.5 per cent of the population, though an unknown number of prisoners and military personnel have contributed many more. What this signifies for the concept of autonomy for the minority regions appears not to have been addressed.

The impact of reform

China's leadership now recognizes that because religious belief is often an integral part of the culture of national minority peoples, it is impossible to be good communists and suppress or diminish the role of religion without also being bad communists and repressing national rights. Despite this post-Cultural Revolution awareness, recognition of the ethnic dimension of the distinct economic systems operated by the different nationalities has been slow in coming. Where such awareness exists, the tendency is primarily to bemoan the lack of consciousness about commodity production among the minority nationalities, and to suggest this is a handicap to economic growth.

The more general attitude is that unless the Western Region experiences a reasonable rate of economic growth, then an intensification of poor relations between the Han and other nationalities will occur. A recent book published in Sichuan and devoted to a discussion of the development of the Western Region and minority nationality areas argued that

> China's ethnic unity and social stability is closely tied up with the economic growth and prosperity of these regions. The yawning gulf in the level of economic development which exists between developed regions on the coast and those in the interior and backward border regions populated by ethnic minorities may bring with it a series of delicate social problems, of a nationalist character, for instance.[18]

There has been little recognition that the process of development itself is something which increases — or can increase — minority nationalist rejection of Han intervention in local economies. Instead, the Western Region is clearly to be seen as a resource-base fortuitously located within Chinese territory. In 1983 this attitude was mobilized behind the slogan 'to tap the Great North-west'. According to another recent study of West China:

> Looking at the natural resources and economic situation of present-day China, two . . . trends emerge: in one the east surpasses the west in terms of levels of economic, technical, scientific and cultural development, while in the other the west surpasses the east in terms of reserves of natural resources, and whereas in the east resource exploitation is maximal, in the west it has scarcely begun.[19]

The main debate is over the method by which economic integration between East and West China is best achieved.

In one view, the Western Region will respond best to the use of market forces, the promotion of commercial rather than state-led forms of investment, and commercialization of new and existing products. The alternative is to retain some form of state-dominated economy, based on the types of financial controls, budgetary aid and central investment in use before the 1980s. It would presumably require subsidy through taxation of efficient enterprises in the Eastern Coastal Region. In reality, China's polity is so disparate and varied that elements of both policies seem to have been in operation simultaneously. However, the dominant model is clearly that which reduces direct state involvement and promotes commercialization of the Western Region. It also allows for greater provincial-level control over revenues (including the right to seek foreign investment independently of central government) and more local level decision-making over the use and allocation of central funds.

One of the early proposals of the post-Mao reform period for promoting the development of the Western Region was termed the 'East-West dialogue'. This is a rather unsophisticated proposal for the wealthier units in the Eastern Coastal Region to transfer skills, technology and capital to the Central and Western Regions. The proposal was predicated on the greater autonomy which enterprises and provinces have experienced since 1978, allowing factories to do deals between themselves, and provinces to seek other sources of funding rather than go through the cumbersome planning system. Initially it also appears to have entailed a high-profile role for the Western Region in national modernization. *Beijing Review* in 1985 mentioned central government plans 'to shift the centre of its economic construction efforts to the west at the turn of the century'.

The East-West dialogue was soon modified. By April 1988 Zhao Ziyang insisted on the need to allow the Eastern Coastal Region to develop as rapidly as possible, with the Western Region as a provider of scarce raw materials.[20] The change does not negate the idea of an East-West dialogue; rather it demonstrates that it was really a non-policy, a phrase that could be used to describe any form of inter-regional co-operation. Such links are continuing, though more in terms of regional comparative advantage as suggested in the Seventh FYP. To quote Tonur Dawamat, the head of the Xinjiang Uighur Autonomous Region (himself an Uighur):

> the development of China's eastern coastal areas complements that of its central and western parts. In the years up to the 1990s, the state will accelerate the development of its east and stress energy and raw materials in the central part to prepare for future development in the west. Xinjiang, located as it is in the west, will become an important base of China's economic construction in the twenty-first century. This well-considered strategy not only conforms with the objective reality of China's economic construction but reflects to the full the aspirations of the people of various nationalities in Xinjiang.[21]

Examples of East-West dialogue that appear in the official media to demonstrate its success in the West indicate rather slow progress. They include a plant which assembles trucks for a Hubei factory; a fruit-juice factory which relies on a huge expansion of fruit output in the fragile environment of the Turpan oasis; and a textile factory which will use more local raw materials and import its machinery from Japan. In total, the 2,600 joint ventures set up with the other regions during 1983–5 are producing a total output value of only 300 million yuan RMB.[22]

On the other hand, such projects indicate the direction of development. They suggest a combination of intensified traditional production by national minority peoples, and the linking of manufacturing and raw material production with the economy elsewhere in China. The former is likely to create growing environmental problems, as minority nationalities respond to the commercial dictates of the new system. The latter will increase conflicts with minorities over the use of resources by Han settlers, including water, minerals and other raw materials, as in the Tarim basin. These too are likely to cause environmental problems, and the lack of sensitivity to that issue has serious implications for the long-term development of the Western Region in areas already seriously damaged by policies designed to create growth for the country as a whole. For example, the growth in livestock in pastoral areas has already led to environmental degradation of the steppe.[23] Worse is likely to follow, as local leaders follow Beijing's dictates. Xinjiang's leadership, for instance, has stated its desire to establish itself as 'a major base for animal by-products and cash crops in China'.[24] The impact on already depleted water resources, plus the associated spoliation of existing reclaimed land through salination caused by inappropriate irrigation is potentially devastating.[25]

The provinces and autonomous regions of Western China are funded by the retained taxation levied within their area, to which are added transfers of funds from the centre to cover budget deficits. Because the Western Region includes border areas with large-scale military activity, and the establishment of other facilities designed for the benefit of the Han economy, it is not really appropriate to consider all state transfers in support of provincial-level budgets as aiding the development of those areas. These subsidies are a cause of resentment in the provinces of the Eastern Coastal Region, whose taxes are used to provide them, and central government has recently announced its ending of the automatic annual 10 per cent increase in the subsidies to which the Western Region had become accustomed.[26]

This policy heralds other changes for the funding of the Western Region, though it is likely (since it is specified in the Seventh FYP) that the minority nationality and border areas will continue to receive the special funding established since 1949 to aid the poorer parts of the country. Change has centred on the notion of making the provinces more responsible for dealing with their own funds, and seeking other sources of finance both within and outside China. Special investment funds allocated by central government — for instance, to finance infrastructural projects in irrigation or transport, such as the new rail link from

Urumqi to the Soviet border due to open in 1989 — have been a particular target of reform. Loans are increasingly to replace grants. Such changes, if fully implemented, will have serious consequences for the provinces and autonomous regions of West China. Xinjiang is reliant on central subsidies and investment grants for about half of its budgetary and capital expenditure.[27]

Reforms in the treatment of minorities and their cultural and religious activities have had some interesting side effects, not least for the mainstream economy. The religious freedoms now permitted to minority nationalities, after at least a decade during which worship was forced underground, have produced curious connections. For instance, the revival of Islamic practices in the Western Region has had security and investment consequences. The growth of Islamic fundamentalism in the Middle East poses a threat through its potential attraction for China's discontented Muslims, who number around fifteen million. In diplomacy China wants to improve its relations with various Islamic states, particularly Saudi Arabia, which still recognizes Taiwan. To demonstrate better treatment of the Muslims is a step towards those ends. In recent years thousands have been permitted to perform *Hadj* in Mecca. Finally, there have been the benefits of improved relations with the Islamic countries in terms of potential investment (including areas inhabited by China's Islamic peoples); and the greater prospects for trade, especially in arms exports (a large Saudi order was hoped for in 1988, and sales to both Iran and Iraq have been reported).

Conclusion

Empires which expand into contiguous territory are soon liable to claim the colonies as an integral part of their national territory. This proved much more difficult to argue where, as with the European powers in the nineteenth century, most of the colonies were separate and overseas. As China's modernization continues, it is necessary to recognize that many non-Han people have found that their lands are now useful to another people. Past tensions are thus likely to be rekindled in new forms.

It is often assumed that colonial relations are demonstrated by economic neglect, yet it can happen that development brings with it greater domination over the colonized people. Change is clearly inevitable for the minority nationalities, but the experience of similar situations elsewhere in the world suggests that they may find it random, undirected and painful. Given the long history of Han domination, the prospects of a sufficiently enlightened central government to act as a useful and sympathetic midwife for the commercial transformation of the Western Region are not auspicious.

As the commercialization of the Western Region intensifies during modernization there will undoubtedly be variations in the responses of different groups among the minority nationalities depending on their perceptions of the benefits (or otherwise) each might reasonably expect to gain. Variations in response will also depend on the proportion of Han settlers in any particular area. The incomers are likely to have a greater interest in the growth process than the locals, whose indigenous economy may be further disrupted. However, even among the minority nationalities, there will be potential for 'compradors' to emerge, seeking to enjoy the benefits of joining the national system. New 'proletarianized' groups of workers may also form, whose allegiance to minority cultures is diminished. Existing economic systems will be transformed, disrupted or destroyed. Precisely how far the benefits of country-wide economic development will actually 'trickle down' to the Western Region, and be accepted by people for whom Han patterns of development may not really be appropriate, are two of the more interesting questions for the future.

Notes

1 *The Guardian*, 17 May 1988, p. 10.
2 *Beijing Review*, no. 31, 1979.
3 See, for a partial explanation of the difference, Grunfeld, A.T. (1987) *The making of Modern Tibet*, London: Zed Press/Armonk: Sharpe, M.E. A map of one Tibetan group's claim is given in *Tibet Foundation Newsletter*, no. 1, 1987, p. 8, based on Chinese government-designated Tibetan Autonomous Prefectures in the neighbouring provinces. According to China's own census figures, these seem to be populated by a slight majority of minority peoples (see *Statistical Yearbook of China 1986*, p. 64).
4 In the National People's Congresses, however, the number of deputies of national minority origin has always been higher than the proportion in the total population, and in 1983 was over 14 per cent (see *Statistical Yearbook of China 1986*, p. 2).
5 See Newby, L.J. (1988) ' "The pure and true religion" in China', *Third World Quarterly*, no. 10, 2 April, p. 939, for information on these two points.
6 Mackerras, C. (1985) 'The minority nationalities: modernization and integration', chapter 6 in Young, G. (ed.) *China: Dilemmas of Modernization*, London: Croom Helm, p. 244.
7 This is not to suggest that the impact of modernization on the non-Han peoples is genocidal, as can be argued, for instance, in the case of Latin America's indigenous peoples or the Aborigines of Australia. But the analogy of contradictory economic and social objectives among different peoples is valid.
8 Reports of demonstrations against nuclear facilities and testing in Xinjiang have emerged in recent years, for example, *South China*

Morning Post, 10 January 1986. *The Economist* has noted the apparent willingness of China to sell nuclear waste storage facilities to foreign countries (18 February 1984).

9 There is, though, one massive area previously under Chinese suzerainty — Outer Mongolia — which was detached in 1921 when a People's Republic was established as a result of increased Soviet influence after 1917.

10 Newby, op. cit., p. 935.

11 Mackerras, op. cit., p. 240.

12 Vermeer, E.B. (1986) 'China's Seventh Five Year Plan 1986–1990', *China Information*, vol. 1, part 1, Leiden, p. 23.

13 Mackerras, C. (op. cit.); The *Guardian*, 18 May 1988.

14 Zhao Ziyang (1988) 'Zhao Ziyang on Nationality Issue', *Beijing Review*, 16–22 May, p. 17.

15 Ibid.

16 Further details on the economic systems of minority nationalities are given in Griffen, K. (1986) 'Rural development in an arid region', *Third World Quarterly*, no. 8, 3 July; Griffen, K. (1987) *World Hunger and the World Economy*, London: Macmillan; and Clarke, G.E. (1987) 'China's reforms of Tibet, and their effects on pastoralism', Brighton: Institute of Development Studies Discussion Paper no. 237.

17 Mackerras, op. cit., p. 249.

18 Wang Xiaoqing and Bai Nanfeng (1985) *The Poverty of Plenty*, Sichuan People's Publishing House, chapter 1, section 3. Translation made available by Angela Knox.

19 Shi Zhengyi (1986) in National Minority Economic Research Unit (ed.) chapter 1, *The western regions: an exploration into economic development in national minority regions*, Beijing: Central Institute of Nationalities. Translation made available by Angela Knox.

20 This view is expressed in *Beijing Review*, 26 August 1985. Zhao's 'pro-coast' speech is in *Beijing Review*, 8 February 1988. He maintains that the Eastern Coastal Region will continue to promote development in the Western Region through a revised model referred to as the 'Two Fannings-out' — the coast will advance while promoting trade with the outside world through its use of foreign technology and growth in exports, while transferring capital and technology to the interior as a result of its advances.

21 *Beijing Review*, 3 November 1986, p. 20.

22 Ibid., 26 January 1987.

23 Shen Chang-jiang (1982) 'Pastoral systems in arid and semi-arid zones of China', London: Overseas Development Institute, Pastoral Network Paper, no. 13b, p. 20.

24 *Beijing Review*, 3 November 1986, p. 20.

25 A useful description of the background to such problems since 1949 may be found in Hoppe, T. (1986) 'An essay on reproduction: the example of Xinjiang Uighur Autonomous Region', in Glaeser, B. (ed.) *Learning from China? Development and environment in Third World countries*, London: Allen & Unwin. A less pessimistic but perhaps

rather uncritical report on Xinjiang alone is given by Griffen (1987) op. cit.

26 *Guardian*, 18 May 1988.
27 See Griffen (1987) op cit., p. 149, and Mackerras, op. cit., p. 253, for information on previous patterns of support for provinces and autonomous regions in the Western Region.

Appendix: Maps

Map 1: Major relief regions

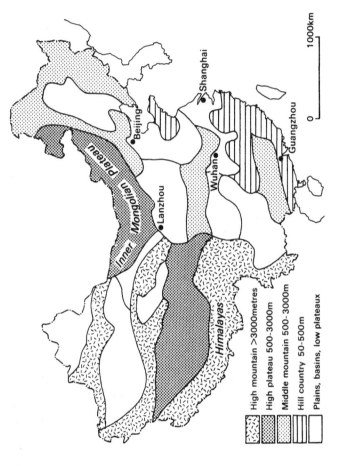

High mountain >3000metres

High plateau 500-3000m

Middle mountain 500-3000m

Hill country 50-500m

Plains, basins, low plateaux

Inner Mongolian Plateau

Himalayas

Beijing

Shanghai

Lanzhou

Wuhan

Guangzhou

0   1000km

Source: Cole, J.P. (1985) *China 1950–2000: Performance and prospects*, Nottingham: Department of Geography, University of Nottingham, Nottingham.

Map 2: Desert lands

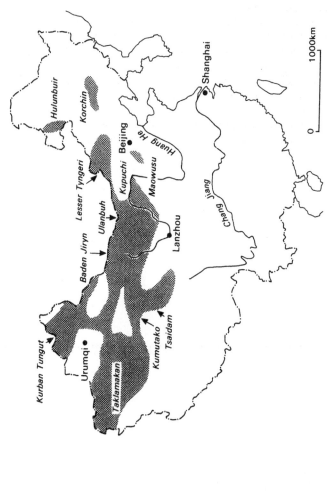

Source: Cole, J.P. (1985) *China 1950–2000: Performance and Prospects*, Nottingham: Department of Geography, University of Nottingham.

Map 3: Annual precipitation

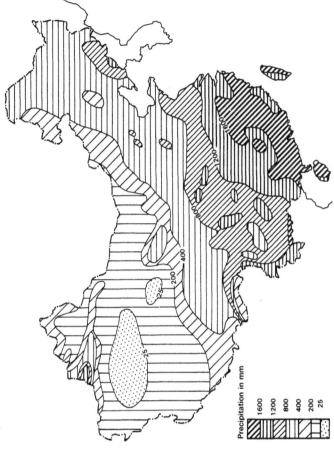

Precipitation in mm

	1600
	1200
	800
	400
	200
	25

Source: Leeming, F. (1984) *Selected Chinese Maps*, Leeds: Department of Geography, University of Leeds.

Map 4: Rural population density

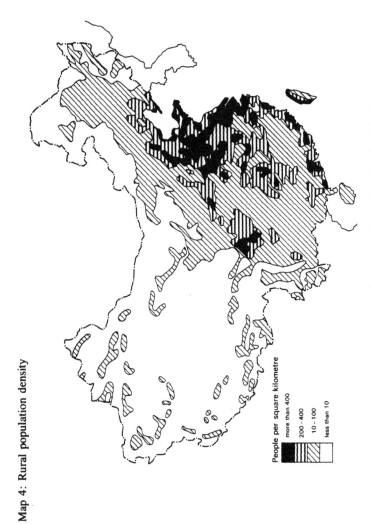

People per square kilometre

more than 400
200 - 400
10 - 100
less than 10

Source: Leeming, F. (1984) *Selected Chinese Maps* Leeds: Department of Geography, University of Leeds.

Map 5: Military Regions

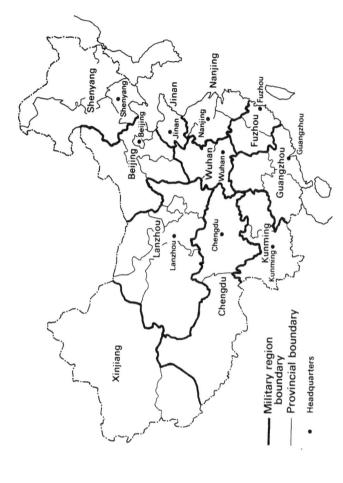

Map 6: Administrative regions and provinces

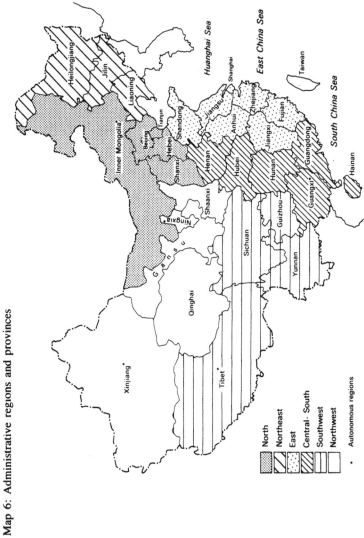

North

Northeast

East

Central- South

Southwest

Northwest

• Autonomous regions

Map 7: The Aihui-Tengchong division

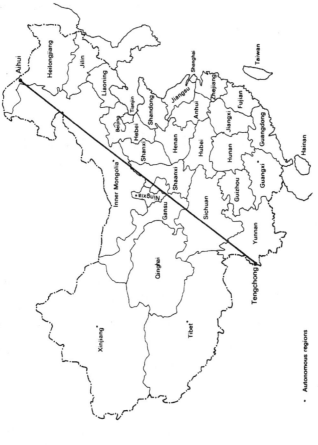

ng line links Aihui County in Heilongjiang and Tengchong County in Yunnan. To the west of this line are six province-level authorities. The six account for over 60 per cent of China's land area, but contain only about 6 per cent of total population, and produced 5 per ' and agricultural output in 1982.

· Autonomous regions

Map 8: The coastal, inland, and border regionalization

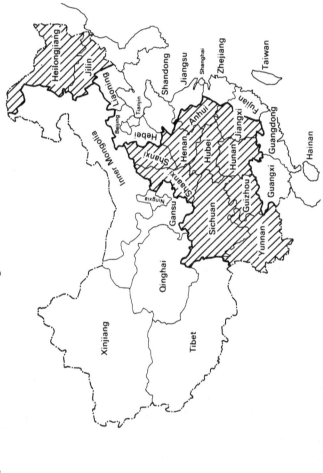

Note: This regionalization (used by Chinese geographers in the early 1980s) differs from that used officially in the Seventh Five-Year Plan (see Map 9): the Central Region includes Sichuan, Shaanxi, and Guizhou, whose fortunes are now linked with those of the Western Region. Inner Mongolia is here included in the West; the 7th Plan puts it in the Central Region.

Map 9: The tripartite regionalization of the Seventh Five-Year Plan

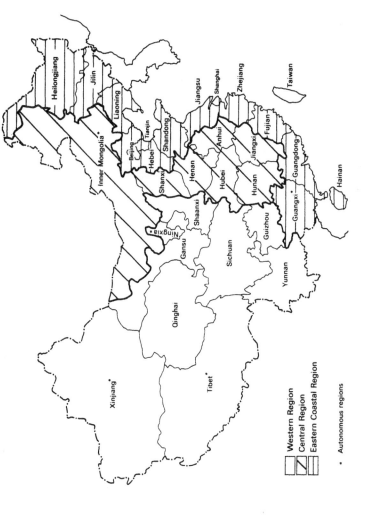

Map 10: Economic development regions

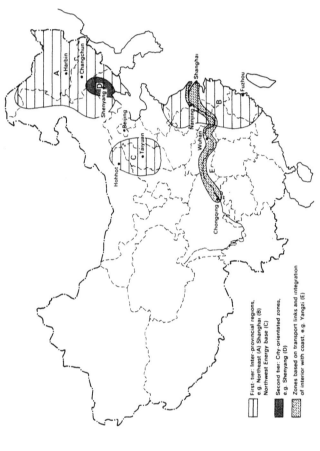

Note: This is an indicative map of the various types of economic policy region defined in the Seventh Five-Year Plan. No definitive maps have been published, and there are many more regions than shown here, active or notional. This merely indicates their varied spatial scale and hierarchy; note too the inter-provincial nature of their focus, a shift from the previous much greater provincial isolationism.

First-tier Inter-provincial regions, e.g. Northeast (A) Shanghai (B) Northwest Energy base (C)

Second tier: City-orientated zones, e.g. Shenyang (D)

Zones based on transport links and integration of interior with coast, e.g. Yangzi (E)

Map 11: China's railway network, 1985

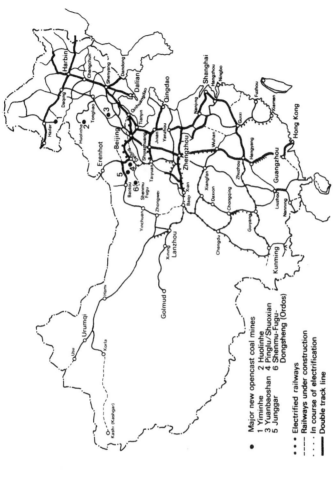

Major new opencast coal mines
1 Yiminhe   2 Huolinhe
3 Yuanbaoshan   4 Pinglu/Shuoxian
5 Junggar   6 Shenmu-Fugu-
          Dongsheng (Ordos)

• • • Electrified railways
----- Railways under construction
· · · · In course of electrification
▬▬▬ Double track line

Source: China Reconstructs, January, 1985.

Map 12: Mineral deposits

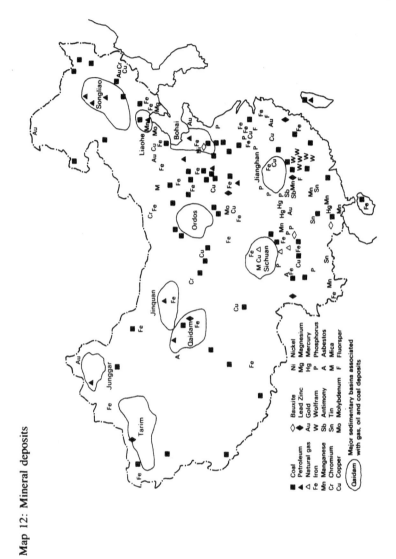

Glossary
of Chinese terms used in the text

Chinese term	Meaning
Changjiang	The Yangtze river, as it is commonly termed in the west.
diqu	District: usually applied to the administrative level immediately below the province.
fushengji	Semi-provincial level: used of cities treated as provinces in China's budgetary relations, despite being sub-provincial units for other administrative purposes.
mu	An area of land: 1 mu is 0.0667 of an hectare or 0.1647 of an acre.
ribao	Daily — used in newspaper titles, eg *Renmin Ribao* (People's Daily).
san xian	The 'Third Front' or 'Third Line'. During the years from the late 1950s to the 1970s regional policy was shaped by fear of invasion. The Third Front was part of the policy to defend in depth, and involved the economic development of west-central China.
xian	County.
xiancheng	County town.
yuan (¥)	Unity of currency: there are approximately seven Chinese yuan to the pound sterling (1988). Yuan Renminbi (RMB) is analogous with pounds sterling.

Select bibliography

Cannon, T.G. and Jenkins, A. (eds) (1989) *The Geography of Contemporary China: the impact of Deng's decade*, London: Routledge.

Feuchtwang, S., Hussein, A. and Pairrault, T. (eds) (1988) *Transforming China in the Eighties*, 2 vols, London: Zed Press.

Goodman, D.S.G. (ed) (1988) *Communism and Reform in East Asia*, London: Frank Cass.

Harding, H. (1987) *China's Second Revolution: Reform after Mao*, Washington: Brookings Institution.

Jao, Y.C. and Leung, C.K. (eds) (1986) *China's Special Economic Zones: Policies, Problems and Prospects*, Hong Kong: Oxford University Press.

Leeming, F. (1985) *Rural China Today*, Harlow: Longman.

Johnson, T.M. (1987) *China: Energy Sector Outlook*, London: Economist Intelligence Unit.

Lampton, D. (ed) (1987) *Policy Implementation in Post-Mao China*, Berkeley: University of California Press.

Perry, E.J. and Wong, C. (1985) *The Political Economy of Reform in Post-Mao China*, Cambridge, Mass.: Harvard University Press.

Pye, L. (1981) *The Dynamics of Chinese Politics*, Cambridge, Mass.: Oelgeschlager, Gunn and Hain.

Riskin, C. (1987) *China's Political Economy*, Oxford and New York: Oxford University Press.

Schram, S.R. (1984) *Ideology and Policy in China since the Third Plenum, 1978–84*, London: Contemporary China Institute.

State Statistical Bureau (1986) *Statistical Yearbook of China 1986*, Oxford: Oxford University Press and Hong Kong: Economic Information and Agency.

State Statistical Bureau, People's Republic of China (1986) *China: A Statistical Survey in 1986*, Beijing: New World Press.

World Bank (1985) *China: Long-Term Development Issues and Options*, Baltimore: The Johns Hopkins University Press.

Index

For Product Safety Concerns and Information please contact our EU
representative GPSR@taylorandfrancis.com Taylor & Francis Verlag GmbH,
Kaufingerstraße 24, 80331 München, Germany

Batch number: 08158919

Printed by Printforce, the Netherlands